Alice B. McCleary
Winter Embertide - 1964

The Showing Forth of Christ

The Showing Forth of Christ

 Sermons of John Donne

SELECTED AND EDITED
WITH AN INTRODUCTION
BY
EDMUND FULLER

Harper & Row, Publishers

NEW YORK, EVANSTON, AND LONDON

To

Chad

and

Eva Walsh

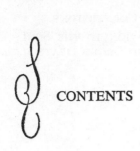 CONTENTS

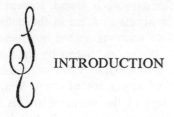

INTRODUCTION

A VISITOR TO ST. PAUL'S CATHEDRAL CHURCH, London, will find, a short way inside the gates of the South Choir Aisle, the fire-damaged statue of a shrouded man. It is the figure of John Donne, Dean of the Cathedral from 1621 until his death in 1631. The statue is the only monument surviving from the old cathedral, destroyed in the great fire of London in 1666. As the monument survived flame, so Donne has survived time. Poet and priest, one of the greatest preachers in the history of the English Church, he has enjoyed an extraordinary revival of interest in this century.

W. B. Yeats and T. S. Eliot were key persons in the renewed attention to Donne as a metaphysical poet, and his name has been on the lips of critics since the first world war. On the heels of this rediscovery as a poet came fresh attention to his prose, especially in its simplest and most accessible form in the Devotions. In the 1930's, Ernest Hemingway popularized the passage beginning "No man is an island . . ." from which he took the title of *For Whom the Bell Tolls*. In 1959, the novelist William Styron derived a title, *Set This House on Fire,* from a great passage in a less consistently distinguished sermon preached before the Earl of Carlisle in 1622. These are small matters in themselves, but they are indications that much in Donne's thought and expression speaks with extraordinary directness and aptness to our own condition today. We find such indications throughout the sermons. There are analogies between his age and ours: both are animated and disturbed by breakthroughs of scientific knowledge and revolutions of thought. Donne's mind and spirit also often show a psychic harmony with twentieth-century man.

It is in the sermons that his finest prose is found. Recent years
have offered a great advantage in access to them in the definitive,
ten-volume edition of the complete sermons, edited by Evelyn M.
Simpson and the late George R. Potter, published by the Univer-
sity of California Press. It is a monumental work of meticulous
scholarship with exhaustive critical apparatus of every kind, and
has been of great aid in the editing of the sermons in this book.
It answers the student's need, perhaps once for all, but because
it is costly and obtainable only as a set, it does not reach the
general reading public. Also, wading through its mazes of sev-
enteenth-century spelling, punctuation, paragraphing, italicizing,
and copious Latin quotations is hard labor for any but the special-
ist. Amidst it all, for the general reader, the roll and sweep of
Donne's eloquence is all but impossible to hear, his forceful exposition difficult to follow.

Yet Donne has many cogent things to say—and to say marvel-
ously well—to modern readers of apologetical, devotional, and
homiletic writing. They are the ones to whom the present book is
addressed. It contains sixteen sermons, from the one hundred and
sixty extant, totaling as herein abridged and edited, something over
one hundred thousand words—the largest selection from the sermons now in print. More important, it is the only selection that
presents the sermons in modern spelling, punctuation, and paragraphing, shorn of the lengthy Latin quotations from Scripture
and the Church Fathers. I have abridged each of the sermons by
some degree, often very little but occasionally by as much as a
third. In that respect it resembles the Logan Pearsall Smith volume of selections, but from among all the sermons Smith culled
only brief passages, paragraphs or a page or two. The selections in
this book are not excerpts, but are still sermons, pruned of elab-
orations, recapitulations, special contemporary controversies, and
other matter which might come between the reader and the heart
of Donne's magnificent expositions of his texts. The selection is
personal, as any such proceeding must be, but the purpose was to
present a wide cross-section of Donne's preaching upon a broad
range of themes, throughout his whole ministry. True representa-

tion has been the aim, not an attempt to select and stress any one element of Donne's theological thought to the minimizing of another. The sixteen sermons in this volume will be read with profit and pleasure by many who might otherwise never read them at all.

Donne was born in London, in 1573. His father, a prosperous merchant, died when the boy was about four years old. His mother, Elizabeth Heywood, was the daughter of the playwright, John Heywood, and her mother was the daughter of Sir Thomas More's sister. It is a good guess that Donne's genius in letters came through the More-Heywood lines. The family was Roman Catholic—through the Mores, notably so. Donne, who had Jesuit schooling as a boy, conformed to the Church of England some time after his law studies at Lincoln's Inn. Earlier he had left Oxford, upon concluding his education there, but without a degree because, as a Roman Catholic, he could not take the required oath. In the early years of Donne's reading at Lincoln's Inn, his younger brother Henry died, at the age of nineteen, of fever contracted in prison where he had been sent for sheltering a Roman priest. Elizabeth Heywood's two brothers were exiled Jesuits. She herself lived in the Deanery at St. Paul's with her son, but still clung to the Roman Church. Thus the bitter and dangerous religious controversies of the day touched the Donne family closely.

Jack Donne, the law student, was described by a friend as "not dissolute, but very neat, a great visitor of ladies, a great frequenter of plays, a great writer of conceited verses." As to the latter, "conceited" did not mean what it does in common usage today, but refers to the mode of the verses rather than to the character of their writer. Donne's verses are full of "conceits," ingenious play with form and word. We should be wary of taking his secular, amorous poetry as a serious clue to his life or personality, for it is largely conventional variations on familiar themes that were the accepted stock-in-trade of the genre. To express caution is not to deny that there was in Donne a fascinating complex of the worldly and the devout, the sensual and the spiritual. His candid searching within himself, as every artist must do, for the understanding of human sin, is one of the qualities that drew people to hear him preach and that draw us still to all that he wrote.

At the end of his law studies, he went on the Earl of Essex's expedition to Cadiz, in 1596, and on another the following year. Afterward he became secretary to Sir Thomas Egerton, one of several important associations with great families, but he ended all prospects for the diplomatic career that might have lain before him by marrying, in 1601, Ann More, a niece of Egerton's wife. She was a minor, and for wedding her without her father's consent he incurred a brief imprisonment and a long period of disfavor and poverty. In time the father relented, the dowry was granted, and Donne began his gradual advancement. Ann More bore him twelve children, seven of whom survived her death in 1617, two years after Donne's ordination.

He aided Thomas Morton, later Bishop of Durham, in controversies with Roman Catholics. He was befriended by Lucy, countess of Bedford, and made valuable associations with Sir Robert Drury, Viscount Rochester, and others. In 1614, he was elected to Parliament.

Essentially, thus far, he had played the game of courtier on a minor scale. It was his polemics on the Roman question that proved to be the decisive factor in his life. Elizabeth had died, and James I, a scholarly king, became keenly interested in Donne through one of his publications, *Pseudo-Martyr*. Earlier, Morton had urged Donne to take holy orders as a path to preferment, but he had clung to the secular life. Now King James pressed him urgently to take orders. Such a counsel could not lightly be declined. Donne accepted it and was ordained in 1615, at the age of forty-two.

Jack Donne had become Dr. Donne. A well-known portrait of about that period shows a man of pale, grave, sensitive face. The pallor is accentuated by black clothing and his dark hair, mustache, and beard. The beard is trimmed to a sharp, wedgelike point forming a black V against the broad, white, pleated ruff. This was he who had turned, in his own words, from "the mistress of my youth, Poesy, to the wife of mine age, Divinity." Whatever the circumstances, the turning was deep and genuine, not expedient; it was an acceptance of a true vocation, perhaps resisted so long because of the rigors his spirit sensed in it. His inward commitment is clear from the riches of his devotional writings and sermons, and the testimony of his personal influence and ministry as priest. Though poetry was for the most part put aside, he wrote in these years some of his finest spiritual poems.

There was no uncertainty or indirection about his career now. For a few years he was Reader in Divinity to the "benchers" of Lincoln's Inn, familiar and congenial precincts to him, though he had never been admitted to the bar. In 1621 came the appointment as Dean of St. Paul's.

He was both an Elizabethan and a Jacobean—a contemporary in the dynamic age of Shakespeare, Marlowe, Jonson (who called him "first poet in the world in some things"), Bacon, Spenser, and at the beginning of another age, the young John Milton. Among his friends were Izaak Walton, his first biographer, and George Herbert. Other great preachers of his time were Richard Hooker, Lancelot Andrewes, and following soon after, Jeremy Taylor.

As Marjorie Hope Nicolson has observed, however, Donne was an Elizabethan who became a modern, in the sense of his response to the great breakthroughs of scientific knowledge and the expanding world sense of his age. For this was the time, too, of Kepler and Galileo, following on the heels of Copernicus, of the opening of the Western hemisphere and the first circumnavigations of the world.

Donne's response to all these stimuli was very marked in his poems, especially in the famous passage from "The First Anniversary" in "An Anatomy of the World," one of his funeral elegies (1610).

> And new Philosophy [science] calls all in doubt,
> The Element of fire is quite put out;
> The Sun is lost, and th' earth, and no man's wit
> Can well direct him where to look for it.
> And freely men confess that this world's spent,
> When in the Planets, and the Firmament
> They seek so many new; then see that this
> Is crumbled out again to his Atomies.
> 'Tis all in pieces, all coherence gone;
> All just supply, and all Relation.

The theological implications of such matters were touchy issues, for there was deep suspicion of heresy in the new cosmology. Donne did not explore scientific subjects widely in the sermons, thus it is all the more notable that we find, at the beginning of the first sermon in this volume, on Genesis 1:26, his use of the new astronomy as a source of images in discussing Creation. There he reflects awareness both of science and the great explorations, as he speaks of

That Earth, which in some thousands of years men could not look over, nor discern what form it had . . . that earth, which no man in his person is ever said to have compassed till our age . . . all that earth, and then that heaven, which spreads so far as that subtle men have, with some appearance of probability, imagined that in that heaven, in those manifold spheres of the planets and the stars, there are many earths, many worlds, as big as this which we inhabit. . . .

And in the sermon on Proverbs 8:17, he speaks of "the merit and passion of Christ Jesus, sufficient to save millions of worlds. . . ."

So we encounter, here, numerous reflections of an age of new horizons—reflections which echo forcefully in our own age, as in the first sermon:

. . . remember that a frame may be thrown down in much less time than it was set up. A child, an ape, can give fire to a cannon: and a vapor can shake the earth: and these fires, and these vapors can throw down cities in a minute.

We can append to this, for pondering today, words from his sermon on the conversion of Paul (Acts 9:4):

[God] can choose his way, he can call in nation against nation, he can cast a damp upon any nation, and make them afraid of one another, he can do an execution upon them by themselves. . . .

Of the sixteen sermons herein, eight are on texts from the Old Testament, eight from the New. Two are from Genesis, one from Job, three from the Psalms (on which he loved to preach, calling them "the manna of the church"), one from Proverbs, and one from Hosea. There are two from Matthew, two from Luke, one from John, one from Acts, and two from I Timothy. Whether from

Old or New Testament, Christ is the center of all. Between the two Testaments he makes the nice distinction:

. . . that which was but a matter of prophecy to them (in the Old Testament they knew not when it should be done) to us in the New is matter of history, and we know when it was done. (Sermon on St. John 14:20)

Something of Donne's characteristic thought on all the great doctrines of Catholic Christianity is represented. He preaches on the Trinity, on Creation, the Incarnation and general Christology, on the doctrine of Man, on the Sacraments, on prayer, repentance, redemption, conversion, on birth, death and marriage, and the necessity for Christian life and worship to be fulfilled within the fold of the Church.

We must not let the controversies of his age confuse us about Donne's preaching within the great, historic Catholic continuity of theology. The Church of England was in conflict with Rome on the one hand and with nonconformist Puritanism on the other. Donne was clearly closer to Rome than to Puritanism; he was more anti-Jesuit than anti-Roman Catholic. In one of his letters he says:

You know I never fettered nor imprisoned the word Religion; not straightening it Frierly . . . nor immuring it in a *Rome,* or a *Wittemberg,* or a *Geneva;* they are all virtual beams of one Sun . . . Religion is Christianity.

In his age, the controversies were inescapable, yet we find him looking beyond them in a spirit which is relevant to today's concern with Christian unity.

If we would but make Christ Jesus and his peace the life and soul of all our actions and all our purposes; if we would mingle that sweetness and suppleness which he loves and which he is, in all our undertakings; if in all controversies, book controversies and sword controversies, we would fit them to him and see how near they would meet in him, that is how near we might come to be friends and yet both sides be good Christians. . . . (Sermon on St. Matt. 21:44)

In his sermon on Psalm 63:7, he summarizes the sources of his faith and preaching.

If he [God] ask me an idea of my religion and my opinions, shall I not be able to say, It is that which thy word and thy Catholic Church hath imprinted in me? If he ask me an idea of my prayers, shall I not be able to say, It is that which my particular necessities, that which the form prescribed by thy Son, that which the care and piety of the Church in conceiving fit prayers hath imprinted in me? If he ask me an idea of my sermons, shall I not be able to say, It is that which the analogy of faith, the edification of the congregation, the zeal of thy work, the meditations of my heart have imprinted in me?

In his sermon on St. Matthew 9:13, in response to a rhetorical question, he asserts

We answer with St. Chrysostom and St. Jerome and St. Ambrose and all the stream of the Fathers. . . .

There we have him, in a position impregnable for his age or ours, in "all the stream of the Fathers."

Though he is far from Puritan theology, there is still a dark, occasionally even morbid, tone to much of his preaching, which reflects aspects of his temperament as well as the dramatic contrasting of lights and darks so typical of his age. Death and disease and pain and danger hovered close to men in Donne's time; 1625 saw one of the great plagues that assailed London. I need not cite only the somber notes; rather I would emphasize his celebrations of joy and of the happiness of religious fellowship. In the sermon on Proverbs 8:17 he says:

And let no man be afraid to seek or find him [God] for fear of the loss of good company; religion is no sullen thing, it is not a melancholy, there is not so sociable a thing as the love of Christ Jesus.

His rejection of a doctrine that would cast out sinners from the congregation is shown in the compassion of a passage from the sermon on St. Matthew 9:13.

. . . howsoever we have a perfect hatred and a religious despite against a sinner, as a sinner; yet if Christ Jesus shall have been pleased to have come to his door, and to have stood, and knocked, and entered, and supped, and brought his dish, and made himself that dish, and sealed a reconciliation to that sinner in admitting him to that table, to that Communion, let us forget the name of publican, the vices of any particular profession; and forget the name of sinner, the history of any man's former life; and be glad to meet that man now in the arms, and to grow up with that man now in the bowels of Christ Jesus. . . .

Donne's preaching is not only great exposition, but reveals a great prose master, whose prose in turn reveals the poet. It is the prose of a Latinist, like Milton's after him. He is able to construct huge, balanced, perfectly controlled, architectonic sentences, clause built upon clause, image upon image, parallel upon parallel, to soaring climaxes. These qualties are seen abundantly in all these sermons, yet perhaps nowhere more notably than in his tenderly compassionate discussion of God's love for us in the sermon on Proverbs 8:17.

His imagery and all his rhetorical resources are displayed in his marriage sermon, on Hosea 2:19. After a discourse on earthly marriage, he develops the metaphor of the marriage of the soul of man to Christ, and culminates it in a rolling surge of language as he depicts the joy and glory of the soul's ultimate union with God in Heaven, at the time of the Last Things, in part freely adapted from burning images in the 6th chapter of the Revelation of St. John the Divine:

I shall see the sun black as sackcloth of hair, and the moon become as blood, and the stars fall as a fig tree casts her untimely figs, and the heavens rolled up together as a scroll. I shall see a divorce between princes and their prerogatives, between nature and all her elements, between the spheres and all their intelligences, between matter itself and all her forms, and my marriage shall be forever.

I shall see an end of faith, nothing to be believed that I do not know; and an end of hope, nothing to be wished that I do not enjoy, but no end of that love in which I am married to the Lamb forever.

For all the savoring of such noble periods, for all the wish that we might have heard the music of the voice that uttered them, these delights of style are no more the prime purpose of this book than they were of Donne when he composed the sermons. It is a fine thing and "a good art to deliver deep points in a holy plainness, and plain points in a holy delightfulness" (Sermon on Job 16:17-19). Yet we must not suppose him to have preached chiefly for the display of skill, or chiefly to give aesthetic satisfaction to the hearers who

thronged to him. This is no liberal, permissive, comfortable sooth-
ing, but rather a firm, sometimes stern, preaching on the demands
of the Faith and the obligations that go with professing it.

In one of his discourses on the right preparation for receiving the
Sacrament (in the lovely Christmas sermon, gravely joyous, on St.
Luke 2:29, 30) Donne says of prayers and sermons:

He that brings any collateral respect to prayers loses the benefit of the
prayers of the congregation; and he that brings that to a sermon loses
the blessings of God's ordinance in that sermon; he hears but the logic,
or the rhetoric, or the ethic, or the poetry of the sermon, but the sermon
of the sermon he hears not.

We should approach the following pages with this counsel in
mind. It is for the sermons of the sermons that we owe most to
Donne.

EDMUND FULLER

London

The Showing Forth of Christ

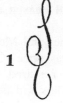

1 OF CREATION, THE TRINITY AND THE NATURE OF MAN, I

And God said, Let us make man, in our Image, after our likeness. GENESIS 1:26

NEVER SUCH A FRAME, SO SOON SET UP, AS THIS, IN this chapter. For, for the thing itself, there is no other thing to compare it with. For it is all, it is the whole world. And for the time, there was no other time to compare it with, for this was the beginning of time, "In the beginning God created Heaven and Earth." That Earth, which in some thousands of years men could not look over, nor discern what form it had (for neither Lactantius, almost three hundred years after Christ, nor St. Augustine, more than one hundred years after him, would believe the earth to be round): that earth, which no man in his person is ever said to have compassed till our age; that earth which is too much for man yet (for as yet a very great part of the earth is unpeopled), that earth which if we will cast it all but into a map costs many months' labor to grave it, nay if we will cast but a piece of an acre of it into a garden, costs many years' labor to fashion and furnish it: all that earth, and then that heaven, which spreads so far as that subtle men have, with some appearance of probability, imagined that in that heaven, in those manifold spheres of the planets and the stars, there are many earths, many worlds, as big as this which we inhabit; that earth and that heaven, which spent God himself,

1

Almighty God, six days in furnishing; Moses sets up in a few syllables, in one line, "In the beginning God created heaven and earth."

God did no more but say, let this and this be done; and Moses does no more but say that upon God's saying it was done. God required not nature to help him to do it: Moses required not reason to help him to be believed. The Holy Ghost hovered upon the waters, and so God wrought. The Holy Ghost hovered upon Moses too, and so he wrote. And we believe these things to be so, by the same Spirit in Moses' mouth, by which they were made so, in God's hand. Only, beloved, remember that a frame may be thrown down in much less time than it was set up. A child, an ape can give fire to a cannon: and a vapor can shake the earth: and these fires, and these vapors can throw down cities in minutes. When Christ said, "Throw down this temple, and in three days I will raise it," they never stopped upon the consideration of throwing it down; they knew that might be soon done; but they wondered at the speedy raising of it.

Now if all this earth were made in that minute, may not all come to the general dissolution in this minute? Or may not your acres, your miles, your shires shrink into feet, and so few feet as shall but make up your grave? When he who was a great lord must be but a cottager; and not so well; for a cottager must have so many acres to his cottage; but in this case, a little piece of an acre, five foot, is become the house itself, the house and the land; the grave is all; lower than that; the grave is the land, and the tenement, and the tenant too. He that lies in it becomes the same earth that he lies in. They all make but one earth, and but a little of it. But then raise yourself to a higher hope again. God has made better land, the land of promise; a stronger city, the new Jerusalem; and inhabitants for that everlasting city, us; whom he made not by saying, let there be men, but by consultation, by deliberation; "God said, Let us make Man in our Image, after our likeness."

Since we have the whole world in contemplation, consider in these words the four quarters of the world, by application, by fair and just accommodation of the words. In the first word that God speaks here, "Let us," in the plural (a denotation of divers Persons in one Godhead), we consider our East where we must begin at the knowledge and confession of the Trinity. For though in the way to heaven we be travelled beyond the Gentiles, when we come to confess but one God, yet we are still among the Jews if we think that one God to be but one Person. Christ's name is *Oriens,* the East; if we will be named by him (called Christians) we must look to this East, the confession of the Trinity. There's then our East, in "Let us make man."

And then our West is in the next word. Though we be thus made, made by the counsel, made by the concurrence, made by the hand of the whole Trinity; yet we are made but men: and man but in the appellation in this text: and man there is but Adam: and Adam is but earth, but red earth, earth dyed red in blood, in soul blood, the blood of our own souls. To that west we must all come, to the earth. "The sun knoweth his going down." Even the sun for all his glory and height has a going down, and he knows it. The highest cannot divest mortality, nor the discomfort of mortality. "When you see a cloud rise out of the west, straightway you say there cometh a storm," says Christ. When out of the region of your west, that is, your later days, there comes a cloud, a sickness, you feel a storm, even the best moral constancy is shaked. But this cloud, and this storm, and this west there must be.

Then the next words design a North, a strong and powerful North, to scatter and dissipate these clouds: that we are made according to a pattern, to an image, to a likeness, which God proposed to himself for the making of man. This consideration, that God did not rest in that pre-existent matter out of which he made all other creatures and produced their forms out of their matter, for the making of man; but took a form, a pattern, a model for that work. This is the North wind, that is called upon to carry out the perfumes of the garden, to spread the goodness of God abroad. This is that which is intended in Job, "Fair weather cometh out of the North." Our West, or declination, is in this, that we are but earth; our North, our dissipation of that darkness, is in this, that we are not all earth: though we be of that matter, we have another form, another image, another likeness.

And then, whose image and likeness it is, is our meridional height, our noon, our south point, our highest elevation; "Let us make man in our Image." Though our sun set at noon, as the Prophet Amos speaks; though we die in our youth, or fall in our height: yet even in that sunset we shall have a noon. For this Image of God shall never depart from our soul; no, not when that soul departs from our body. And that's our South, our meridional height and glory.

When I am gone over this East, and West, and North, and South here in this world, I should be as sorry as Alexander was, if there were no more worlds. But there is another world, which these considerations will discover and lead us to, in which our joy and our glory shall be to see that God essentially, and face to face, after whose Image and likeness we were made before. But as that pilot which had harbored his ship so far within land as that he must have change of winds, in all the points of the compass, to bring her out, cannot hope to bring her out in one day, so being to transport you, by occasion of these words, from this world to the next; and in this world through all the compass, all the four quarters thereof; I cannot hope to make all this voyage today. Today we shall consider only our longitude, our East and West; and our North and South at another tide and another gale.

First then we look towards our East, the fountain of light and of life. There this world began; the Creation was in the east. And there our next world began too. There the gates of heaven opened to us; and opened to us in the gates of death; for our heaven is the death of our Savior, and there he lived, and died there, and there he looked into our west, from the east, from his terrace, from his pinnacle, from his exaltation (as himself calls it) the cross. The light which arises to us, in this east, the knowledge which we receive in this first word of our text, "Let us" (where God speaking of himself speaks in the plural) is the manifestation of the Trinity; the Trinity, which is the first letter in his alphabet that ever thinks to read his name in the book of life; the first note in his gamut that ever thinks to sing his part in the choir of the Triumphant Church. He has not learned to spell that has not learned the Trinity; nor learned to pronounce the first word that cannot bring three Persons into one God. The subject of natural philosophy are the four elements, which God made; the subject of supernatural philosophy, divinity, are the three elements, which God is; and (if we may so speak) which make God, that is, constitute God, notify God to us, Father, Son, and Holy Ghost.

The natural man that harkens to his own heart and the law written there, may produce actions that are good, good in the nature and matter and substance of the work. He may relieve the poor, he may defend the oppressed. But yet he is but as an open field; and though he be not absolutely barren, he bears but grass. The godly man, he that has taken in the knowledge of a great and a powerful God, and enclosed and hedged in himself with the fear of God, may produce actions better than the mere natural man, because he refers his actions to the glory of his imagined God. But yet this man, though he be more fruitful than the former, more than a grassy field; yet he is but a ploughed field, and he bears but corn, and corn, God knows, choked with weeds. But that man who has taken hold of God by those handles by which God has delivered and manifested himself in the notions of Father, Son, and Holy Ghost; he is no field, but a garden, a Garden of God's planting, a Paradise in which grow all things good to eat, and good to see (spiritual refection, and spiritual recreation too), and all things good to cure. He has his being, and his diet, and his physic there, in the knowledge of the Trinity; his being in the mercy of the Father; his physic in the merits of the Son; his diet, his daily bread, in the daily visitations of the Holy Ghost.

God is not pleased, not satisfied, with our bare knowledge that there is a God. For "it is impossible to please God without faith"; and there is no such exercise of faith, in the knowledge of a God, but that reason and nature will bring a man to it. When we profess God in the Creed, by way of belief, "I believe in God," in the same article we profess him to be a Father too, "I believe in God the Father Almighty." And that notion, the Father, necessarily implies a second Person, a Son. And then we profess him to be "maker of heaven and earth." And in the Creation, the Holy Ghost, the Spirit of God, is expressly named. So that we do but exercise reason and nature in directing ourselves upon God. We exercise not faith (and "without faith it is impossible to please God") till we come to that which is above nature, till we apprehend a Trinity. We know God, we believe in the Trinity.

The Gentiles multiplied gods. There were almost as many gods as men that believed in them. And I am got out of that thrust, and out of that noise, when I am come into the knowledge of one God. But I am got above stairs, got into the bedchamber, when I am come to see the Trinity, and to apprehend not only that I am in the care of a great and a powerful God, but that there is a Father, that made me, a Son that redeemed me, a Holy Ghost that applies this good purpose of the Father and Son upon me, to me. The root of all is God. But it is not the way to receive fruits, to dig to the root, but to reach to the boughs. I reach for my Creation to the Father, for my redemption to the Son, for my sanctification to the Holy Ghost: and so I make the knowledge of God a tree of life unto me; and not otherwise.

I hope it cannot be said of any of us that he believes not the Trinity, but who amongst us thinks of the Trinity, considers the Trinity? Father and Son do naturally imply and induce one another; and therefore they fall oftener into our consideration. But for the Holy Ghost, who feels him, when he feels him? Who takes knowledge of his working, when he works? Indeed our Fathers provided not well enough for the worship of the whole Trinity, nor of the Holy Ghost in particular, in the endowments of the Church, and consecrations of Churches, and possessions in their names.

Which of us does truly and considerately ascribe the comforts that he receives in dangers, or in distresses, to that God of all comfort, the Comforter, the Holy Ghost? We know who procured us our presentation, and our dispensation: you know who procured you your offices and your honors. Shall I ever forget who gave me my comfort in sickness? Who gave me my comfort in the troubles, and perplexities, and diffidencies of my conscience? The Holy Ghost brought you hither. The Holy Ghost opens your ears and your hearts here. Till in all your distresses you can say, "Come Holy Ghost," and that you feel a comfort in his coming, you can never say, "Come Lord Jesus, come to judgment." Never to consider the day of judgment is a fearful thing. But to consider the day of judgment without the comfort of the Holy Ghost is a thousand times more fearful.

This seal then, this impression, this notion of the Trinity being set upon us, in the first Creation; this notion of the Trinity being our distinctive character from Jew and Gentile; this being our specific form: why does not this our form, this soul of our religion denominate us? Why are we not called Trinitarians, a name that would embrace the profession of all the Persons, but only Christians, which limits and determines us upon one?

Why so? Beloved, the name of Christ involved all: not only because it is a name that has a dignity in it, more than the rest (for Christ is an anointed person, a King, a Messiah, and so the profession of that name confers an unction, a regal and a holy unction upon us, for we are thereby a royal priesthood); but because in the profession of Christ, the whole Trinity is professed. How often does the Son say that the Father sent him? And how often that the Father will, and that he will send the Holy Ghost? "This is the life eternal," says he, "to know thee, the only true God, and Jesus Christ, whom thou hast sent"; and sent with all power in heaven and in earth. This must be professed, Father and Son. And then no man can profess this; no man can call Jesus the Lord, but by the Holy Ghost. So that, as in the persecutions, in the primitive Church, the martyrs which were hurried to tumultuary executions, and could not be heard for noise, in excusing themselves of treason, and sedition, and crimes imputed to them, to make their cause odious, did use in the sight of the people (who might see a gesture, though they could not hear a protestation), to sign themselves with the sign of the cross, to let them know for what profession they died, so that the sign of the cross, in that use thereof, in that time, was an abridgement and a catechism of the whole Christian religion, so is the professing of the name of Christ, the professing of the whole Trinity. As he that confesses one God is got beyond the mere natural man; and he that confesses a Son of God, beyond him: so is neither got to the full truth till he confess the Holy Ghost too. It is antichristian to deny, or not to confess, the Holy Ghost. For as Christ is the manifestation of the Father, so the Holy Ghost is the application of the Son. Therein only are we

Christians, that in the profession of that name of Christ, we profess all the three Persons. In Christ is the whole Trinity; because, as the Father sent him, so he sent the Holy Ghost. And that's our specific form, that's our distinctive character, from Jews and Gentiles, the Trinity.

So he speaks in our text; not only as the Lord our King, intimating his providence, and administration; but as the Lord our maker, and then a maker so as that he made us in a council, "Let us"; and that he speaks as in a council is another argument for reverence. For what interest or freedom soever I have, by his favor, with any counsellor of state: yet I should surely use another manner of behavior towards him at the council table than at his own table. So does there belong another manner of consideration to this plurality in God, to this meeting in council, to this intimation of a Trinity, than to those other actions in which God is presented to us, singly, as one God, for so he is presented to the natural man, as well as to us. And here enters the necessity of this knowledge: without a second birth no salvation; and no second birth without baptism; no baptism but in the name of Father, Son, and Holy Ghost.

It was the entertainment of God himself, his delight, his contemplation, for those infinite millions of generations when he was without a world, without creatures, to joy in one another, in the Trinity. It was the Father's delight to look upon himself in the Son; and to see the whole Godhead, in a threefold and an equal glory. It was God's own delight, and it must be the delight of every Christian, upon particular occasions to carry his thoughts upon the several persons of the Trinity. If I have a bar of iron, that bar in that form will not nail a door; if a sow of lead, that lead in that form will not stop a leak; if a wedge of gold, that wedge will not buy my bread. The general notion of a mighty God may less fit my particular purpose. But I coin my gold into current money when I apprehend God in the several notions of the Trinity. That if I have been a prodigal son, I have a Father in heaven, and can go to him and say, "Father, I have sinned," and be received by him. That if I be a decayed father, and need the sustentation of mine own children, there is a Son in heaven, that will do more for me than mine own (of what good means or what good nature soever they be) can or will do. If I be dejected in spirit, there is a Holy Spirit in heaven, which shall bear witness to my spirit, that I am the child of God. And if the ghosts of those sinners whom I made sinners haunt me after their deaths, in returning to my memory, and re-proaching to my conscience, the heavy judgments that I have brought upon them: if after the death of mine own sin, when my appetite is dead to some particular sin, the memory and sinful delight of past sins, the ghosts of those sins haunt me again; yet there is a Holy Ghost in heaven, that shall exorcise these, and shall overshadow me, the God of all comfort and consolation. God is the God of the whole world, in the general notion as he is God; but he is my God, most especially and most appliably, as he receives me in the several notions of Father, Son, and Holy Ghost.

This is our East, here we see God, God in all the persons, consulting, concurring to the making of us. But then my West presents itself, that is, an occasion to humble me in the next words. He makes but man; a man that is but Adam, but earth. Now God did not say of man, as of other creatures, let the earth bring forth herbs, and fruits, and trees, as upon the third day; nor let the earth bring forth cattle, and worms, as upon the sixth day, the same day that he made man. God calls not man out with an imperious command, but he leads him out with a familiar, with his own hand. And it is not "Let there be," but "Let us make man." Man is but an earthen vessel, 'tis true, but when we are upon that consider-ation, God is the potter: if God will be that, I am well content to be this: let me be anything, so that that I am be from my God. I am as well content to be a sheep as a lion, so God will be my shepherd: and the Lord is my shepherd: to be a cottage, as a castle, so God will be the builder; and the Lord builds, and watches the city, the house, this house, this city, me: to be rye, as wheat, so God will be the husbandman; and the Lord plants me, and waters, and weeds, and gives the increase: and to be clothed in leather as well as in silk, so God will be the merchant; and he clothed me in Adam, and assures me of clothing, in clothing the lilies of the field, and is fitting the robe of Christ's righteousness to me now, this minute; Adam is as good to me as a clod of earth, as a hill of earth, so God be the potter.

God made man of earth, not of air, not of fire. Man has many offices that appertain to this world, and while he is here, must not withdraw himself from those offices of mutual society, upon a pretense of zeal, or better serving God in a retired life. A ship will no more come to the harbor without ballast than without sails; a man will no more get to heaven without discharging his duties to other men, than without doing them to God himself. "Man liveth not by bread only," says Christ, but yet he lives by bread too. Every man must do the duties, every man must bear the incumbrances of some calling.

You are earth; he whom you tread upon is no less, and he that treads upon you is no more. Positively, it is a low thing to be but earth, and yet the low earth is the quiet center. There may be rest, acquiescence, content in the lowest condition. But comparatively, earth is as high as the highest. Challenge him, that magnifies himself above you, to meet you in Adam; there bid him, if he will have more nobility, more greatness, than you, take more original sin than you have. If God have submitted you to as much sin, and penalty of sin, as him, he has afforded you as much, and as noble earth as him. And if he will not try it in the root, in your equality in Adam, yet in another test, another furnace, in the grave he must. There all dusts are equal. Except an epitaph tell me who lies there, I cannot tell by the dust; nor by the epitaph know which is the dust it speaks of, if another have been laid before, or after, in the same grave. Nor can any epitaph be confident in saying, here lies; but, here was laid. For so various, so vicissitudinary is all this world, as that even the dust of the grave has revolutions. As the motions of an upper sphere imprint a motion in a lower sphere, other than naturally it would have; so the changes of this life work after death. And as envy supplants and removes us alive, a shovel removes us, and throws us out of our grave, after death. No limbeck, no weights can tell you, this is dust royal, this plebeian dust; no commission, no inquisition can say, this is Catholic, this is heretical dust. All lie alike; and all shall rise alike: alike, that is, at once, and upon one command. The Saint cannot accelerate, the reprobate cannot return the Resurrection. And all that rise to the right hand, shall be equally kings; and all at the left, equally, what? The worst name we can call them by, or affect them with, is devil;

and then they shall have bodies to be tormented in, which devils have not. Miserable, unexpressible, unimaginable, macerable condition, where the sufferer would be glad to be but a devil; where it were some happiness, and some kind of life, to be able to die; and a great preferment, to be nothing.

He made us all of earth, and all of red earth. Our earth was red, even when it was in God's hands: a redness that amounts to a shamefacedness, to a blushing at our own infirmities, is imprinted in us by God's hand. For this redness is but a conscience, a guiltiness of needing a continual supply and succession of more and more grace. And we are all red, red so, even from the beginning, and in our best state. Adam had, the Angels had thus much of this infirmity, that though they had a great measure of grace, they needed more. The prodigal child grew poor enough, after he had received his portion: and he may be wicked enough, that trusts upon former, or present grace, and seeks not more. This redness, a blushing, that is, an acknowledgment, that we could not subsist with any measure of faith except we pray for more faith, nor of grace except we seek more grace, we have from the hand of God. And another redness from his hand too, the blood of his Son, for that blood was effused by Christ, in the value of the ransom for all, and accepted by God in the value thereof for all: and this redness is, in the nature thereof, as extensive as the redness derived from Adam is; both reach to all.

So we were red earth in the hands of God, as redness denotes our general infirmities, and as redness denotes the blood of his Son, our Savior, all have both. But that redness, which we have contracted from blood shed by ourselves, the blood of our own souls, by sin, was not upon us when we were in the hands of God. That redness is not his tincture, not his complexion. No decree of his is writ in any such red ink. Our sins are our own, and our destruction is from ourselves. We are not as accessories, and God as principal in this soul murder: God forbid. We are not as executioners of God's sentence, and God the malefactor, in this soul damnation: God forbid. Cain came not red in his brother's blood out of God's hands; nor David red with Uriah's blood; nor Achitophel with his own; nor Judas with Christ's, or his own. That that

Pilate did illusorily, God can do truly; wash his hands from the blood of any of these men. It were a weak plea to say, I killed not that man; but 'tis true, I commanded one who was under my command to kill him.

God is innocency; and the beams that flow from him are of the same nature and color. Christ when he appeared in heaven, was not red but white. His head and hair were white as white wool, and as snow; not head only, but hair too. He and that that grows from him; he, and we, as we come from his hands, are white too. His Angels that provoke us to the imitation of that pattern are so, in white. Two men, two Angels stood by the Apostles in white apparel. The imitation is laid upon us by precept too: "At all times let thy garments be white"; those actions in which you appear to the world, innocent. It is true, that Christ is both. "My beloved is white and ruddy," says the Spouse. But the white was his own: his redness is from us. That which Zipporah said to her husband Moses in anger, the Church may say to Christ in thankfulness, "Thou art truly a bloody husband to me."

This was a mercy to the Militant Church, that even the Triumphant Church wondered at it. They knew not Christ, when he came up to heaven in red. "Who is this that cometh in red garments? Wherefore is thy apparel red, like him that treadeth in the winepress?" They knew he went down in white, in entire innocency: and they wondered to see him return in red. But he satisfies them; you think I have trodden the winepress, and you mistake it not: "I have trodden the winepress"; and I have trodden it alone, all the redness, all the blood of the whole world is upon me. And as he adds, of all people there was none with me, with me so as to have any part in the merit; so of all people there was none without me; without me so as to be excluded by me, without their own fault, from the benefit of my merit.

Be pleased to receive this note at parting, that there is a spot, and yet white, as well as a red spot: a whiteness, that is an indication of a leprosy, as well as a redness. It is whole Pelagianism to think nature alone sufficient; half Pelagianism to think grace once received to be sufficient; super Pelagianism to think our actions can bring God in debt to us by merit and supererogation, and

Catharism, imaginary purity, in canonizing ourselves as present Saints and condemning all that differ from us, as reprobates. All these are white spots, and have the color of goodness, but are indications of leprosy.

The good works that are done openly to please men have their reward, says Christ, that is, shall never have reward. To pretend to do good and not mean it; to do things, good in themselves, but not to good ends; to go towards good ends, but not by good ways; to make the deceiving of men your end; or the praise of men your end: all this may have a whiteness, a color of good: but all this is a barking of the bough, and an indication of a mischievous leprosy. There is no good whiteness but a reflection from Christ Jesus, in an humble acknowledgment that we have none of our own, and in a confident assurance that in our worst estate we may be made partakers of his. We are all red earth. In Adam we would not, since Adam we could not, avoid sin, and the concomitants thereof, miseries; which we have called our West, our cloud, our darkness. But then we have a North that scatters these clouds, in the next word; that we are made to another pattern, in another likeness, than our own. So far are we gone, East and West; which is half our compass, and all this day's voyage. For we are struck upon the sand; and must stay another tide, and another gale for our North and South.

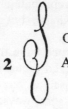

2 OF CREATION, THE TRINITY
AND THE NATURE OF MAN, II

And God said, Let us make man, in our Image, after our likeness. GENESIS 1:26

IN THIS POINT, THE NORTH, WE PLACE OUR FIRST comfort. The North is not always the comfortablest clime: nor is the North always a type of happiness in the Scriptures. Many times God threatens storms from the North. But even in those Northern storms, we consider that action, that they scatter, they dissipate those clouds that were gathered, and so induce a serenity. And so, fair weather comes from the North. And that's the use which we have of the North in this place. The consideration of our West, our low estate; that we are but earth, but red earth, dyed red by ourselves: and that imaginary white, which appears so to us, is but a white of leprosy: this West enwraps us in heavy clouds of murmuring, in this life, that we cannot live so freely as beasts do; and in clouds of desperation for the next life, that we cannot die so absolutely as beasts do; we die all our lives, and yet we live after our deaths. These are our clouds; and then the North shakes these clouds.

"The North wind driveth away the rain," says Solomon. There is a North in our text, that drives all those tears from our eyes. Christ calls upon the North, as well as the South, to blow upon his Garden, and to diffuse the perfumes thereof. Adversity, as well as

14

prosperity, opens the bounty of God unto us; and oftentimes better. But that's not the benefit of the North in our present consideration. But this is it, that first our sun sets in the West. The Eastern dignity, which we received in our first Creation, as we were the work of the whole Trinity, falls under a Western cloud, that that Trinity made us but earth. And then blows our North, and scatters this cloud; that this earth has a nobler form than any other part or limb of the world. For we are made by a fairer pattern, by a nobler Image, by a higher likeness. Though we make but a man, "Let us make him in our Image, after our likeness."

The variety which the Holy Ghost uses here, in the pen of Moses, has given occasion to divers, to raise divers observations upon these words, which seem divers, "Image" and "likeness," as also in the variety of the phrase. For it is thus conceived, and laid, "in our Image," and then "after our likeness." I know it is a good rule that Damascen gives, "Nothing is to be neglected as little, from which great things may arise." If the consequence may be great, the thing must not be thought little. When our Savior said that we shall give an account of every idle word in the day of judgment; what great hills of little sands will oppress us then? And if substances of sin were removed, yet what circumstances of sin would condemn us? If idle words have this weight, there can be no word thought idle in the Scriptures. And therefore I blame not in any, I decline not in mine own practice, the making use of the variety and copiousness of the Holy Ghost, who is ever abundant, and yet never superfluous in expressing his purpose in change of words. And so no doubt we might do now, in observing a difference between these words in our text, Image, and likeness; and between these two forms of expressing it, "in our Image," and "after our likeness." This might be done: but that that must be done, will possess all our time; that is, to declare (taking the two words for this time to be but a farther illustration of one another, Image and likeness, to our present purpose, to be all one) what this Image and this likeness imports; and how this North scatters our former cloud; what our advantage is, that we are made to an Image, to a pattern; and our obligation to set a pattern before us, in all our actions.

God appointed Moses to make all that he made according to a pattern. God himself made all that he made according to a pattern. God had deposited and laid up in himself certain forms, patterns, ideas of everything that he made. He made nothing of which he had not preconceived the form, and predetermined in himself, I will make it thus. And when he had made any thing, he saw it was good; good because it answered the pattern, the Image; good, because it was like to that. And therefore, though of other creatures, God pronounced they were good, because they were presently like their pattern, that is, like that form which was in him for them, yet of man he forbore to say that he was good; because his conformity to his pattern was to appear after in his subsequent actions.

Now as God made man after another pattern, and therefore we have a dignity above all, that we had another manner of creation than the rest: so have we comfort above all, that we have another manner of providence upon man than upon other creatures. "A sparrow falls not without God," says Christ: yet no doubt God works otherwise in the fall of eminent persons than in the fall of sparrows. "For ye are of more value than many sparrows," says Christ there of every man; and some men single, are of more value than many men. God does not thank the ant for her industry and good-husbandry in providing for herself. God does not reward the foxes for concurring with Samson in his revenge. God does not fee the lion which was the executioner upon the prophet which had disobeyed his commandment: nor those two she-bears which slew the petulant children who had calumniated and reproached Elisha. God does not fee them before, nor thank them after, nor take knowledge of their service.

But for those men that served God's execution upon the idolaters of the golden calf, it is pronounced in their behalf that therein they consecrated themselves to God; and for that service God made that tribe, the tribe of Levi, his portion, his clergy, his consecrated tribe. So, says God to Abraham, "By myself I have sworn; because thou hast done this thing, and hast not withheld thy son, thine only son: that in blessing, I will bless thee; and in multiplying, I will multiply thee." So neither is God angry with the dog that turns to his vomit, nor with the sow, that after her wash-

ing wallows in the mire. But of man in that case, he says, "It is
impossible for those who were once enlightened, if they fall away,
to renew them again by repentance." The creatures live under his
law; but a law imposed thus, this they shall do, this they must do.
Man lives under another manner of law; this you shall do; that is,
this you should do, this I would have you do; and do this, and you
shall live; disobey, and you shall die. But yet, the choice is yours:
choose you this day life or death. So that this is God's administration in the creature, that he has imprinted in them an instinct, and
so he has something to preserve in them. In man his administration
is this, that he has imprinted in him a faculty of will, and election;
and so has something to reward in him.

That instinct in the creature God leaves to the natural working
thereof in itself. But the free will of man God visits, and assists
with his grace to do supernatural things. When the creature does
an extraordinary action above the nature thereof (as when Balaam's Ass spake), the creature exercises no faculty, no will in
itself; but God forced it to that it did. When man does anything
conducing to supernatural ends, though the work be God's, the will
of man is not merely passive. The will of man is but God's agent;
but still an agent it is: and an agent in another manner than the
tongue of the beast. For the will considered, as a will (and grace
never destroys nature, nor though it make a dead will a live will, or
an ill will a good will, does it make the will, no will), might refuse
or omit that that it does. So that because we are created by another
pattern, we are governed by another law, and another providence.

Go you then the same way. If God wrought by a pattern, and
writ by a copy, and proceeded by a precedent, do you so too.
Never say, there is no Church without error: therefore I will be
bound by none; but frame a Church of mine own, or be a Church
to myself. What greater injustice, than to propose no Image, no
pattern to yourself to imitate; and yet propose yourself for a pattern, for an Image to be adored? You will have singular opinions,
and singular ways differing from all other men; and yet all that are
not of your opinion must be heretics; and all reprobates that go not
your ways. Propose good patterns to yourself; and thereby become
a fit pattern for others. God we see was the first that made Images;

and he was the first that forbade them. He made them for imitation; he forbade them in danger of adoration. For what a drowsiness, what a laziness, what a cowardliness of the soul is it to worship that which does but represent a better thing than itself? Worship belongs to the best; know your distance, and how far to go, and where to stop.

Dishonor not God by an Image in worshiping it; and yet benefit yourself by it, in following it. There is no more danger out of a picture than out of a history, if you intend no more in either than example. Though you have a West, a dark and a sad condition, that you are but earth, a man of infirmities, and ill counselled in yourself: yet you have herein a North, that scatters and dispels these clouds, that God proposes to you in his Scriptures and otherwise, Images, patterns of good and holy men to go by. But beyond this North, this assistance of good examples of men, you have a South, a meridional height, by which you see your Image, your pattern, to be no copy; no other man, but the original itself, God himself: "Let us make man in our Image, after our likeness."

Here we consider first where this Image is, and then what it does: first, in what part of man God has imprinted this his Image; and then what this Image confers and derives upon man; what it works in man. And as when we seek God in his essence we are advised to proceed by negatives, God is not mortal, not passible: so when we seek the Image of God in man, we begin with a negative; this Image is not in his body.

Nor that way neither, which some have assigned, that God, who has no body as God, yet in the creation did assume that form which man has now, and so made man in his Image, that is, in that form which he had then assumed. The Image of God is not in man's body this way. Nor that third way, which others have imagined; that is, that when God said, "Let us make man after our likeness," God had respect to that form which in the fullness of time his Son was to take upon him, upon earth. Let us make him now (says God at first) like that which I intend hereafter my Son shall be. For though this were spoken before the fall of man, and so before any occasion of decreeing the sending of Christ: yet in the school a great part of great men adhered to that opinion that

God from all eternity had a purpose that his Son should become man in this world, though Adam had not fallen. Though Christ had not come as a redeemer, if man had not needed him by sin, but had kept his first state; yet as a prince that desired to heap honor upon him whom he loves, to do man an honor, by his assuming that nature, Christ, say they, should have come, and to that Image, that form, which he was to take then was man made in his text, say these imaginers.

But alas, how much better were wit and learning bestowed to prove to the Gentiles that a Christ must come (that they believe not); to prove to the Jews that the Christ is come (that they believe not); to prove to our own consciences that the same Christ may come again this minute to judgment (we live as though we believed not that), than to have filled the world, and torn the Church, with frivolous disputations whether Christ should have come if Adam had not fallen? Woe unto fomenters of frivolous disputations. None of these ways, not because God has a body; not because God assumed a body, not because it was intended that Christ should be born, before it was intended that man should be made, is the Image of God in the body of man. Nor has it in any other relation, respect to the body, but as we say in the school, that because God has given man a body of a nobler form than any other creature; we infer, and argue, and conclude from thence, that God is otherwise represented in man than in any other creature.

So far is this Image of God in the body above that in the creatures, that as you see some pictures, to which the very tables are jewels; some watches, to which the very cases are jewels, and therefore they have outward cases too; and so the picture and the watch is in that outward case, of what meaner stuff soever that be: so is the Image in this body as in an outward case; so as that you may not injure, nor enfeeble this body, neither by sinful intemperance and licentiousness, nor by inordinate fastings or other disciplines of imaginary merits, while the body is alive; for the Image of God is in it: nor defraud your body of decent burial, and due solemnities after death; for the Image of God is to return to it. But yet the body is but the out-case, and God looks not for the gilding, or enamelling, or painting of that; but requires the labor and cost therein to be bestowed upon the table itself, in which this Image is immediately, that is the soul. And that's truly the place where this Image is. And there remains only now the operation thereof, how this Image of God in the soul of man works.

The sphere then of this intelligence, the gallery for this picture, the arch for this statue, the table and frame and shrine for this Image of God is inwardly and immediately the soul of man. Not immediately so, as that the soul of man is a part of the essence of God; for so essentially, Christ only is the Image of God. But this Image is in our soul, as our soul is the wax, and this Image the seal. The comparison is St. Cyril's, and he adds well, that no seal but that which printed the wax at first can fit that wax and fill that impression after. No Image, but the Image of God can fit our soul. Every other seal is too narrow, too shallow for it. The magistrate is sealed with the lion; the wolf will not fit that seal: the magistrate has a power in his hands, but not oppression. Princes are sealed with the crown; the miter will not fit that seal. Powerfully and graciously they protect the Church, and are supreme heads of the Church; but they minister not the Sacraments of the Church. They give preferments; but they give not the capacity of preferment. They give order who shall have; but they give not orders, by which they are enabled to have, that have.

Men of inferior and laborious callings in the world are sealed with the cross; a rose, or a bunch of grapes will not answer that seal. We should wonder to see a mother in the midst of many sweet children passing her time in making babies and puppets for her own delight. We should wonder to see a man whose chambers and galleries were full of curious masterpieces, thrust in a village fair to look upon sixpenny pictures and three-farthing prints.

We have all the Image of God at home, and we all make babies, fancies of honor, in our ambitions. The masterpiece is our own, in our own bosom; and we thrust in country fairs, that is, we endure the distempers of any unseasonable weather, in night journeys and watchings: we endure the oppositions and scorns and triumphs of a rival and competitor, that seeks with us and shares with us: we endure the guiltiness and reproach of having deceived the trust which a confident friend reposes in us, and solicit his wife, or daughter: we endure the decay of fortune, of body, of soul, of honor, to possess lower pictures; pictures that are not originals, not made by that hand of God, nature, but artificial beauties. And for that body, we give a soul, and for that drug, which might have been bought, where they bought it, for a shilling, we give an estate. The Image of God is more worth than all substances; and we give it for colors, for dreams, for shadows.

But the better to prevent the loss, let us consider the having of this Image: in what respect, in what operation, this Image is in our soul. For whether this Image be in those faculties which we have in nature; or in those qualifications which we may have in grace; or in those super-illustrations, which the blessed shall have in glory; has exercised the contemplation of many. Properly this Image is in nature; in the natural reason and other faculties of the immortal soul of man. For thereupon does St. Bernard say, "Till the soul be burnt to ashes, to nothing" (which cannot be done, no not in Hell) "the Image of God cannot be burnt out of that soul." For it is radically, primarily, in the very soul itself. And whether that soul be infused into the elect, or into the reprobate, that Image is in that soul, and as far as he has a soul by nature, he has the Image of God by nature in it. But then the seal is deeper cut, or harder pressed, or better preserved in some than in others; and in some other considerations than merely natural.

Therefore we may consider man who was made here to the Image of God; and of God in three Persons, to have been made so in God's intendment, three ways. Man had this Image in nature, and does deface it; he has it also in grace here, and so does refresh it; and he shall have it in glory hereafter, and that shall fix it, establish it. And in every of these three, in the Trinity in man, nature, grace, and glory, man has not only the Image of God, but the Image of the Holy Ghost in nature; and all these also in grace; capacities. He has the Image of the Father, the Image of the Son, the Image of the Holy Ghost in nature; and all these also in grace; and all in glory too. How all these are in all, I cannot hope to handle particularly; not though I were upon the first grain of our sand, upon the first dram of your patience, upon the first flash of my strength. But a clear repeating of these many branches, that

these things are thus, that all the Persons of the heavenly Trinity
are (in their Image) in every branch of this human Trinity, in
man, may, at least must, suffice.

In nature then, man, that is, the soul of man has the Image of
God, of God considered in his unity, entirely, altogether, in this,
that this soul is made of nothing, proceeds of nothing. All other
creatures are made of that pre-existent matter, which God had
made before, so were our bodies too; but our souls of nothing.
Now, not to be made at all is to be God himself; only God himself
was never made. But to be made of nothing, to have no other
parent but God, no other element but the breath of God, no other
instrument but the purpose of God, this is to be the Image of God.
For this is nearest to God himself, who was never made at all, to
be made of nothing. And then man (considered in nature) is
otherwise the nearest representation of God too. For the steps
which we consider are four. First, being; for some things have only
a being, and no life, as stones. Secondly, living; for some things
have life, and no sense, as plants. And then, thirdly, sense; for
some things have sense, and no understanding. Which understanding and reason, man has with his being, and life, and sense;
and so is in a nearer station to God than any other creature, and
a livelier Image of him who is the root of being, than all they,
because man only has all the declarations of beings. Nay if we
consider God's eternity, the soul of man has such an Image of that,
as that though man had a beginning, which the original, the eternal
God himself had not; yet man shall no more have an end than the
original, the eternal God himself shall have.

He has this Image as God is considered in his unity (for as God
is, so the soul of man is, indivisibly one, entire), and he has it also
as God is notified to us in a Trinity. For as there are three Persons
in the essence of God: so there are three faculties in the soul of
man. The attributes, and some kind of specification of the Persons
of the Trinity are, power to the Father, wisdom to the Son, and
goodness to the Holy Ghost. And the three faculties of the soul
have the Images of these three. The understanding is the Image of
the Father, that is, power. For no man can exercise power, no man
can govern well without understanding the natures and dispositions
of them whom he governs. And therefore in this consists the

power, which man has over the creature, that man understands the nature of every creature, for so Adam did, when he named every creature according to the nature thereof. And by this advantage of our understanding them, and comprehending them, we master them, and so says St. Ambrose, the lion, the bear, the elephant have forgot what they were born to. They invest and put on such a disposition, and such a nature, as we enjoin them, and appoint to them. They wait upon us as servants; who, if they understood us as well as we understand them, might be our masters: and they receive correction from us, as though they were afraid of us; when, if they understood us, they would know that we were not able to stand in the teeth of the lion, in the horn of the bull, in the heels of the horse. And they counterfeit a weakness, that they might be beholden to us for help: and they are content to thank us if we afford them any rest, or any food; who, if they understood us as well as we do them, might tear our meat out of our throats; nay tear out our throats for their meat.

So then in this first natural faculty of the soul, the understanding, stands the Image of the first Person, the Father, power: and in the second faculty which is the will, is the Image, the attribute of the second Person, the Son, which is wisdom: for wisdom is not so much in knowing, in understanding, as in electing, in choosing, in assenting. No man needs go out of himself, nor beyond his own legend, and the history of his own actions for examples of that, that many times we know better, and choose ill ways. Wisdom is in choosing, in assenting. And then, in the third faculty of the soul, the memory, is the Image of the third Person, the Holy Ghost, that is, goodness. For to remember, to recollect our former understanding and our former assenting, so far as to do them, to crown them with action, that's true goodness. The office that Christ assigns to the Holy Ghost, and the goodness which he promises in his behalf is this, that he shall bring former things to our remembrance. The Wiseman places all goodness in this faculty, the memory: properly nothing can fall into the memory but that which is past, and yet he says, "Whatsoever thou takest in hand, remember the end, and thou shalt never do amiss." The end cannot be yet come, and yet we are bid to remember that.

Certainly, beloved, if a man were like the king but in countenance and in proportion, he himself would think somewhat better of himself, and others would be the less apt to put scorns or injuries upon him than if he had a vulgar and coarse aspect. With those who have the Image of the king's power (the magistrate), the Image of his wisdom (the council), the Image of his goodness (the clergy), it should be so too. There is a respect due to the Image of the king in all that have it. Now in all these respects man, the mere natural man, has the Image of the King of Kings. And therefore respect that Image in yourself, and exalt your natural faculties. Emulate those men, and be ashamed to be outgone by those men, who had no light but nature. Make your understanding, and your will, and your memory (though but natural faculties) serviceable to your God; and auxiliary and subsidiary for your salvation. For though they be not naturally instruments of grace; yet naturally they are susceptible of grace, and have so much in their nature as that by grace they may be made instruments of grace; which no faculty in any creature but man can be. And do not think that because a natural man cannot do all, therefore he has nothing to do for himself.

This then is the Image of God in man, the first way, in nature; and most literally this is the intention of the text. Man was the Image thus; and the room furnished with this Image was Paradise. But there is a better room than that Paradise for the second Image (the Image of God in man by grace), that is the Christian Church. For though the most part this text be understood of our natural faculties; yet Origen, and not only such allegorical expositors, but St. Basil, and Nyssen, and Ambrose, and others, who are literal enough, assign this Image of God to consist in the gifts of God's grace exhibited to us here in the Church. A Christian then in that second capacity as a Christian and not only as a man, has this Image of God; of God first considered entirely. And those expressions of this impression, those representations of this Image of God, in a Christian by grace, which the Apostles have exhibited to us; that we are "the sons of God; the seed of God; the offspring of God; and partakers of the divine nature," are high and glorious exaltations.

And whereas the humiliation of my Savior is in all things to be

imitated by me; yet herein am I bound to depart from his humiliation; that whereas he being in the form of God, took the form of a
servant; I being in the form of a servant may, nay must take upon
the form of God, in being a man made in Christ, the Image of
God. So have I the Image of God entirely, in his unity, because I
profess that faith, which is but one faith; and under the seal of that
baptism, which is but one baptism. And then, as of this one God,
so I have also the Image of the several persons of the Trinity, in
this capacity, as I am a Christian, more than in my natural faculties.

The attribute of the first Person, the Father, is power, and none
but a Christian has power over those great tyrants of the world,
sin, Satan, death, and Hell. For thus my power accrues and grows
unto me. First, I have a power to judge; a judiciary, a discretive
power; a power to discern between a natural accident and a judgment of God, and will never call a judgment an accident; and
between an ordinary occasion of conversation and a temptation of
Satan. When I find it to be a temptation, I am able to resist it: I
am able, not only to withstand, but to stand out this battle of
temptations to the end. And then, that which Christ proposes for a
trial of his Disciples, "Let him that is able to receive it, receive it,"
I shall have power or receive the gift of continency against all
temptations of that kind. Bring it to the highest act of power, that
with which Christ tried his strongest Apostles, I shall be able to
drink of Christ's cup; even to drink his blood, and be the more
innocent for that, and to pour out my blood and be the stronger for
that. There's the fulness of power, in Christ I can do all things, I
can want, or I can abound, I can live, or I can die. And yet there is
an extension of power beyond all this, in this, being born of God in
Christ, I cannot sin. This that seems to have a name of impotence,
I cannot, is the fullest omnipotence of all, I cannot sin; not sin to
death; not sin with a desire to sin; not sin with a delight in sin; but
that temptation that overthrows another, I can resist, or that sin
which being done, casts another into desperation, I can repent.
And so I have the Image of the first Person, the Father, in power.

The Image of the second Person, whose attribute is wisdom, I
have in this, that wisdom being the knowledge of this world and

the next, I embrace nothing in this world but as it leads me to the next. For thus my wisdom, my knowledge grows. First, I know whom I have believed in: I have not mislaid my foundation; my foundation is Christ; and then my foundation cannot sink, I know that "Christ being raised from the dead, dies no more"; again, I know what my spirit, enlightened by the Spirit of God, desires; I am not transported with illusions and singularities of private spirits. And as in the attribute of power, we found an omnipotence in a Christian, so in this, there is an omniscience, "We know that we have all knowledge," for all St. Paul's universal knowledge was but this, "I determined not to know any thing, save Jesus Christ, and him crucified." And then, the way by which he would proceed, and take degrees in this wisdom, was the way that God had ordained when the world by wisdom knew not God, it pleased God by the foolishness of preaching to save them that believe. These then are the steps of Christian wisdom, my foundation is Christ, of Christ I enquire no more but fundamental doctrines, him crucified, and this I apply to myself, by his ordinance of preaching. And in this wisdom, I have the image of the second Person.

And then of the third also in this, that his attribute being goodness, I, as a true Christian, call nothing good that conduces not to the glory of God in Christ Jesus, nor anything ill that draws me not from him. Thus I have an express Image of his goodness, that all things work together for my good, if I love God. I shall thank my fever, bless my poverty, praise my oppressor, nay thank, and bless, and praise, even some sin of mine which by the consequences of that sin, which may be shame, or loss, or weakness, may bring me to a happy sense of all my former sins; and shall find it to have been a good fever, a good poverty, a good oppression, yea a good sin. "You thought evil," says Joseph to his brethren, "but God meant it unto good"; and I shall have the benefit of my sin, according to his transmutation, that is, though I meant ill in that sin, I shall have the good that God meant in it. And so as in nature I have the Image of God, in my whole soul, and of all the three Persons, in the three faculties thereof, the understanding, the will, and the memory, so in grace, in the Christian Church, I have the same Images of the power of the Father, of the wisdom of the Son, of the goodness of the Holy Ghost, in my Christian profession. And all this we shall have in a better place than Paradise, where we considered it in nature, and a better place than the Church, as it is Militant, where we considered it in grace, that is, in the kingdom of heaven, where we consider this Image in glory; which is our last word.

There we shall have this Image of God in perfection; for, if Origen could lodge such a conceit, that in heaven, at last, all things should ebb back into God, as all things flowed from him, at first, and so there should be no other essence but God, all should be God, even the Devil himself; how much more may we conceive an unexpressible association (that's too far off), an assimilation (that's not near enough), an identification (the school would venture to say so), with God in that state of glory. Where, as the sun by shining upon the moon, makes the moon a planet, a star, as well as itself, which otherwise would be but the thickest and darkest part of that sphere, so those beams of glory which shall issue from my God and fall upon me, shall make me (otherwise a clod of earth, and worse, a dark soul, a spirit of darkness), an Angel of light, a star of glory, a something that I cannot name now, not imagine now, nor tomorrow, nor next year, but, even in that particular, I shall be like God, that as he, that asked a day to give a definition of God, the next day asked a week, and then a month, and then a year, so undeterminable would my imaginations be, if I should go about to think now, what I shall be there. I shall be so like God, as that the Devil himself shall not know me from God, so far as to find any more place to fasten a temptation upon me, than upon God; nor to conceive any more hope of my falling from that kingdom than of God's being driven out of it; for, though I shall not be immortal, as God, yet I shall be as immortal as God. And there's my Image of God; of God considered altogether, and in his unity, in the state of glory.

I shall have also then, the Image of all the three Persons of the Trinity. Power is the Father's; and a greater power than he exercises here, I shall have there: here he overcomes enemies; but yet here he has enemies; there, there are none; here they cannot prevail, there they shall not be. So wisdom is the Image of the Son;

and there I shall have better wisdom than spiritual wisdom itself is here: for here our best wisdom is but to go towards our end, there it is to rest in our end; here it is to seek to be glorified by God, there it is that God may be everlastingly glorified by me. The Image of the Holy Ghost is goodness, here our goodness is mixed with some ill; faith mixed with scruples and good works mixed with a love of praise, and hope of better, mixed with fear of worse. There I shall have sincere goodness, and indeterminate goodness; so good a place as no ill accident shall annoy it; so good company, as no impertinent, no importune person shall disorder it; so full a goodness, as no evil of sin, no evil of punishment for former sins, can enter; so good a God, as shall no more keep us in fear of his anger, nor in need of his mercy, but shall fill us first, and establish us in that fulness in the same instant; and give us a satiety, that we can wish no more, and an infallibility, that we can lose none of that, and both at once.

The holy nobleness and the religious ambition that I would imprint in you, for attaining of this glory, makes me dismiss you with this note, for the fear of missing that glory; that as we have taken just occasion to magnify the goodness of God towards us, in that he speaks plurally, and so pours out the blessings of the whole Trinity upon us, in this Image of himself, in every Person of the three, and in all these three ways which we have considered: so when the anger of God is justly kindled against us, God collects himself, and threatens plurally too. So that God carries himself so equally herein, as that no soul, no Church, no state, may any more promise itself patience in God, if it provoke him, than suspect anger in God, if we conform ourselves to him. For from them that set themselves against him, God shall withdraw his Image, in all the Persons, and all the attributes. The Father shall withdraw his power, and we shall be enfeebled in our forces, the Son his wisdom, and we shall be infatuated in our counsels, the Holy Ghost his goodness, and we shall be corrupted in our manners, and corrupted in our religion, and be a prey to temporal and spiritual enemies, and change the Image of God into the Image of the beast. And as God loves nothing more than the Image of himself, in his Son, and then the Image of his Son Christ Jesus, in us, so he hates nothing more than the Image of Antichrist, in them in whom he had imprinted his Son's Image, that is, declinations towards Antichrist, or concurrencies with Antichrist in them who were born, and baptized, and catechised, and blessed in that profession of his truth.

That God who has hitherto delivered us from all cause or color of jealousies, or suspicions thereof, in them whom he has placed over us, so conform us to his Image, in a holy life, that sins continued and multiplied by us against him do not so provoke him against us, that those two great helps, the assiduity of preaching, and the personal and exemplary piety and constancy in our princes, be not by our sins made unprofitable to us. For that's the height of God's malediction upon a nation, when the assiduity of preaching, and the example of a religious prince, does them no good, but aggravates their fault.

ON THE MYSTERY OF THE TRINITY AND WHAT WE MAY KNOW OF THE GODHEAD; A WHITSUNDAY SERMON

3

At that day shall ye know, that I am in the Father, and you in me, and I in you.

JOHN 14:20

THE TWO VOLUMES OF THE SCRIPTURES ARE JUSTLY and properly called two Testaments, for they are the attestation, the declaration of the will and pleasure of God, how it pleased him to be served under the Law, and how in the state of the Gospel. But to speak according to the ordinary acceptation of the word, the Testament, that is, the last Will of Christ Jesus is this speech, this declaration of his to his Apostles, of which this text is a part. For it was spoken as at his deathbed, his last supper. And it was before his agony in the garden, so that (if we should consider him a mere man) there was no inordinateness, no irregularity in his affections. It was testified with sufficient witnesses, and it was sealed in blood in the institution of the Sacrament. By this Will then, as a rich and abundant and liberal testator, having given them so great a legacy as "a place in the kingdom of heaven," yet he adds a codicil, he gives more, he gives them the evidence by which they should maintain their right to that kingdom, that is, the testimony of the Spirit, the Comforter, the Holy Ghost, whom he promises to send to them. And still more and more abundant, he promises them that that assurance of their right shall not be taken from them till he himself return again to give them an everlasting possession, "That he may receive us unto himself, and that where he is, we may also be." The main legacy, the body of the gift is before. That which is given in this text is part of that evidence by which it appears to us that we have right, and by which that right is maintained, and that is knowledge, that knowledge which we have of our interest in God and his kingdom here: "At that day ye shall know, etc."

And in the giving of this we shall consider first the legacy itself, this knowledge, "Ye shall know." And secondly the time when this legacy grows due to us, "At that day ye shall know." And thirdly how much of this treasure is devised to us, what portion of this heavenly knowledge is bequeathed to us, and that is in three great sums, in three great mysteries. First ye shall know the mystery of the Trinity, of distinct persons in the Godhead: "that I am in my Father." And then the mystery of the Incarnation of God, who took our flesh, "that you are in me." And lastly, the mystery and working of our redemption in our sanctification, that Christ (by his Spirit, the Holy Ghost) is in us.

The iniquity of the soul, says Trismegistus—he does not say it is the infirmity of the soul, or the impotency of the soul, but the iniquity—the wickedness of the soul consists in this, that we are ignorant of those ways and those ends upon which we should direct and by which we should govern our purposes. And if ignorance be the corruption and dissolution, certainly knowledge is the redintegration and consolidation of the soul. From this corruption, from this ignorance God delivered his people at first, in some measure, by the Law; that is, he gave them thereby a way to get out of this ignorance; he put them to school. "The Law was their schoolmaster," says the Apostle. But in the state of the Gospel, in the shedding of the beams, of the streams of his grace in the blood of Christ Jesus we are graduates and have proceeded so far as to a manifestation of things already done, and so our faith is brought in a great part to consist in matter of fact, and that which was but a matter of prophecy to them (in the Old Testament they knew not when it should be done) to us in the New is matter of history, and we know when it was done.

In the old times God led his people sometimes with clouds,

sometimes with fire; some lights they had, but some hidings, some withdrawings of those lights too; the mysteries of their salvation were not fully revealed unto them. To us, all is holy fire, all is evident light, all is in the Epiphany, in the manifestation of Christ, and in the presence of the Holy Ghost, who is delivered over to us to remain with us, till the end of the world. God has buried and hidden from us the body of Moses; he has removed that cloud, that veil, the ceremony, the letter of the Law. Yes, he has hidden that which benighted us more and kept us in more ignorance of him, our infinite sins, which are clouds of witnesses to our consciences, he has hidden them in the wounds of his Son our Savior, so that there remains nothing but clearness, evident clearness. The Gospel being brought to us all, in that Christ is actually and really come, and Christ being brought to me, in that he is appliable in the Church to every particular soul; so this legacy that is given in this text is not only in a possibility, and in a probability, and in a verisimilitude, but in an assurance, and in an infallibility, in a knowledge, we know it thus and thus.

We shall therefore consider this knowledge first as it is opposed to ignorance, secondly as it is opposed to inconsideration, and thirdly as it is opposed to concealing, to smothering. First we must have it, and then we must know that we have it, and after that we must publish it and declare it, so that others may know that we know it. Now as there is a profitable, a wholesome, a learned ignorance, which is a modest and a reverent abstinence from searching into those secrets which God has not revealed in his word (whereupon St. Augustine says usefully, "Let not us desire to know that which God has no will to reveal"), so also there is an unprofitable, an infectious, indeed an ignorant knowledge, which puffs and swells us up; that of which the prophet says, every man's knowledge makes him a fool when it makes him undervalue and despise another. And this is one strange and incurable effect of this opinion of wit and knowledge, that whereas every man murmurs and says to himself, such a man has more land than I, more money than I, more custom, more practice than I (when perchance in truth it is not so), yet every man thinks that he has more wit, more knowledge than all the world beside, when God knows it is very far from being so.

When the prophet in that place calls this confident believer in his own wisdom, fool, he has therein fastened upon him a name of the greatest reproach to man, which the Holy Ghost, in the mouth of a prophet, could choose; as it appears best in those gradations which Christ makes where, "Whosoever is angry, is made culpable of judgment, whosoever says Racha" (that is, expresses his anger in any contumelious speech), "is subject to a council, but whosoever shall say, fool, shall be worthy to be punished in hell fire." For by calling him fool, says St. Chrysostom, he takes from him that understanding by which he is a man and so, says he, despoils him of all interest in the creature in this life, and all interest in God in the life to come. It is the deepest indignation, the highest abomination that Job in his anguish conceived, "They that are but fools themselves, despised me." And after that again, "They are the children of fools, and yet I am their song and their talk." And in that comparison which God himself instituted and proposed in Deuteronomy, "They have moved me to jealousy, with that which is not God, and I will move them to jealousy with those who are no people, I will provoke them to anger with a foolish nation," God intimates so much, that a fool is no more a man than an idol is a God.

Now this foolishness which we speak of, against which God gives us this legacy of knowledge, is not that bluntness, that dullness, that narrowness of understanding which is opposed to sharpness of wit, or readiness of expressing and delivering any matter, for very many very devout and godly men lack that sharpness and that readiness, and yet have a good portion of spiritual wisdom and knowledge. Neither is this foolishness that weakness or inability to amass and gather together particulars, as they have fallen out in former times and in our times, and thereby to judge of future occurrences by former precedents (which is the wisdom of statesmen, and of civil contemplation, to build up a body of knowledge from reading stories or observing actions), for this wisdom Solomon calls vanity and vexation. Nor is this foolishness that precipitation, that overearnestness, that animosity, that heat which some men have, and which is opposed to discretion; for sometimes zeal itself has such a heat and such a precipitation in it, and yet that zeal may not be absolutely condemned, but may be sometimes of some use. The dull man, the weak man, the hasty man is not this fool but (as the Wiseman who knew best has told us), "The fool is he that trusteth in his own heart." And therefore against this foolishness of trusting in our own hearts, of confiding and relying upon our own plots and devices, and from sacrificing to our own nets (as the Prophet Habakkuk speaks), from this attributing of all to our own industry, from this ignorance that all blessings, spiritual and temporal too, proceed from God, and from God only, and from God manifested in Christ, and from Christ explicated in the Scriptures, and from the Scriptures applied in the Church (which is the sum of all religion), God has given us this legacy of knowledge, "At that day ye shall know," as knowledge is opposed to ignorance.

As it is opposed to inconsideration, it is a great work that it does too. For as God has made himself like man in many things, in taking upon him, in Scriptures, our lineaments and proportion, our affections and passions, our apparel and garments, so has God made himself like man in this also, that as man does, so he also takes it worse to be neglected than to be really injured. Some of our sins do not offend God so much as our inconsideration, a stupid passing him over, as though that we did, that which we had, that which we were, appertained not to him, had no emanation from him, no dependence upon him. As God says in the prophet of lame, blemished and unperfect sacrifices, "Offer it unto any of your princes, and see if they will accept it at your hands"; so I say to them that pass their lives thus inconsiderately, offer that to any of your princes, any of your superiors. Dares an officer that receives instructions from his prince, when he leaves his commandments unperformed, say, I never thought of it? Dares a subject, a servant, a son say so?

Now beloved, this knowledge, as it is opposed to inconsideration, is in this, that God by breeding us in the visible Church, multiplies unto us so many helps and assistances in the word preached, in the Sacraments, in other sacramental and ritual and ceremonial things which are auxiliary, subsidiary reliefs and refreshings to our consideration, as that it is almost impossible to fall into this inconsideration. Here God shows this inconsiderate man

his book of creatures, which he may run and read; that is, he may
go forward in his vocation and yet see that every creature calls him
to a consideration of God. Every ant that he sees asks him, Where
had I this providence and industry? Every flower that he sees asks
him, Where had I this beauty, this fragrancy, this medicinal virtue
in me? Every creature calls him to consider what great things God
has done in little subjects. But God opens to him also, here in his
Church, his book of Scriptures, and in that book every word cries
out to him, every merciful promise cries to him, Why am I here to
meet you, to wait upon you, to perform God's purpose towards
you, if you never consider me, never apply me to yourself? Every
judgment of his anger cries out, Why am I here if you respect me
not, if you make not your profit of performing those conditions
which are annexed to those judgments and which you might perform if you would consider it?

Yes, here God opens another book to him, his manual, his
bosom, his pocketbook, the abridgement of all nature and all law,
his own heart and conscience. And this book, though he shut it up,
and clasp it never so hard, yet it will sometimes burst open of
itself. Though he interline it with other studies and knowledges, yet
the text itself, in the book itself, the testimonies of the conscience,
will shine through and appear. Though he load it, and choke it
with commentaries and questions, that is perplex it with circumstances and disputations, yet the matter itself which is imprinted
there will present itself. Yes, though he tear some leaves out of the
book, that is, wilfully, yes studiously, forget some sins that he has
done and discontinue the reading of this book, the survey and
consideration of his conscience, for some time, yet he cannot lose,
he cannot cast away this book, that is so in him, as that it is
himself, and evermore calls upon him to deliver him from this
inconsideration by remembering that even that only perfect man,
Christ Jesus, who had that great way of making him a perfect man,
as that he was perfect God too, even in that act of deepest devotion, in his prayer in the garden, by permitting himself out of that
human infirmity which he was pleased to admit in himself (though
far from sin), to pass one petition in that prayer without a debated
and considered will, in his "If it be possible, let this cup pass," he

was put to a reconsideration, and to correct his prayer, "Yet not my will, but thine be done." And if then our best acts of praying and hearing need such an exact consideration, consider the richness and benefit of the legacy, knowledge, as this knowledge is opposed to inconsideration.

It is also opposed to concealing and smothering; it must be published to the benefit of others. Virtue that is never produced into action is scarce worthy of that name. For that is it which the Apostle, in his Epistle to that Church which was in Philemon's house, does so much praise God for, "That the fellowship of thy faith may be made fruitful and that whatsoever good thing is in you through Jesus Christ, may be known": that according to the nature of goodness, and to the root of goodness, God himself, this knowledge of God may be communicated, and transfused, and shed, and spread, and derived, and digested upon others. And therefore certainly, as the Philosopher said of civil actions, that it was some degree of wisdom to be able to seem wise; so, though it be no degree of religion to seem religious, yet even that may be a way of reducing others, and perchance themselves. When a man makes a public, an outward show of being religious, by coming ordinarily to Church and doing those outward duties, though this be hypocrisy in him, yet sometimes other men receive profit by his example and are religious in earnest. And sometimes (as St. Augustine confesses that it was his case, when he came out of curiosity and not out of devotion, to hear St. Ambrose preach) what respect soever brought that man hither, yet when God finds him here in his house, he takes hold of his conscience and shows him to himself, though he came not to see him. And if God do thus produce good out of the hypocrite, and work good in him, much more will he provide a plentiful harvest by their labors, who, having received this knowledge from God, assist their weaker brethren, both by the example of their lives and the comfort of their doctrine.

This knowledge then, which to work the intended effect in us is thus opposed to ignorance, and to inconsideration, and to concealing (which were the pieces that constitute our first part), in the second part, which is the time when this legacy accrues to us, is to

be given us at that day: "At that day shall ye know, etc." It is the
illumination, the illustration of our hearts, and therefore well re-
ferred to the day. The word itself affords cheerfulness. For when
God inflicted that great plague to kill all the firstborn in Egypt,
that was done at midnight. And when God would intimate both
deaths at once, spiritual and temporal, he says, "O fool, this night
they will fetch away thy soul." Against all supply of knowledge, he
calls him fool; and against all sense of comfort in the day, he
threatens night.

It was in the day, and at a certain day, and at a short day. For
after Christ had made his Will at this supper, and given strength to
his Will by his death, and proved his Will by his Resurrection, and
left the Church possessed of his estate by his Ascension, within ten
days after that he poured out this legacy of knowledge. That day
we celebrate this day; and we can never find the Christian Church
(so far as we can judge by the evidence of story) to have been
without this festival day. The reason of all festivals in the Church
was and is, lest after many ages involved and wrapped up in one
another, God's particular benefits should be involved and wrapped
up in unthankfulness. And the benefits received this day were such
as should never be forgotten, for without this day all the rest had
been evacuated and ineffectual. If the Apostles by the coming of
the Holy Ghost had not been established in an infallibility in themselves, and in an ability to deal with all nations by the benefit of
tongues, the benefit of Christ's passion had not been derived upon
all nations. And therefore to this day, and to Easter day, all public
baptisms in the Primitive Church were reserved. None were baptized (except in cases of necessity) but upon one of these two
days: for as there is an exaltation, a resurrection given us in baptism, representing Easter, so there belongs to us a confirmation, an
establishing of grace and the increase thereof, represented in Pentecost in the coming of the Holy Ghost. As the Jews had an Easter
in the memory of their deliverance from Egypt, and a Pentecost in
the memory of the Law given at Mount Sinai; so at Easter we
celebrate the memory of that glorious Passover, when Christ
passed from the grave and Hell, in his Resurrection, and at this
feast of Pentecost we celebrate his giving of the Law to all nations,

and his investing and possessing himself of his Kingdom, the Church. For this is, as St. Chrysostom calls it, "The cheerful feast of our adoption," in which the Holy Ghost conveying the Son of God to us, enables us to be the Sons of God, and to cry, "Abba, Father."

This then is that day when the Apostles being "with one accord and in one place" (that is, in one faith, and in one profession of that faith, not only without heresy but without schism too) "the Holy Ghost as a mighty wind, filled them all, and gave them utterance." As a wind, to note a powerful working. And he filled them, to note the abundance. And he gave them utterance, to infer that which we spoke of before, the communication of that knowledge which they had received, to others. This was that Spirit whom it concerned the Apostles so much to have as that Christ himself must go from them to send him to them. "If I go not away," says Christ, "the Comforter will not come to you." How great a comfort must this necessarily be, which must so abundantly recompense the loss of such a comfort as the presence of Christ was? This is that Spirit, who though he were to be sent by the Father, and sent by the Son, yet he comes not as a messenger from a superior, for he was always equal to Father and Son. But the Father sent him, and the Son sent him, as a tree sends forth blossoms and as those blossoms send forth a sweet smell, and as the sun sends forth beams by an emanation from itself.

St. Chrysostom says he has him not that does not see he has him, nor is any man without him who, in a rectified conscience, thinks he has him. The prophets, as high as their calling was, says the same Father, saw nothing without this Spirit, and with this Spirit a simple man understands the prophets. And therefore does St. Basil attribute that to the Holy Ghost which seems to be peculiar to the Son; he calls him Word of God, because, says he, as the Son has revealed to us the will of the Father, and so is the Word of God to us, so the Holy Ghost applies the promises and the merits of the Son to us, and so is the Word of God to us too, and enables us to come to God. In that voice of his blessed servant, St. Augustine, though nothing be more mysterious than the knowledge of God in the Trinity, yet nothing is more manifest unto

us than, by the light of this person, the Holy Ghost, so much of
both the other Persons as is necessary for our salvation, is.

Now it is not only to the Apostles that the Holy Ghost is descended this day. This day if you be all in this place (concentered,
united here in one faith and one religion), if you be of one accord
(that is, in perfect charity), the Holy Ghost shall fill you all (according to your measure and his purpose) and give you utterance,
in your lives and conversations. He that loves the exercise of
prayer so earnestly as that in prayer he feels this vehemence of the
Holy Ghost, that man dwells in an everlasting Whitsunday: for so
he does, he has it always that ever had it aright. God hates that
man, says Origen also, that celebrates any holy day of his but one
day: that never thinks of the Incarnation of Christ but upon
Christmas day, nor upon his passion and Resurrection but upon
Easter and Good Friday. If you deal so with your souls as with
your bodies, and as you clothe yourselves with your best habits
today, but return again to your ordinary apparel tomorrow: so for
this day, or this hour, you divest the thought of your sins, but
return after to your vomit, you have not celebrated this day of
Pentecost. You have not been truly in this place, for your hearts
have been visiting your profits or pleasures. You have not been
here with one accord, you have not truly and sincerely joined with
the Communion of Saints. Christ has sent no Comforter to you this
day, neither will he send any, till you be better prepared for him.
But if you have brought your sins hither in your memory, and
leave them here in the blood of your Savior, always flowing in his
Church and ready to receive them; if you be come to that heavenly
knowledge that there is no comfort but in him, and in him abundant consolation, then you are this day capable of this great
legacy, this knowledge, which is all the Christian religion, That
Christ is in the Father, and you in him, and he in you.

We are now come to our third part, our portion in this legacy,
the measure of the knowledge of these mysteries which we are to
receive: of which St. Chrysostom says well, "It is a good argument, that that man knows much, who desires not to know all." In
pursuing true knowledge, he is gone a good way that knows where
to give over. When that great Manichean Felix would needs prove

to St. Augustine that Manes was the Holy Ghost, because it was
said that the Holy Ghost should teach all truths, and that Manes
did so because he taught many things that they were ignorant of
before, concerning the frame, and motion, and nature of the heavens and their stars, St. Augustine answered, "The Holy Ghost
makes us Christians, not mathematicians."

If any man think, by having his station at court, that it is enough
for him to have studied that one book, and that if in that book, the
knowledge of the court, he be come to an apprehension by what
means and persons businesses are likeliest to be carried; if he by
his foresight have provided perspective glasses, to see objects afar
off, and can make almanacks for next year and tell how matters
will fall out then, and think that so he has received his portion, as
much knowledge as he needs, he must remember that the Holy
Ghost makes Christians, and not politicians. So if a man have a
good foundation of a fortune from his parents, and think that all
his study must be to proceed in that and still to add a cipher more
to his accounts, to make tens, hundreds, and hundreds, thousands,
the Holy Ghost makes Christians, and not such arithmeticians.

If a man know ways enough to disguise all his sins; if no ex-
chequer take hold of his usurious contracts, no high commission of
his licentiousness, no star-chamber of his misdemeanors; if he will
not to sleep till he can hold up his eyes no longer, for fear his sins
should meet him in his bed and vex his conscience there; if he will
not come to the Sacrament but at that time of the year when laws
compel him, or good company invite him, or other civil respects
and reasons provoke him; if he have avoidances, to hide his sins
from others, and from himself too, by such disguisings, this is all
but a blinding of his own internal eyes. The Holy Ghost makes
Christians, and not jugglers.

This knowledge then which we speak of, is to know the end and
the way, Heaven and Christ, the Kingdom to which he is gone, and
the means which he has taught us to follow. Now in all our ways,
in all our journeys, a moderate pace brings a man most surely to
his journey's end, and so does a sober knowledge in matters of
divinity and in the mysteries of religion. And therefore the Fathers
say that this coming of the Holy Ghost upon the Apostles, this

day, though it were a vehement coming, did not give them all kind of knowledge, a knowledge of particular arts and sciences. But he gave them enough for their present work, and withal a faithful confidence that if at any time they should have to do with learned heathens, with philosophers, the Holy Ghost would either instantly furnish them with such knowledge as they had not before (as we see in many relations in the ecclesiastical story that men spoke upon the sudden in divers cases otherwise than in any reason their education could promise or afford), or else he would blunt the sharpness of the adversaries' weapons, and cast a damp upon their understandings, as we see he did in the Council of Nicea, when after many disputations amongst the great men of great estimation, the weakest man in the council rose up, and he, of whom his own party were afraid lest his discourse should disadvantage the cause, overthrew and converted that great advocate and defender of Arius, whom all the rest could never shake. For though this man said no more than other men had said, yet God at this time disposed the understanding and the abilities of the adversaries otherwise than before; sometimes God will have glory, in arming his friends, sometimes in disarming his enemies, sometimes in exalting our abilities, and sometimes in evacuating or enfeebling theirs.

And so, as the Apostles were, as many of us as celebrate this day as they did, are filled with the Holy Ghost, that is, with so much knowledge as is necessary to God's purpose in us. Enough for ourselves, if we be private men, and enough for others, if we have charge of others. Private men shall have knowledge enough where to seek for more, and the priest shall have enough to communicate his knowledge to others. And though this knowledge were delivered to the Apostles as from a print, from a stamp, all at once, and to us but as by writing, letter after letter, syllable after syllable, by catechisms and sermons, yet both are such knowledges as are sufficient for each. As the glory of heaven shall fall upon us all, and though we be not all of equal measure and capacity, yet we shall be equally full of that glory. So the way to that glory, this knowledge, shall be manifest to us all, and infallible to us all, though we do not all know alike. The simplest soul that hears me shall know the way of his salvation as well as the greatest of those

Fathers whom he hears me cite. And upon us all (so disposed) the Holy Ghost shall fall as he did here, in fire and in tongues; in fire, to inflame us in a religious zeal, and in tongues to utter that in confession, and in profession, that is to glorify God both in our words and in our actions. This then is our portion in this legacy, a sober seeking after those points of knowledge which are necessary for our salvation, and these, in this text, Christ derived into these three, "That I am in my Father, that you are in me, that I am in you."

The first of these is the knowledge of distinction of persons, and so of the Trinity. Origen says the principal use and office of my knowledge, is to know the Trinity. For to know an unity in the Godhead, that there is but one God, natural reason serves our turn. And to know a creation of the world of nothing, reason serves us too; we know by reason, that either neither of them is infinite, if there be two Gods (and then neither of them can be God), or if both be infinite (which is an impossibility), one of them is superfluous, because whatsoever is infinite can alone extend to all. So also we can collect infallibly, that if the world were not made of nothing, yet that of which the world shall be pretended to have been made of must have been made of nothing, or else it must be something eternal and uncreated; and whatsoever is so must necessarily be God itself. To be sure of those two, an unity in the Godhead, and a creation of the world, I need no Scriptures; but to know this distinction of Persons, that the Son is in the Father, I need the Scriptures, and I need more than the Scriptures, I need this Pentecost, this coming, this illustration of the Holy Ghost, to inspire a right understanding of these Scriptures into me. For if this knowledge might be had without Scriptures, why should not the heathen believe the Trinity as well as I, since they lack no natural faculty which Christians have? And if the Scriptures themselves, without the operation of the Holy Ghost, should bring this clearness, why should not the Jews and the Arians conform themselves to this doctrine of the Trinity as well as I, since they accept those Scriptures out of which I prove the Trinity to mine own conscience? We must then attend his working in us; we must not admit such a vexation of spirit as either to vex our spirit, or the Spirit of God, by inquiring farther than he has been pleased to reveal.

If you consider that Christ says here, "You shall know that I am in the Father," and does not say, "You shall know *how* I am in the Father," and this to his Apostles themselves, and to the Apostles after they were to be filled with the Holy Ghost, which should teach them all truth, it will cut off many perplexing questions and impertinent answers which have been produced for the expressing of the manner of this generation, and of the distinction of the persons in the Trinity. You shall know *that* it is, you shall not ask *how* it is. It is enough for a happy subject to enjoy the sweetness of a peaceable government, though he know not the ways by which the prince governs. So is it for a Christian to enjoy the working of God's grace, in a faithful believing the mysteries of religion, though he inquire not into God's bedchamber, nor seek into his unrevealed decrees. It is, says Luther, a hateful, a damnable monosyllable, how, how God does this or that: for if a man come to the boldness of proposing such a question to himself, he will not give over till he find some answer: and then, others will not be content with his answer, but every man will have a several one.

When the Church fell upon the *Quomodo* in the Sacrament, *how,* in what manner the body of Christ was there, we see what an inconvenient answer it fell upon, that it was done by transubstantiation. That satisfied not (as there was no reason it should), and then they fell upon others, *In, Sub,* and *Cum,* and none could, none can give satisfaction. And so also have our times, by asking *Quomodo,* how Christ descended into Hell, produced so many answers, as that some have thought it no article at all, some have thought that it is all one thing to have descended into Hell and to have ascended into Heaven, and that it amounts to no more than a departing into the state of the dead.

Make much of that knowledge which the Holy Ghost has trusted you withal, and believe the rest. No man knows how his soul came into him; whether by infusion from God, or by generation from parents, no man knows so, but that strong arguments will be produced on the other side; and yet no man doubts but he has a soul. No man knows so, as that strong arguments may not be brought on the other side, how he sees, whether by reception of species from without, or by emission of beams from within; and yet no man doubts whether he see or no. The Holy Ghost shall tell you, when he tells you the most that ever he shall tell you, in that behalf, that the Son is in the Father, but he will not tell you how.

Our second portion in this legacy of knowledge is, that we are in Christ; and this is the mystery of the Incarnation. For since the Devil had so surprised us all, as to take mankind all in one lump, in a corner, in Adam's loins, and poisoned us all there in the fountain, in the root; Christ, to deliver us as entirely, took all mankind upon him, and so took every one of us, and the nature, and the infirmities, and the sins, and the punishment of every singular man. So that the same pretense which the Devil has against every one of us, you are mine, for you sinned in Adam, we have also for our discharge, we are delivered, for we paid our debt in Christ Jesus. In all his temptations, send him to look upon the records of that process, of Christ's passion, and he shall find there the names of all the faithful recorded: that such a day, that day when Christ died, I, and you, and all that shall be saved, suffered, died, and were crucified, and in Christ Jesus satisfied God the Father for those infinite sins which we had committed. And now second death, which is damnation, has no more title to any of the true members of his mystical body, than corruption upon natural, or violent, death could have upon the members of his natural body.

The assurance of this grows from the third part of this knowledge, that Christ is in us; for that is such a knowledge of Christ's general Redemption of mankind, as that it is also an application of it to us in particular. For his Incarnation, by which we are in him, may have given a dignity to our human nature; but what great benefit (however the dignity had been great to all mankind) had mankind had if Christ had saved no more than that one person whom he assumed? The largeness and bounty of Christ is to give us of his best treasure, knowledge, and to give us most at last, to know Christ in me. For to know that he is in his Father, this may serve me to convince another, that denies the Trinity. To know that we are in Christ, so as that he took our nature, this may show me an honor done to us, more than the angels. But what gets a

lame wretch at the pool, how sovereign soever the water be, if
nobody puts him in? What gets a naked beggar by knowing that a
dead man has left much to pious uses, if the executors take no
knowledge of him? What get I by my knowledge of Christ in the
Father, and of us in Christ so, if I find not Christ in me?

How then is Christ in us? Here the question *De modo,* how it is,
is lawful, for he has revealed it to us. It is by our obedience to his
inspiration, and by our reverent use of those visible means which
he has ordained in his Church, his Word and Sacraments. As our
flesh is in him, by his participation thereof, so his flesh is in us, by
our communication thereof. And so is his divinity in us, by making
us one spirit with himself, which he does at this Pentecost, that is,
whensoever the Holy Ghost visits us with his effectual grace: for
this is an union in which Christ in his purpose has married himself
to our souls inseparably and without any intention of divorce on
his part. But if we will separate him, if either we take the bed of
licentiousness, or the board of voluptuousness, or if when we eat
and drink, or sleep or wake, we do not all to the glory of God, if
we separate, he will divorce.

If then we be thus come to this knowledge, let us enlarge science
into conscience: for conscience is a syllogism that comes to a
conclusion. Then only has a man true knowledge when he can
conclude in his own conscience that his practice and conversation
has expressed it. Who will believe that we know there is a ditch,
and know the danger of falling into it and drowning in it, if he see
us run headlong towards it, and fall into it, and continue in it?
Who can believe that he that separates himself from Christ, by
continuing in his sin, has any knowledge, or sense, or evidence, or
testimony of Christ's being in him? As Christ proceeds by enlarging your knowledge, and making you wiser and wiser, so enlarge your testimony of it by growing better and better, and let him
that is holy be more holy. If you have passed over the first heats of
the day, the wantonnesses of youth, and the second heat, the fire of
ambition, if these be quenched in you by preventing grace, or by
repenting grace, be more and more holy, for your age will meet
another sin of covetousness, or of indevotion, that needs as much
resistance.

God stayed not in any less degree of knowledge toward you than in bringing himself to you. Do not you stay by the way neither; not in the consideration of God alone, for all creatures declare it. Stay not at the Trinity; every coming to Church, nay your first being brought to Church at your baptism is and was a profession of that. Stay not at the Incarnation; that the Devil knows and testifies. But come to know that Christ is in you and express that knowledge in a sanctified life. For though he be in us all, in the work of his Redemption, so as that he has poured out balm enough in his blood to spread over all mankind, yet only he can enjoy the cheerfulness of this unction, and the inseparableness of this union, who (as St. Augustine pursues this contemplation) always remembers that he stands in the presence of Christ, and behaves himself worthy of that glorious presence; that has Christ always at his tongue's end, and always at his finger's ends, that loves to discourse of him, and to act his discourses; that hears God's will here in his house, and does his will at home in his own house; who having done well from the beginning, perseveres in well doing to the end, he and he only shall find Christ in him.

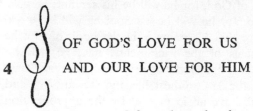

OF GOD'S LOVE FOR US
AND OUR LOVE FOR HIM

4

> *I love them that love me, and they that
> seek me early shall find me.*
>
> PROVERBS 8:17

AS THE PROPHETS AND THE OTHER SECRETARIES OF
the Holy Ghost in penning the books of Scriptures do for the most
part retain, and express in their writings, some impressions and
some air of their former professions; those that had been bred in
courts and cities, those that had been shepherds and herdsmen,
those that had been fishers, and so of the rest; ever inserting into
their writings some phrases, some metaphors, some allusions taken
from that profession which they had exercised before; so that soul
that has been transported upon any particular worldly pleasure,
when it is entirely turned upon God and the contemplation of his
all-sufficiency and abundance, does find in God fit subject and just
occasion to exercise the same affection piously and religiously,
which had before so sinfully transported and possessed it.

A covetous person who is now truly converted to God will
exercise a spiritual covetousness still. He will desire to have him
all, he will have good security, the seal and assurance of the Holy
Ghost. And he will have his security often renewed by new testimonies, and increases of those graces in him; he will have witnesses enough; he will have the testimony of all the world, by his
good life and conversation. He will gain every way at God's hand.

He will have wages of God, for he will be his servant; he will have a portion from God, for he will be his Son; he will have a reversion, he will be sure that his name is in the book of life; he will have pawns, the seals of the sacraments, nay, he will have a present possession; all that God has promised, all that Christ has purchased, all that the Holy Ghost has the stewardship and dispensation of, he will have all in present by the appropriation and investiture of an actual and applying faith. A covetous person converted will be spiritually covetous still.

So will a voluptuous man who is turned to God find plenty and deliciousness enough in him to feed his soul as with marrow and with fatness, as David expresses it. And so an angry and passionate man will find zeal enough in the house of God to eat him up.

All affections which are common to all men, and those too which particular men have been addicted unto, shall not only be justly employed upon God, but also securely employed, because we cannot exceed nor go too far in employing them upon him. According to this rule, St. Paul, who had been so vehement a persecutor, had ever his thoughts exercised upon that; and thereupon after his conversion he fulfils the rest of the sufferings of Christ in his flesh; he suffers most, he makes most mention of his suffering of any of the Apostles.

And according to this rule, too, Solomon, whose disposition was amorous and excessive in the love of women, when he turned to God, he departed not utterly from his old phrase and language, but having put a new and a spiritual tincture and form and habit into all his thoughts and words, he conveys all his loving approaches and applications to God, and all God's gracious answers to his amorous soul, into songs and epithalamions, and meditations upon contracts and marriages between God and his Church, and between God and his soul; as we see so evidently in all his other writings and particularly in this text, "I love them that love me . . ."

In which words is expressed all that belongs to love, all which is to desire and to enjoy; for to desire without fruition is a rage, and to enjoy without desire is a stupidity. In the first alone we think of nothing but that which we then would have; and in the second alone, we are as good as if we were without it, for we have no pleasure in it. Nothing then can give us satisfaction but where those two concur, to love and to enjoy.

In sensual love it is so; "I took no joy in this world but in loving and in being beloved." In sensual love it is so, but in sensual love, when we are come so far, there is no satisfaction in that. The same Father [Augustine] confesses more of himself than any commission, any oath, would have put him to. "I had all I desired, and I had it with that advantage of having it secretly; but what got I by all that; nothing but to be scourged with burning iron rods, rods of jealousy, of suspicion and of quarrels." But in the love and enjoying of this text, there is no room for jealousy, nor suspicion, nor quarrelsome complaining.

In this text then you may be pleased to consider these two things: what the affection of this love is, what is the blessedness of this enjoying. In the first of these we must first consider the persons who are the lovers in this text; for there are persons that are incredible, though they say they love, because they are accustomed to falsehood; and there are persons which are unrequitable, though they be believed to love, because they love not where and as they should. When we have found the persons, in a second consideration we shall look upon the affection itself, what is the love in this text; and then after that, upon the bond and union and condition of this love, that it is mutual: "I love them that love me." And having passed those three branches of the first part, we shall in the second, which is enjoying, consider first that this enjoying is expressed in the word finding; and then that this finding requires two conditions, a seeking, and an early seeking: "And they that seek me early shall find me."

The person that professes love in this place is wisdom herself, as appears at the beginning of the chapter; so that to be wise and to love, which perchance never met before nor since, are met in this text. But whether this wisdom, so frequently mentioned in this book of Proverbs, be wisdom created or uncreated, whether it be the virtue wisdom, or the root of wisdom Christ Jesus, has been diversely debated. But since there is nothing said of wisdom in all this book which has not been by good expositors applied to Christ, much more may we presume the lover in this text (though presented in the name of wisdom) to be Christ himself, and so we do.

To show the constancy and durableness of this love, the lover is a he: that is Christ. To show the vehemency and earnestness of it, the lover is a she: that is wisdom, as it is often expressed in this chapter, "She crieth, she uttereth her voice." Yes, in one place of the Bible (and only in that one place I think) where Moses would express an extraordinary and vehement and passionate indignation in God against his people, when as it is in that text, "his wrath was kindled," and grievously kindled, there and only there does Moses attribute even to God himself the feminine sex, and speaks to God in the original language, as if he should have called him an angry she God. All that is good then, either in the love of man or woman, is in this love; for he is expressed in both sexes, man and woman; and all that can be ill in the love of either sex is purged away, for the man is no other man than Christ Jesus, and the woman no other woman than wisdom herself, even the uncreated wisdom of God himself.

Now all this is but one person, the person that professes love. Who is the other, who is the beloved of Christ, is not so easily discerned. In the love between persons in this world, and of this world, we are often deceived with outward signs; we often miscall and misjudge civil respects and mutual courtesies; and a delight in one another's conversation, and such other indifferent things as only malignity, and curiosity, and self-guiltiness makes to be misinterpretable, we often call these love; but neither among ourselves, much less between Christ and ourselves, are these outward appearances always signs of love.

This person then, this beloved soul, is not everyone, to whom Christ sends a loving message, or writes to; for his letters, his Scriptures, are directed to all; not everyone he wishes well to and swears that he does so, for so he does to all; "As I live [saith the Lord] I would not the death of a sinner"; not everyone that he sends jewels and presents to, for they are often snares to corrupt, as well as arguments of love; not though he admit them to his table and supper, for even there the Devil entered in Judas with a sop;

not though he receive them with a kiss, for even with that familiarity Judas betrayed him; not though he betroth himself as he did to the Jews; not though he make an everlasting covenant; not though he have communicated his name to them, which is an act of marriage; for to how many has he said, "I have said you are gods," and yet they have been reprobates. Not all these outward things make us discern who is this beloved person; for himself says of the Israelites, to whom he had made all these demonstrations of love, yet after, for their abominations, divorced himself from them; "I have forsaken mine house, I have left mine heritage, I have given the dearly beloved of my soul into the hands of her enemies." To contract this, the person beloved of Christ is only that soul that loves Christ.

Having found the person, we are to consider the affection itself, the love of this text. It is an observation of Origen's that though these three words—love, and affection, and good will—be all of one signification in the Scriptures, yet says he, wheresoever there is danger of representing to the fancy a lascivious and carnal love, the Scripture forbears the word "love" and uses either "affection" or "good will." Where there is no such danger, the Scripture comes directly to this word "love," of which Origen's examples are, that when Isaac bent his affections upon Rebecca, and Jacob upon Rachel, in both places it is affection and not love; and when it is said in the Canticles, "I charge you daughters of Jerusalem to tell my well-beloved," it is not to tell him that she was in love, but to tell him that I am wounded with an affection and good will towards him. But in this book of Proverbs, in all the passages between Christ and the beloved soul there is evermore a free use of this word "love"; because it is even in the first apprehension a pure, a chaste, and an undefiled love. All the words of the Lord, and all their words that love the Lord, all discourses, all that is spoken to or from the soul, is all full of chaste love and of the love of chastity.

Now though this love of Christ to our souls be too large to shut up or comprehend in any definition, yet if we content ourselves with the definition of the schools, "love is nothing but a desire that they whom we love should be happy," we may easily discern the

advantage and profit which we have by this love in the text, when
he that wishes us good, by loving us, is author of all good himself
and may give us as much as pleases him without impairing his own
infinite treasure. He loves us as his ancient inheritance, as the first
among his creatures in the creation of the world, which he created
for us. He loves us more as his purchase, whom he has bought with
his blood; for even man takes most pleasure in things of his own
getting. But he loves us most for our improvement, when by his
ploughing up of our hearts, and the dew of his grace, and the seed
of his word, we come to give a greater rent in the fruits of sanctification than before. And since he loves us thus, and that in him
this love is a desire that his beloved should be happy, what soul
among us shall doubt that when God has such an abundant and infinite treasure as the merit and passion of Christ Jesus, sufficient
to save millions of worlds, and yet many millions in this world (all
the heathen) excluded from any interest therein; when God has a
kingdom so large as that nothing limits it, and yet he has banished
many natural subjects thereof, even those legions of Angels which
were created in it and are fallen from it; what soul among us shall
doubt but that he that has this much and loves this much will not
deny her a portion in the blood of Christ or a room in the kingdom
of heaven? No soul can doubt it except it have been a witness to
itself, and be so still, that it love not Christ Jesus, for that's a
condition necessary. And that is the third branch to which we are
come now in our order; that this love be mutual; "I love them that
love me."

"If any man love not our Lord Jesus, let him be accursed," says
the Apostle. Now the first part of this curse is upon the indisposition to love; he that loves not at all is first accursed. That stupid
inconsideration, which passes on drowsily and negligently upon
God's creatures, that sullen indifferency in one's disposition, to
love one thing no more than another, not to value, not to choose,
not to prefer; that stoniness, that inhumanity, not to be affected,
not to be tender toward those things which God has made objects
and subjects of affections; that which St. Paul places in the bottom
and lees and dregs of all the sins of the Jews, to be without natural
affections, this distemper, this ill complexion, this ill nature of the

soul is under the first part of this curse, if any man love not; for he that loves not, knows not God, for God is love.

But this curse determines not upon that, neither is it principally directed upon that, not loving; for as we say in the schools, the first thing that the will of man does is to affect, to choose, to love something; and it is scarce possible to find any man's will so idle, so barren, as that it has produced no act at all; and therefore the first act being love, scarce any man can be found that does not love something. But the curse extends, yes is principally intended, upon him that loves not Christ Jesus. Though he love the creature, and orderly enough; yes, though he love God as a great and incomprehensible power, yet if he love not Christ Jesus, if he acknowledge not that all that passes between God and him is in and for Christ Jesus, let him be accursed for all his love.

Now there are but two that can be loved, God and the creature: and of the creatures, that must necessarily be best loved which is nearest us, which we understand best and reflect most upon, and that's ourselves. For the love of other creatures is but a secondary love; if we love God, we love them for his sake; if we love ourselves, we love them for our sakes. Now to love oneself is only allowable, only proper to God himself; for this love is a desire that all honor, and praise, and glory should be attributed to oneself, and it can be only proper to God to desire that. To love ourselves then is the greatest treason we can commit against God; and all love of the creatures determines in the love of ourselves. For though sometimes we may say that we love them better than ourselves; and though we give so good (that is indeed, so ill testimony) that we do so, that we neglect ourselves, both our religion and our discretion for their sakes, whom we pretend to love, yet all this is but a secondary love, and with relation still to ourselves and our own contentment. For is this love which we bear to other creatures within that definition of love, "to wish that which we love happy"? Does any ambitious man love honor or office because he thinks that title or that place should receive a dignity by his having it, or an excellency by his executing it? Does any covetous man love a house or horse because he thinks that house or horse should be happy in such a master or such a rider? Does any licentious man covet or solicit a woman because he thinks it is a happiness to her to have such a servant? No, it is only himself that is within the definition; he wishes well (as he mistakes it) to himself, and he is content that the slavery and dishonor and ruin of others should contribute to make up his imaginary happiness.

What a perverse madness is it to love a creature and not as a creature, that is, with all the adjuncts and circumstances and qualities of a creature, of which the principal is that love raise us to the contemplation of the Creator. For if it do so, we may love ourselves as we are the Images of God; and so we may love other men, as they are the Images of us and our nature; yes, as they are the members of the same body; for all men make up but one mankind, and so we love other creatures, as we all meet in our Creator, in whom princes and subjects, Angels and men and worms are fellow servants. If you have loved yourself or anybody else principally; or so, that when you do any act of love you cannot say to your own conscience, I do this for God's sake and for his glory; if you have loved so, you have hated yourself, and him whom you have loved, and God whom you should love.

If you have hated as you should hate, if you have hated your own internal temptations and the outward solicitations of others, then you have expressed a manifold act of love; of love to your God, and love to his Image yourself, and love to your image, that man whom your virtue and your example have declined, and kept from offending his and your God.

And as this affection, love, belongs to God principally, that is, rather than to anything else, so does it also principally another way, that is, rather than any affection else; for "the fear of God is the beginning of wisdom," but the love of God is the consummation, that is, the marriage and union of your soul and your Savior.

But can we love God when we will? Do we not find that in the love of some other things, or some courses of life, of some ways in our actions, and of some particular persons, that we would fain love them and cannot? when we can object nothing against it, when we can multiply arguments why we should love them, yet we cannot. But it is not so towards God; every man may love him that will. But can every man have this will, this desire? Certainly we cannot begin this love; except God love us first we cannot love him. But God does love us all so well, from the beginning, as that every man may see the fault was in the perverseness of his own will, that he did not love God better. If we look for the root of this love, it is in the Father; for though the death of Christ be towards us, as a root, as a cause of our love, and of the acceptableness of it, yet the death of Christ was but an effect of the love of God towards us: "So God loved the world that he gave his Son." If he had not loved us first, we had never had his Son. Here is the root, then, the love of the Father, and the tree, the merit of the Son. Except there be fruit too, love in us, to them again, both root and tree will wither in us, howsoever they grew in God. "I have loved thee with an everlasting love, therefore with mercy I have drawn thee." If therefore we do not perceive that we are drawn to love again by this love, 'tis not an everlasting love that shines upon us.

All the sunshine, all the glory of this life, though all these be testimonies of God's love to us, yet all these bring but a winter's day, a short day, and a cold day, and a dark day, for except we love too, God does not love with an everlasting love. God will not suffer his love to be idle, and since it profits him nothing if it profits us nothing neither, he will withdraw it. "The sun has no benefit by his own light, nor the fire by his own heat, nor a perfume by the sweetness thereof, but only they who make their use, and enjoy this heat and fragrancy" [Ambrose]. And this brings us to our other part, to pass from loving to enjoying.

"They have taken away my Lord, and I know not where they have laid him." This was one strain of Mary Magdalen's lamentation when she found not her Savior in the monument. It is a lamentable case to be fain to cry so, "They have taken"; other men have taken away Christ, by a dark and corrupt education. But when the casting away of God which is so often complained of by God in the prophets is pronounced against you, when you have had Christ offered to you by the motions of his grace and sealed to you by his sacraments, and yet will cast him so far from you that you know not where to find him; when you have poured him out at your eyes in profane and counterfeit tears which should be your soul's rebaptizing for your sins; when you have blown him away in corrupt and ill intended sighs, which should be the voice of the turtle to sound your peace and reconciliation with your God; yes, when you have spit him out of your mouth in execrable and blasphemous oaths; when you have not only cast him so far as that you know not where to find him, but have made so ordinary and so indifferent a thing of sin as you know not when you did lose him, no nor do not remember that ever you had him; no, nor do not know that there is any such man as Jesus, that is your Lord; the taking away is dangerous, when others hide Christ from you, but the casting away is desperate, when you yourself cast him away.

To lose Christ may befall the most righteous man that is; but then he knows where he left him; he knows at what time he lost his way, and where to seek it again. Even Christ's imagined father and his true mother, Joseph and Mary, lost him, and lost him in the holy city at Jerusalem. They lost him and knew it not. They lost him and went a day's journey without him and thought him to be in the company. But as soon as they comprehended their error, they sought and they found him, when as his mother told him, his father and she had sought with a heavy heart. Alas we may lose him at Jerusalem, even in his own house, even at this present while we pretend to do him service. We may lose him by suffering our thoughts to look back with pleasure upon the sins which we have committed, or to look forward with greediness upon some sin that is now in our purpose and prosecution. We may lose him at Jerusalem, how much more, if our dwelling be a Babylon in confusion and mingling God and the world together, or if it be a Sodom, a wanton and intemperate misuse of God's benefits to us. We may think him in the company when he is not; we may mistake his house; we may take a conventicle for a Church; we may mistake his apparel, that is, the outward form of his worship; we may mistake the person, that is, associate ourselves to such as are no members of his body. But if we do not return to our diligence to seek him, and seek him, and seek him with a heavy heart, though we began with a taking away—other men, other temptations took him away—yet we end in a casting away, we ourselves cast him away since we have been told where to find him and have not sought him. And let no man be afraid to seek or find him for fear of the loss of good company; religion is no sullen thing, it is not a melancholy, there is not so sociable a thing as the love of Christ Jesus.

It was the first word which he who first found Christ of all the Apostles, St. Andrew, is noted to have said, "We have found the Messiah"; and it is the first act that he is noted to have done, after he had found him, to seek his brother Peter and take him to Jesus, so communicable a thing is the love of Jesus when we have found him.

But where are we likeliest to find him? It is said by Moses of the words and precepts of God, "They are not hid from thee, neither are far off." Not in heaven that you should say, Who shall go up to heaven for us to bring them down? Nor beyond the seas, that you should go over the sea for them. But the word is very near you, even in your mouth and in your heart; and so near is Christ Jesus, or you shall never find him. You must not so think him in heaven, as that you cannot have immediate access to him without intercession of others, nor so beyond sea as to seek him in a foreign Church, either where the Church is but an antiquary's cabinet full of rags and fragments of antiquity but nothing fit for that use for which it was first made, or where it is so new built a house with bare walls that it is yet unfurnished of such ceremonies as should make it comely and reverend. Christ is at home with you, he is at home within you, and there is the nearest way to find him.

It is true that Christ in the beginning of this chapter shadowed under the name of wisdom; when he discovers where he may be found, speaks in the person of human wisdom as well as divine. Does not wisdom cry, and understanding utter her voice? where those two words, wisdom and understanding, signify that wisdom whose object is God, and that which concerns our conversation in this world. For Christ has not taken so narrow a dwelling as that he may be found but one way or in one profession; for in all professions, in all stations, in all vocations, when all our actions in our several courses are directed principally upon his glory, Christ is imminent and may easily be found. To that person in that place, Christ, in the person of wisdom, offers himself to be found in the tops of high places and in the gates of cities; to show that this

Christ, and this wisdom which must save our souls, is not confined to cloisters and monasteries and speculative men only, but is also evidently and imminently to be found in the courts of religious princes, in the tops of high places, and in the courts of justice (in the gates of the city).

Both these kinds of courts may have more diversions from him than other places; but yet in these places he is also gloriously and conspicuously to be found; for wheresoever he is, he cries aloud, as the text says there, and he utters his voice. Now temptations to sin are all but whisperings, and we are afraid that a husband, that a father, that a competitor, that a rival, a pretender, at least the magistrate may hear of it. Temptations to sin are all but whisperings; private conventicles and clandestine worshiping of God in a forbidden manner, in corners, are all but whisperings. It is not the voice of Christ except you hear him cry aloud and utter his voice, so as you may confidently do whatsoever he commands you, in the eye of the whole world. He is everywhere to be found, he calls upon you everywhere, but yet there belongs a diligence on your part; you must seek him.

Isaiah is bold (says St. Paul) and says, "I was found of them that sought me not," when that prophet derives the love of God to the Gentiles, who could seek God nowhere but in the book of creatures and were destitute of all other lights to seek him by, and yet God was found by them afterward by the preaching of the Gospel. Isaiah is bold (cries the Apostle) that is, it was a great degree of confidence in Isaiah to say that God was found of them that sought him not. It was a boldness and confidence which no particular man may have, that Christ will be found except he be sought. He gives us light to seek him by, but he is not found till we have sought him.

It is true that in that commandment of his, "First seek the kingdom of God," the "first" is not to prevent God, that we should seek it before he shows it; that's impossible. Without the light of grace we dwell in darkness and in the shadow of death. But the "first" is that we should seek it before we seek anything else, that when the sun of grace is risen to us, the first thing that we do be to seek Christ Jesus. "Seek me and ye shall live." Why? We were alive before, else we could not seek him; but it is a promise of another life, of an eternal life, if we seek him, and seek him early, which is our last consideration.

The word there used for "early" signifies properly "the morning," and is usually transferred in Scriptures to any beginning of any action. Therefore this text is elegantly translated by one, "They that have their break of day towards me, they that send forth their first morning beams towards me, their first thoughts, they shall be sure to find me." St. Jerome expresses this early diligence required in us well, in his translation, "They that wake betimes in the morning shall find me"; but the Chaldee Paraphrase better, "They that rise betimes in the morning shall find me." For which of us does not know that we waked long ago, that we saw day and had heretofore some motions to find Christ Jesus? But though we were awake, we have kept our bed still, we have continued still in our former sins; so that there is more to be done than waking. We see the Spouse herself says, "In my bed, by night, I sought him whom my soul loved, but I found him not." Christ may be sought in the bed and missed; other thoughts may exclude him; and he may be sought there and found, we may have good meditations there; and Christ may be nearer us when we are asleep in our beds than when we are awake. But howsoever, the bed is not his ordinary station; he may be, and he says he will be, at the making of the bed of the sick, but not at the marring of the bed of the wanton and licentious.

The circumstance only required here is that he be sought early; and to invite you to it, consider how early he sought you. It is a great mercy that he stays so long for you. It was more to seek you so early. Do you not feel that he seeks you now, in offering his love and desiring yours? Can you not remember that he sought you yesterday, that is, that some temptations besieged you then and he sought you out by his grace and preserved you? And has he not sought you so, so early as from the beginning of your life? Do you not remember that after you had committed that sin, he sought you by imprinting some remorse, some apprehension of his judgments, and so by a miraculous and powerful working of his Spirit he threatened you when he comforted you, he loved you when he chid you, he sought you when he drove you from him? He has sought you among the infinite numbers of false and fashionable Christians, that he might bring you out from the hypocrite, to serve him in earnest, and in holiness, and in righteousness.

He sought you before that among the herd of the nations and Gentiles, who had no Church, to bring you into his enclosures and pastures, his visible Church, and to feed you with his word and sacraments. He sought you before that in the catalogue of all his creatures, where he might have left you a stone, or a plant, or a beast; and then he gave you an immortal soul, capable of all his future blessings. Yes, before this he sought you, when you were nowhere, nothing, he brought you then the greatest step of all, from being nothing to be a creature. How early did he seek you when he sought you in Adam's confused loins, and out of that leavened and sour loaf in which we were all kneaded up, out of that refuse and condemned lump of dough, he sought and severed out that grain which you should be. Yes, millions of millions of generations before all this he sought you in his own eternal decree. And in that first Scripture of his, which is as old as himself, in the book of life he wrote your name in the blood of that Lamb which was slain for you, not only from the beginning of this world, but from the writing of that eternal decree of your salvation. Thus early had he sought you in the Church among hypocrites; out of the Church among heathen; in his creatures among creatures of an ignoble nature, and in the first vacuity when you were nothing he sought you so early as in Adam, so early as in the Book of Life, and when will you think it a fit time to seek him?

There is an earliness which will not serve your turn, when afflictions and anguish shall come upon you. "They shall seek me early and shall not find me," early in respect of the punishment, at the beginning of that. But this is late in respect of your fault, or of your age, when you are grown old in the custom of sin. For thus we may misuse this early and make it serve all ill uses, if we will say we will leave covetousness early, that is, as soon as we are rich enough; incontinence early, that is, as soon as we are old or sick; ambition early, that is, as soon as we have overthrown and crushed our enemies irrecoverably; for thus, we shall by this habit carry on this early to our late and last hour, and say we will repent early, that is, as soon as the bell begins to toll for us.

It is good for a man that he bear his yoke in his youth, that he seek Christ early, for even God himself, when he had given over his people to be afflicted by the Chaldeans, yet complains of the Chaldeans that they laid heavy loads upon old men. Though this yoke of this amorous seeking of Christ be a light yoke, yet it is too heavy for an old man that has never used himself in all his life to bear it; even this spiritual love will not suit well with an old man, if he never began before, if he never loved Christ in his youth, even this love will be an unwieldy thing in his age.

Yet if we have omitted our first early, our youth, there is one early left for us; this minute; seek Christ early, now, now, as soon as his Spirit begins to shine upon your hearts. Now as soon as you begin your day of regeneration, seek him the first minute of this day, for you know not whether this day shall have two minutes or no, that is, whether his Spirit, that descends upon you now will tarry and rest upon you or not, as it did upon Christ at his baptism.

Therefore shall every one that is godly make his prayer unto thee, O God, in a time when you may be found. We acknowledge this to be that time, and we come to you now early, with the confession of your servant Augustine: O glorious beauty, infinitely reverend, infinitely fresh and young, we come late to your love if we consider the past days of our lives, but early if you be pleased to reckon with us from this hour of the shining of your grace upon us. And therefore, O God, as you have brought us safely to the beginning of this day, as you have not given us over to a final perishing in the works of night and darkness, as you have brought us to the beginning of this day of grace, so defend us in the same with your mighty power, and grant that this day, this day of your visitation, we fall into no sin, neither run into any kind of danger; no such sin, no such danger as may separate us from you, or frustrate us of our hopes in that eternal kingdom which your Son our Savior Jesus Christ has purchased for us, with the inestimable price of his incorruptible blood.

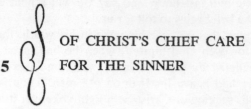

5 OF CHRIST'S CHIEF CARE
FOR THE SINNER

*I am not come to call the righteous, but
sinners to repentance.* MATTHEW 9:13

SOME THINGS THE SEVERAL EVANGELISTS RECORD
severally; one, and no more. Some things are severally recorded
by the several evangelists. Now our text had neither this singularity
nor this universality. It is neither in one only, nor in all the evangelists, but it has (as they speak in the law) an interpretative universality, a presumptive universality, for that which has a plurality of
voices is said to have all. Three of the four evangelists have recorded this text. Only St. John, who especially extends himself
about the divine nature of Christ, pretermits it. But in all the rest,
who insist more upon his assuming our nature and working our
salvation in that, the Holy Ghost has recorded and repeated this
protestation of our Savior's, "I came to call not the righteous, but
sinners to repentance." Which words, being spoken by Christ upon
occasion of the Pharisees murmuring at his admitting of publicans
and sinners to the table with him, at that feast which St. Matthew
made him, at his house, soon after his calling to the apostleship,
direct our consideration upon the whole story.

First, then, Christ justified feasting, festival and cheerful conversation. For, as St. Ambrose says, God, who made the world primarily for his own glory, had made light in vain if he had made no

62

creatures to see and to be seen by that light, wherein he might receive glory. So God, who intended secondarily man's good in the Creation, had made creatures to no purpose if he had not allowed man a use and an enjoying of those creatures. Our mythologists, who think they have conveyed a great deal of moral doctrine in their poetical fables (and so indeed they have) had mistaken the matter much when they made it one of the torments of Hell to stand in a fresh river and not be permitted to drink, and amongst pleasant fruits and not to be suffered to eat, if God required such a forbearing, such an abstemiousness in man, as that being set to rule and govern the creatures he might not use and enjoy them. Privileges are lost by abusing, but so they are by not using, too.

When Christ came to Jairus's house and commanded away the music and all the funeral solemnities, it was not because he disallowed those solemnities, but because he knew there was no funeral to be solemnized in that place, to which he came with an infallible purpose to raise that maid which was dead. Civil recreations, offices of society and mutual entertainment, and cheerful conversation; and such a use of God's creatures as may testify him to be a God not of the valleys only but of the mountains too, not a God of necessity only but of plenty too, Christ justified by his personal presence at a feast in an Apostle's house.

The Apostle then had a house, and means to keep a house and to make occasional feasts in his house, though he had bound himself to serve Christ in so near a place as an Apostle. The profession of Christ's service in the ministry does not take from any man the use of God's creatures, nor cheerfulness of conversation. As some of the other Apostles are said to have followed Christ: "They left their nets, and followed him"; and yet upon occasion they did at times return to their nets and fishing after that, for Christ found them at their nets after his Resurrection. So St. Matthew followed Christ, as St. Luke expresses it: "He left all, and followed Christ." But not so absolutely all that he did not only neglect the gain of his place, but the danger of displeasure by such a leaving of his place: for St. Matthew was a publican, and so a public officer and an accountant to the state. But though he did so far leave all as that nothing retarded him from an immediate following of Christ, yet no doubt but that he returned after to the settling of his office and the rectifying of his accounts.

When God sees it necessary or behooveful for a man to leave all his worldly state that he may follow him, God tells him so. He gives him such a measure of light by his Spirit as lets him see it is God's will. And then, to that man, that is a full commandment and binds him to do it, and not only an evangelical counsel, as they call it, which leaves him at liberty to do it or leave it undone. Christ saw how much was necessary to that young man in the Gospel, and therefore to him he said, "Go and sell all that thou hast, and then follow me." And this was a commandment to that man, though it be not a general commandment to all. Upon Matthew Christ laid no such commandment, but only said to him, "Follow me"; and he did so, but yet not so divest himself of his worldly estate as that he had not a house, and means to keep a house, and that plentifully, after this.

When Elijah used that holy fascination upon Elisha (we may not, I think, call it a fascination; fascination, I think, has never a good sense), but when Elijah used that holy charm and incantation upon him, to spread his mantle over him and to draw him with that as with a net after him; yet after Elisha had thus received a character of Orders, after this imposition of hands in the spreading of the mantle, after he had this new filiation by which he was the son of the prophet, yet Elisha went home and feasted his friends after this. So Matthew began his Apostleship with a feast; and though he in modesty forbear saying so, St. Luke, who reports the story, says that it was a great feast. He began with a great but ended with a greater: for (if we have St. Matthew's history rightly delivered to us) when he was at the greatest feast which this world can present, when he was receiving and administering the blessed Sacrament, in that action was he himself served up as a dish to the table of the Lamb, and added to the number of the martyrs then; and died for that Savior of his, whose death for him he did then celebrate.

Here was Matthew weaned from the breasts of this world; and he made a feast, a feast that was a type of a type, a prevision of a vision, of that vision which St. Peter had after of a sheet with all kind of meats clean and unclean in it. For at this table was the clean and unspotted Lamb, Christ Jesus himself; and at the same table those spotted and unclean goats, the publicans and sinners. He justified feasting, feasting in an Apostle's house, feasting with publicans and sinners.

Christ was in himself a dispensation upon any law, because he was the lawmaker. But here he proceeded not in that capacity; he took no benefit of any dispensation; he fulfilled the intention and purpose of the law. For the laws forbade conversation with sinners lest a man should take infection by such conversation. So the Jews were forbidden to eat with the Gentiles, but it was lest in eating with the Gentiles they might eat of things sacrificed to idols. So they were forbidden conversation with leprous persons, lest by such conversation the disease should be propagated. But where the danger of infection ceased, all conversation might be open. And Christ was always far enough from taking any infection by any conversation with any sinner. He might apply himself to them, because he could take no harm by them; but he did it especially that he might do good upon them.

Some forbear the company of sinners out of a singularity and pride in their own purity and say with those in Isaiah, "Stand by thyself, come not near me, for I am holier than thou." But Christ was a lily though he grew amongst thorns. A lily is not the less a lily, nor the worse, nor the darker a lily because it grows amongst thorns. That man is not so good as he should be that cannot maintain his own integrity and continue good, or that cannot maintain his charity, though others continue bad.

It was St. Paul's way, "I am made all things to all men, that I might save some." And in that place where the Apostle names the persons whom we are to forbear, amongst them he names idolaters; and, as he does the rest, he calls even those idolaters, brethren: "If any that is called a Brother be an idolater, etc." In cases where we are safe from danger of infection (and it lies much in ourselves to save ourselves from infection), even some kind of idolaters are left by St. Paul under the name of Brethren; and some brotherly and neighborly and pious offices belong to them, for all that. These faults must arm me to avoid all danger from them, but not extinguish all charity towards them. And therefore it was an unjust calumny in the Pharisees to impute this for a fault to Christ, that he applied himself to these men.

Now in the manner of this calumny there was a great deal of iniquity, and a great deal in the matter. For the manner: that which they say of Christ they say not to Christ himself, but they whisper it to his servants, to his disciples. A legal and juridical accusation is justifiable, maintainable, because it is the proper way for remedy. A private reprehension done with discretion and moderation should be acceptable too, but a privy whispering is always Pharisaical. The Devil himself, though he be a lion, yet he is a roaring lion; a man may hear him, but for a privy whisperer we shall only hear of him. And in their plot there was more mischief, for when Christ's disciples plucked ears of corn upon the sabbath the Pharisees said nothing to those disciples, but they come to their master, to Christ, and they tell him of it. Here when Christ eats and drinks with these sinners, they never say anything to Christ himself, but they go to his servants, and they tell him of it. By privy whisperings and calumnies they would alienate Christ from his disciples and his disciples from him; the king from his subjects by some tales, and the subjects from the king by other. They took this for the shortest way to disgrace both their preaching, to discredit both their lives; to defame Christ for a wine-bibber and a loose companion, and to defame his disciples for profane men and sabbath-breakers. Discredit a man's life and you disgrace his preaching. Lay imputations upon the person and that will evacuate and frustrate all his preaching; for whether it be in the corruption of our nature, or whether it be in the nature of the thing itself, so it is, if I believe the preacher to be an ill man I shall not be much the better for his good sermons.

Thus they were injurious in the manner of the calumny. They were so too in the matter, to calumniate him therefore because he applied himself to sinners. The Wiseman in Ecclesiasticus institutes his meditation thus: "There is one that hath great need of help, full of poverty, yet the eye of the Lord looked upon him for good, and set him up from his low estate, so that many that saw it, marvelled at it." Many marvelled, but none reproached the Lord, chid the Lord, calumniated the Lord, for doing so. And if the Lord will look upon a sinner and raise that bedrid man; if he will look with that eye that pierces deeper than the eye of heaven, the sun (and yet with a look of that eye the womb of the earth conceives), if he will look with that eye that conveys more warmth than the eye of the ostrich (and yet with a look of that eye that bird is said to hatch her young ones without sitting), that eye that melted Peter into water and made him flow towards Christ; and rarefied Matthew into air and made him flee towards Christ; if that eye vouchsafe to look upon a publican, and redeem a Goshen out of an Egypt, hatch a soul out of a carnal man, produce a saint out of a sinner, shall we marvel at the matter? marvel so, as to doubt God's power? shall anything be impossible to God? or shall we marvel at the manner, at any way by which Christ shall be pleased to convey his mercy? shall we wonder that Christ would live with sinners who was content to die for sinners? wonder that he would eat the bread and wine of sinners, that gave sinners his own flesh to eat and his own blood to drink?

Or if we do wonder at this (as indeed nothing is more wonderful), yet let us not calumniate, let us not misinterpret any way, that he shall be pleased to take, to derive his mercy to any man. But (to use Clement of Alexandria's comparison) as we tread upon many herbs negligently in the field but when we see them in an apothecary's shop we begin to think that there is some virtue in them; so howsoever we have a perfect hatred and a religious despite against a sinner, as a sinner; yet if Christ Jesus shall have been pleased to have come to his door, and to have stood, and knocked, and entered, and supped, and brought his dish, and made himself that dish, and sealed a reconciliation to that sinner in admitting him to that table, to that Communion, let us forget the name of publican, the vices of any particular profession; and forget the name of sinner, the history of any man's former life; and be glad to meet that man now in the arms, and to grow up with that man now in the bowels of Christ Jesus; since Christ does not now begin to make that man his, but now declares to us that he has been his from all eternity. For in the Book of Life the name of Mary Magdalen was as soon recorded, for all her incontinency, as the

name of the Blessed Virgin, for all her integrity; and the name of
St. Paul who drew his sword against Christ, as soon as St. Peter,
who drew his in defence of him. For the Book of Life was not
written successively, word after word, line after line, but delivered
as a print, all together. There the greatest sinners were as soon
recorded as the most righteous; and here Christ comes to call, not
the righteous at all, but only sinners to repentance.

Christ justifies his conversation with these sinners, and he gives
answers proportionable to the men with whom he dealt. First,
because the Pharisees pretended a knowledge and zeal to the
Scriptures, he answers out of the Scriptures, out of the prophet.
"Mercy is better than sacrifice," and an evangelical desire to do
good upon sinners, better than a legal inhibition to come near
them. And Christ seems to have been so full of this saying of
Hosea, as that he says it here, where the Pharisees calumniate him
to his disciples; and when they calumniate the disciples about the
sabbath he says it there too. He answers out of Scriptures because
they pretend a zeal to them; and then because the Pharisees were
learned and rational men, he answers out of reason too. "The
whole have no need of the physician": I come in the quality of a
physician, and therefore apply myself to the sick. For we read of
many blind and lame and deaf and dumb and dead persons that
came or were brought to Christ to be recovered, but we never read
of any man, who being then in a good state of health, came to
Christ to desire that he might be preserved in that state. The whole
never think of a physician, and therefore Christ, who came in that
quality, applied himself to them that needed. And that he might
give full satisfaction, even to calumniators, every way, as he answered them out of Scriptures and out of reason; so because the
Pharisees were statesmen too, and led by precedents and records,
he answers out of the tenor and letter of his commission and
instructions, which is that part of his answer that falls most directly into our text: "I came to call not the righteous, but sinners
to repentance."

First then, he came, he is come; he came in promise, often
ratified before. Now there is no more room for John the Baptist's
question, "Art thou he that should come, or must we look for

another?" For another coming of the same Messiah we do look, but not for another Messiah. We look for none after him, no post-Messiahs. We join none, saints nor angels, with him, no sub-Messiahs, no vice-Messiahs. The Jews may as well call the history of the flood prophetical and ask when the world shall be drowned according to that prophecy; or the history of their deliverance from Babylon prophetical and ask when they shall return from thence to Jerusalem according to that prophecy, as seek for a Messiah now amongst their prophets, so long after all things being performed in Christ which were prophesied of the Messiah; Christ has so fully made prophecy history.

He is really, personally, actually come; and then he is come freely and of his own mere goodness. How freely? Come and not sent? Yes, he was sent: "God so loved the world, as that he gave his only begotten Son for it." There was enough done to magnify the mercy of the Father in sending him. How freely then? Come and not brought? Yes, he was brought: "The Holy Ghost over-shadowed the Blessed Virgin," and so he was conceived: there was enough done to magnify the goodness of the Holy Ghost in bringing him. He came to his prison, he abhorred not the Virgin's womb; and not without a sending; he was sent: he came to the execution; and not without a desire of reprieve, in his "If it be possible, let this cup pass from me"; and yet he came freely, voluntarily, of his own goodness. No more than he could have been left out at the Creation and the world made without him, could he have been sent into this world without his own hand to the warrant, or have been left out at the decree of his sending. As when he was come, no man could have taken away his soul, if he had not laid it down. So (if we might so speak) no God, no person in the Trinity, could have sent him, if he had not been willing to come. He is come; there's our comfort: he came freely; there's his goodness. And so you have the action: He came.

The next is his errand, his purpose, what he came to do. "He came to call." It is not that Christ came when we called upon him to come. Man had no power, no will, no not a faculty to wish that Christ would have come, till Christ did come and call him. For it is not that Christ came to meet them who were upon the way before.

Man had no predisposition in nature to invite God to come to him. How should I pray at first that God should come into me, whenas I could not only not have the spirit of prayer, but not the spirit of life and being except God were in me already? Where was I, when Christ called me out of my rags, nay out of my ordure, and washed me in the sacramental water of baptism, and made me a Christian so? Where was I, when in the loins of my sinful parents, and in the unclean act of generation, Christ called me into the covenant and made me the child of Christian parents? Could I call upon him to do either of these for me? Or if I may seem to have made any step towards baptism, because I was within the covenant; or towards the covenant, because I was of Christian parents: yet where was I when God called me, when I was not, as though I had been, in the eternal decree of my election? What said I for myself, or what said any other for me then, when neither I nor they had any being? "God is found of them that sought him not." He came not to meet them who were, of themselves, set out before.

He came not to force and compel them who would not be brought into the way. Christ saves no man against his will. There is a word crept into the later school that deludes many a man. They call it *Irresistibility* and they would have it mean that when God would have a man, he will lay hold upon him by such a power of grace as no perverseness of that man can possibly resist. There is some truth in the thing, soberly understood: for the grace of God is more powerful than any resistance of any man or devil. But leave the word where it was hatched, in the school, and bring it not home, not into practice. For he that stays his conversion upon that God, at one time or other, will lay hold upon me by such a power of grace as I shall not be able to resist, may stay till Christ come again to "preach to the spirits that are in prison." Christ beats his drum, but he does not press men; Christ is served with voluntaries.

There is a forcing of men to come in and fill the house and furnish the supper, but that was an extraordinary commission and in a case of necessity. Our ordinary commission is, "Go, and preach the Gospel," and bring men in so. It is not, force men to come in; it is not, draw the sword, kindle the fire, wind up the rack; for, when it was come to that, that men were forced to come in (as that parable is reported in this evangelist), "the house was filled," and the supper was furnished (the Church was filled and the Communion table frequented), but it was with good and bad too: for men that are forced to come hither, they are not much the better in themselves, nor we much the better assured of their religion for that. Force and violence, pecuniary and bloody laws, are not the right way to bring men to religion, in cases where there is nothing in consideration but religion merely. But Christ's end being merely spiritual, to constitute a Church, as he came not to meet man, man was not so forward; so he came not to compel man, to deal upon any that was so backward; for, "He came to call."

Now this calling implies a voice, as well as a Word. It is by the Word; but not by the Word read at home, though that be a pious exercise; nor by the Word submitted to private interpretation; but by the Word preached, according to his ordinance, and under the great seal of his blessing upon his ordinance. So that preaching is this calling; and therefore, as if Christ do appear to any man, in the power of a miracle, or in a private inspiration, yet he appears but in weakness, as in an infancy, till he speak, till he bring a man to the hearing of his voice in a settled Church and in the ordinance of preaching. So how long soever Christ have dwelt in any State or any Church, if he grow speechless, he is departing; if there be a discontinuing or slackening of preaching there is a danger of losing Christ. Adam was not made in Paradise but brought thither, called thither: the sons of Adam are not born in the Church, but called thither by baptism. No man is born a Christian, but called into that state by regeneration. And therefore, as the consummation of our happiness is in that we shall be called at last into the Kingdom of Glory, in the "Come ye blessed, and enter into your Master's joy"; so it is a blessed inchoation of that happiness that we are called into the Kingdom of Grace and made partakers of his Word and sacraments and other ordinances by the way. And so you have his action and errand, "he came" and "came to call."

The next is the persons upon whom he works, whom he calls; where we have first the negative, the exclusive, "Not the righteous." In which, Gregory of Nyssa is so tender, so compassionate,

so loath that this negative should fall upon any man, that any man
should be excluded from possibility of salvation, as that he carries
it wholly upon Angels: "Christ took not the nature of Angels,"
Christ came not to call Angels. But this exclusion falls upon men.
What men? Upon the righteous. Who are they? Were there any
that needed not Christ's coming? No, there were none. Who then
are these righteous?

We answer with St. Chrysostom and St. Jerome and St. Ambrose and all the stream of the Fathers. They are those who
thought themselves righteous; those who relied upon their own
righteousness; those who mistook their righteousness, as the
Laodiceans did their riches; they said, "They were rich and had
need of nothing; and they were wretched, and miserable, and poor,
and blind, and naked." So, these men, "being ignorant of God's
righteousness, and going about to establish a righteousness of their
own, have not submitted themselves to the righteousness of God";
that is, depend wholly upon the righteousness of Christ. He calls it
"their righteousness" because they thought they had a righteousness of their own, either in the faculties of nature, or in the exaltation of those faculties by the help of the law. And he calls it "their
righteousness" because they thought none had it but they. And
upon this Pelagian righteousness, it thought nature sufficient without grace. Or upon this righteousness of the Cathari, the Puritans
in the Primitive Church, that thought the grace which they had
received sufficient, and that upon that stock they were safe, and
become impeccable, and therefore left out of the Lord's Prayer
that petition, "Forgive us our trespasses." Upon this Pelagian
righteousness, and this Puritan righteousness Christ does not work.
He left out the righteous, not that there were any such, but such as
thought themselves so; and he took in sinners, not all effectually,
that were simply so, but such as the sense of their sins, and the
miserable state that that occasioned, brought to an acknowledgment that they were so.

Here then enters our affirmative, our inclusive. Who are called:
sinners. For here no man asks the question of the former branch.
There we asked whether there were any righteous, and we found
none. Here we ask not whether there were any sinners, for we can

find no others, no not one. He came to call sinners, and only
sinners; that is, only in that capacity, in that contemplation, as
they were sinners. He came for sinners; for sinners only; else he
had not come. And then he came for all kinds of sinners. For upon
those words of our Savior's to the high priests and Pharisees,
"Publicans and harlots go into the Kingdom of Heaven before
you," good expositors note that in those two notations, "publicans" and "harlots," many sorts of sinners are implied. In the
name of publicans, all such as by their very profession and calling
are led into temptations and occasions of sin, to which some callings are naturally more exposed than other, such as can hardly be
exercised without sin. And then in the name of harlots, and prosti-
tute women, such as cannot at all be exercised without sin; whose
very profession is sin. And yet for these, for the worst of these, for
all these, there is a voice gone out, Christ is come to call sinners,
only sinners, all sinners.

Comes he then thus for sinners? What an advantage had St. Paul
then, to be of this quorum, and the first of them; that when Christ
came to save sinners he should be the greatest sinner, the first in
that election? If we should live to see that acted which Christ
speaks of at the last day, "Two in the field, the one taken, the
other left," should we not wonder to see him that were left lay hold
upon him that were taken and offer to go to Heaven before him,
therefore, because he had killed more men in the field, or robbed
more men upon the highway, or supplanted more in the court, or
oppressed more in the city? to make the multiplicity of his sins his
title to Heaven? Or, "two women grinding at the mill, one taken,
the other left"; to see her that was left offer to precede the other
into Heaven, therefore, because she had prostituted herself to more
men than the other had done? Is that St. Paul's quorum, his dignity,
his prudency; I must be saved because I am the greatest sinner?
God forbid: God forbid we should presume upon salvation because we are sinners, or sin therefore that we may be surer of
salvation.

St. Paul's title to Heaven was not that he was first sinner, but
first confessor; that he first accused himself and came to a sense of
his miserable estate; for that implies that which is our last word,

and the effect of Christ's calling, that whomsoever he calls, or how, or whensoever, it is to repentance. Christ does not come to call us to make satisfaction to the justice of God; he called us to a heavy, to an impossible account, if he called us to that. If the death of Christ Jesus himself be but a satisfaction for the punishment of my sins (for nothing less than that could have made that satisfaction), what can a temporary Purgatory of days or hours do towards a satisfaction? And if the torments of Purgatory itself, sustained by myself, be nothing towards a satisfaction, what can an evening's fast, or an Ave Maria, from my executor or my assignee after I am dead, do towards such a satisfaction? Can you satisfy the justice of God, for all that blood which you have drawn from his Son, in your blasphemous oaths and execrations; or for all that blood of his which you have spilt upon the ground, upon the dunghill, in your unworthy receiving the Sacrament? Can you satisfy his justice for having made his blessings the occasions and the instruments of your sin; or for the delapidations of his temple, in having destroyed your own body by your incontinency and making that the same flesh with a harlot? "If he will contend with thee, thou canst not answer him one of a thousand." Nay, a thousand men could not answer one sin of one man.

Christ does not call us to an immediate possession of glory without doing anything in between. Our glorification was in his intention as soon as our election. In God who sees all things at once, both entered at once. But in the execution of his decrees here God carries us by steps; he calls us to repentance. The Holy Ghost tells us; it is "to repentance." Are you to learn now what that is? He that cannot define repentance, he that cannot spell it, may have it; and he that has written whole books, great volumes of it, may be without it. In one word (one word will not do it, but in two words), it is *Aversio* and *Conversio;* it is a *turning* from our sins, and a *returning* to our God. It is both: for in our age, in our sickness, in any impotency toward a sin, in any satiety of a sin, we turn from our sin, but we turn not to God; we turn to a sinful delight in the memory of our sins and a sinful desire that we might continue in them. So also in a storm at sea, in any imminent calamity at land, we turn to God, to a "Lord, Lord"; but at the next calm, and at the next deliverance, we turn to our sin again. He only is the true Israelite, the true penitent, that has Nathaniel's mark, "In whom there is no deceit." For to sin and think God sees it not because we confess it not; to confess it as sin and yet continue the practice of it; to discontinue the practice of it and continue the possession of that which was got by that sin; all this is deceit and destroys, evacuates, annihilates all repentance.

To recollect all and to end all: Christ justifies feasting; he feasts you with himself. And feasting in an Apostle's house, in his own house; he feasts you often here. And he admits publicans to this feast, men whose full and open life, in court, must necessarily expose them to many hazards of sin.

This Christ, with joy and thanksgiving, we acknowledge to be come; to be come actually; we expect no other after him, we join no other to him. And come freely, without any necessity imposed by any above him, and without any invitation from us here. Come, not to meet us, who were not able to rise without him; but yet not to force us, to save us against our wills, but come to call us by his ordinances in his Church. Us, not as we pretend any righteousness of our own, but as we confess ourselves to be sinners, and sinners led by this call to repentance; which repentance is an everlasting divorce from our beloved sin, and an everlasting marriage and super-induction of our everliving God.

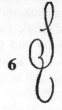

THE SHOWING FORTH OF CHRIST;

6 A CHRISTMAS SERMON

Lord now lettest thou thy servant depart in peace, according to thy word: For mine eyes have seen thy salvation.

LUKE 2:29-30

THE WHOLE LIFE OF CHRIST WAS A CONTINUAL Passion; others die martyrs but Christ was born a martyr. He found a Golgotha (where he was crucified) even in Bethlehem, where he was born; for to his tenderness then the straws were almost as sharp as the thorns after, and the manger as uneasy at first as his cross at last. His birth and his death were but one continual act, and his Christmas day and his Good Friday are but the evening and morning of one and the same day. And as even his birth is his death, so every action and passage that manifests Christ to us is his birth, for *Epiphany* is *manifestation*. And therefore, though the Church do now call Twelfth-day Epiphany, because upon that day Christ was manifested to the Gentiles in those Wise Men who came then to worship him, yet the ancient Church called this day (the day of Christ's birth) the Epiphany, because this day Christ was manifested to the world by being born this day. Every manifestation of Christ to the world, to the Church, to a particular soul, is an Epiphany, a Christmas day. Now there is nowhere a more evident manifestation of Christ than in that which induced this text, "Lord now lettest thou thy servant, etc."

It had been revealed to Simeon (whose words these are) that he should see Christ before he died. And actually, and really, substantially, essentially, bodily, presentially, personally he does see him; so it is Simeon's Epiphany, Simeon's Christmas day. So also this day, in which we commemorate and celebrate the general Epiphany, the manifestation of Christ to the whole world in his birth, all we, we who besides our interest in the universal Epiphany and manifestation implied in the very day, have this day received the Body and Blood of Christ in his holy and blessed Sacrament, have had another Epiphany, another Christmas day, another manifestation and application of Christ to ourselves. And as the Church prepares our devotion before Christmas day with four Sundays in Advent, which brings Christ nearer and nearer unto us and remembers us that he is coming, and then continues that remembrance again with the celebration of other festivals with it, and after it, as St. Stephen, St. John and the rest that follow; so for this birth of Christ in your particular souls, for this Epiphany, this Christmas day, this manifestation of Christ which you have had in the most blessed Sacrament this day, as you were prepared before by that which was said before, so it belongs to the thorough celebration of the day, and to the dignity of that mysterious act, and to the blessedness of worthy and the danger of unworthy receivers, to press that evidence in your behalf and to enable you by a farther examination of yourselves to depart in peace because your eyes have seen his salvation.

To be able to conclude to yourselves that because you have had a Christmas day, a manifestation of Christ's birth in your souls by the Sacrament, you shall have a whole Good Friday, a crucifying and an "it is finished," a measure of corrections, and joy in those corrections, temptations, and the issue with the temptation; and that you shall have a Resurrection and an Ascension, an inchoation and an unremovable possession of heaven itself in this world; make good your Christmas day, that Christ by a worthy receiving of the Sacrament be born in you, and he that died for you will live with you all the year, and all the years of your lives, and inspire into you, and receive from you at the last gasp, this blessed acclamation, "Lord now lettest thou thy servant, etc."

In the first part we collect some marks and qualities in Simeon which prepared him to a quiet death, qualities appliable to us in that capacity as we are fitted for the Sacrament (for in that way only we shall walk throughout this exercise), we consider first the action itself, what was done at this time. At this time our Savior Christ, according to the Law by which all the first born were to be presented to God in the temple at a certain time after their birth, was presented to God in the temple and there acknowledged to be his; and then bought of him again by his parents at a certain price prescribed in the Law. A lord could not exhibit his son to his tenants and say this is your landlord; nor a king his son to his subjects and say this is your prince; but first he was to be tendered to God; his they were all; he that is not God's first is not truly his king's nor his own. And then God does not sell him back to his parents at a racked, at an improved price. He sells a lord or a king back again to the world as cheap as a yeoman; he takes one and the same price for all. God made all mankind of one blood, and with one blood, the blood of his Son, he bought all mankind again. At one price and upon the same conditions he has delivered over all into this world. Believe and live well is the price of all. More he asks not, less he takes not for any man, upon any pretense of any unconditioned decree.

At the time of this presentation there were to be offered a pair of turtles [turtledoves] or a pair of pigeons. The sacrifice was indifferent: turtles that live solitarily and pigeons that live sociably were all one to God. God in Christ may be had in an active and sociable life, denoted in the pigeon, and in the solitary and contemplative life, denoted in the turtle. Let not Westminster despise the Church, nor the Church the exchange, nor the exchange and trade despise arms. God in Christ may be had in every lawful calling. And then, the pigeon was an emblem of fecundity and fruitfulness in marriage. And the turtle may be an emblem of chaste widowhood, for I think we find no bigamy in the turtle. But in these sacrifices we find no emblem of a natural or of a vowed barrenness; nothing that countenances a vowed virginity to the dishonor or undervaluing of marriage.

Thus was our Savior presented to God. And in this especially was that fulfilled: "The glory of the later house shall be greater than the glory of the former." The later temple exceeded the former in this, that the Lord, the God of this house, was in the house bodily as one of the congregation. And the little body of a sucking child was a chapel in that temple, infinitely more glorious than the temple itself. How was the joy of Noah at the return of the dove into the ark multiplied upon Simeon at the bringing of this Dove into the temple? At how cheap a price was Christ tumbled up and down in this world? It does almost take off our pious scorn of the low price at which Judas sold him, to consider that his Father sold him to the world for nothing; and then, when he had him again, by this new title of primogeniture and presentation, he sold him to the world again, if not for a turtle or for a pigeon, yet at most for five shekels, which at most is but ten shillings.

And yet you have had him cheaper than that today in the Sacrament. Whom has Christ cost five shekels there? As Christ was presented to God in the temple so is he presented to God in the Sacrament; not sucking, but bleeding. And God gives him back again to you. And at what price? Upon this exchange: take his first born, Christ Jesus, and give him yours. Who is yours? The heart is the first part of the body that lives; give him that. And then, as it is in nature it shall be in grace too, the last part that dies; for it shall never die. "If a man eat the bread that cometh down from heaven, he shall not die," says Christ. If a man in exchange of his heart receive Christ Jesus himself, he can no more die than Christ Jesus himself can die. That which Aeschines said to Socrates admits a fair accommodation here. He saw everybody give Socrates some present, and he said, "Because I have nothing else to give, I will give you myself." "Do so," says Socrates, "and I will give you back again to yourself better than when I received you." If you have truly given yourself to him in the Sacrament, God has given you yourself back so much mended as that you have received yourself and him too; yourself in a holy liberty to walk in the world in a calling, and himself in giving a blessing upon all the works of your calling and imprinting in you a holy desire to do all those works to his glory.

And so having thus far made this profit of these circumstances in the action itself appliable to us as receivers of the Sacrament,

that as the child Jesus was first presented to God in the temple, so
for your children (the children of your bodies, and the children of
your minds, and the children of your hands, all your actions and
intentions), that you direct them first upon God, and God in the
temple, that is, God manifested in the Church, before you assign
them or determine them upon any other worldly courses, and then,
that as God returned Christ as all other children, at a certain price,
so God delivers man upon certain, and upon the same conditions.
He comes not into the world, nor he comes not to the Sacrament
as to a lottery, where perchance he may draw salvation but it is ten
to one he misses, but upon these few and easy conditions: believe
and love, he may be sure. And then also, that the sacrifice, pigeons
or turtles, was indifferent, so it were offered to God, for any honest
calling is acceptable to God if God's glory be intended in it.

We receive it by general tradition from all, that Simeon was now
come to a great age, a very old man. So then we accept him, a
person in a reverend age. Even in nature age was the center of
reverence, the channel, the valley, to which all reverence flowed. In
this blessed age Simeon was thus dignified, admitted to this Epiphany, this manifestation of Christ. And to be admitted to your
Epiphany and manifestation of Christ in the Sacrament, you must
put off the young man and put on the old. God, to whose table you
are called, is represented as the ancient of days, and his guess
must be of mortified affections. He must be crucified to the world,
that will receive him who was crucified for the world. The lusts of
youth, the voluptuousness of youth, the revengefulness of youth
must have a holy damp shed upon them that come thither. Nay it
is not enough to be suddenly old, to have sad and mortified
thoughts then; no, nor to be suddenly dead, to renounce the world
then, that hour, that morning, but you should have been dead four
days, as Lazarus. You should have passed an examination, an
accusation, a condemnation of yourselves divers days before you
came to that table. God was most glorified in the raising of Lazarus when he was long dead and putrefied. God is most glorified in
giving a resurrection to him who has been longest dead; that is,
longest in the contemplation of his own sinful and spiritual putrefaction. For he that stinks most in his own, by true contrition, is

the best perfume to God's nostrils, and a conscience troubled in itself is, as Noah's sacrifice was, a savor of rest to God.

This assistance we have to the exaltation of our devotion from that circumstance, that Simeon was an old man. We have another from another, that he was a priest, and in that capacity the better fitted for this Epiphany, this Christmas, this manifestation of Christ. We have not this in the letter of the story, nor so constantly in the tradition, that he was a priest, as that he was an old man, but it is rooted in antiquity, too. Accepting him in that quality, a priest, we consider that as the king takes it worse in his household servant than in his subjects at large if they go not his ways, so they who dwell in God's house, whose livelihood grows out of the revenue of his Church, and whose service lies within the walls of his Church, are most inexcusable if they have not a continual Epiphany, a continual manifestation of Christ. All men should look towards God, but the priest should never look off from God. And at the Sacrament every man is a priest.

Consider then that to come to the Communion table is to take Orders. Every man should come to that altar as holy as the priest, for there he is a priest. And no man is truly a priest which is anything else besides a priest; that is, that entangles himself in any other business so as that hinders his function in his priesthood. No man comes to the Sacrament well that is sorry he is there; that is, whom the penalty of the law, or observation of neighbors, or any collateral respect brings thither. There you are a priest, though you be but a layman at home. And then, no man that has taken Orders can deprive himself, or divest his Orders, when he will. You are bound to continue in the same holiness after, in which you present yourself at that table. As the sails of a ship when they are spread and swollen, and the way that the ship makes, shows me the wind, where it is, though the wind itself be an invisible thing; so your actions tomorrow, and the life that you lead all the year, will show me with what mind you came to the Sacrament today, though only God, and not I, can see your mind. Live in remembrance that you were a priest today, for no man has received Christ that has not sacrificed himself. And live as though you were a priest still, and then I say, with Sidonius Apollinaris, I had rather have one man that lives as a priest should do than a hundred priests who live not so. A worthy receiver shall rise in Judgment against an unworthy giver. Christ shall be the sacrifice still, and you the priest, that came but to receive, because you have sacrificed yourself.

It is farther added for his [Simeon's] honor, and for his competency and fitness for this Epiphany, to see his Savior, that he was a just and righteous man. This is a legal righteousness; a righteousness in which St. Paul says he was unreproachable; that is, in the sight of all the world. And this righteousness, even this outward righteousness, he must bring with him that comes to this Epiphany, to this manifestation and application of his Savior to him in the Sacrament. It must stand well between him and all the world. If you bring your gift to the altar, says Christ (if you bring yourself to the altar, says our case), and there remember that your brother has ought against you (it was ill done not to remember it before, but if you remember it then), go your way, says Christ, first be reconciled to your brother and then come and offer your gift; that is, offer yourself for that sacrifice. Better come a month after, with a clear, than kneel it out then with a perplexed, conscience. If your brother have ought against you, how little soever; if you have but scandalized him, though you have not injured him, yet venture not upon this holy action till you have satisfied him. You may be good; good so as that you have intended no ill to him. He may be good, too; good so as that he wishes no ill to you. And yet some negligence and remissness in you may have struck upon a weakness and a tenderness in him, so as that he may be come to think uncharitably of you. And though this uncharitableness be his fault and not yours, yet the negligence that occasioned it was yours. Satisfy him and that rectifies both; it redeems your negligence, it recovers his weakness. Till that be done, neither of you are fit for this holy action. God neither accepts that man that is negligent of his actions and cares not what others think, nor him that is overeasy to be scandalized and misinterpret actions otherwise indifferent. For to them who study not this righteousness, to stand upright in the good opinions of good men, as God says, "Why takest thou my word into thy mouth," so Christ shall say, to the shaking of that conscience, "Why takest thou my Body and Blood into thy hand?"

We cannot pursue this anatomy of good old Simeon, this just

and devout priest, so far as to show you all his parts and the use of them all in particular. His example, and the characters that are upon him, are our alphabet. I shall only have time to name the rest of those characters; you must spell them and put them into their syllables; you must form them and put them into their words; you must compose them and put them into their syntax and sentences; that is, you must pursue the imitation, that when I have told you what he was, you may present yourselves to God such as he was. He was one that had the Holy Ghost upon him, says that story. The testimony given before that he was righteous and fearing God was evidence enough that the Holy Ghost was upon him. This addition is a testimony of a more particular presence and operation of the Holy Ghost, in some certain way; and the way is agreed by all to be, the Holy Ghost was upon him in the spirit of prophecy, so as that he made him, at that time, a prophet.

You are a prophet upon yourself when you come to the Communion. You are able to foretell and to pronounce upon yourself what you shall be forever. Upon your disposition then, you may conclude your eternal state. Then you know which part of St. Paul's distribution falls upon you; whether that tribulation and anguish upon every soul of man that does evil, or that glory, and honor, and peace to every man that works good. You are this prophet; silence not this prophet; do not chide your conscience for chiding you; stone not this prophet; do not petrify and harden your conscience against these holy suggestions. Say not with Ahab to the prophet, "Hast thou found me out, O mine enemy?" When an unrepented sin comes to your memory then, be not sorry that you remember it then, nor do not say, I would this sin had not troubled me now, I would I had not remembered it until tomorrow. For in that action you are a preacher to yourself, and you have your text in St. Paul: "He that eateth and drinketh unworthily, eateth and drinketh damnation to himself." And then, for the application to the particular case, you are a prophet to yourself; you that know in yourself what you do then, can say to yourself what you shall suffer after, if you do ill.

There are more elements in the making up of this man; many more. He waited, says the story, and he waited for the consolation of Israel. It is not an appropriating of hopes, or possessions of those hopes, to himself, but a charitable desire of a communication of this consolation upon all the Israel of God. Therefore is the Sacrament a Communion; therefore is the Church, which is built of us, "Built of lively stones." And in such buildings every stone is supported by another and supports another. As you would be well interpreted by others, interpret others well. And as when you come to Heaven the joy and the glory of every soul shall be your glory and your joy, so when you come to the porch of the triumphant Church, the door of Heaven, the Communion table, desire that that joy which you feel in your soul then may then be communicated to every communicant there.

To this purpose, to testify his devotion to the communion of saints, Simeon came into the temple, says the story; to do a holy work in a holy place. When we say that God is no accepter of persons, we do not mean but that they which are within his covenant, and they that have preserved the seals of his grace, are more acceptable to him than they which are not, or have not. When we say that God is not tied to places, we must not mean but that God is otherwise present, and works otherwise, in places consecrated to his service than in every profane place. When I pray in my chamber I build a temple there, that hour. And that minute, when I cast out a prayer in the street, I build a temple there. And when my soul prays without any voice, my very body is then a temple. And God, who knows what I am doing in these actions, erecting these temples, he comes to them, and prospers and blesses my devotions. And shall not I come to his temple where he is always resident? My chamber were no temple, my body were no temple, except God came to it. But whether I come hither or no, this will be God's temple. I may lose by my absence; he gains nothing by my coming.

He that has a cause to be heard will not go to Smithfield, nor he that has cattle to buy or sell to Westminster. He that has bargains to make or news to tell should not come to do that at Church; nor he that has prayers to make walk in the fields for his devotions. If I have a great friend, though in cases of necessity, as sickness or other restraints, he will vouchsafe to visit me, yet I must make my suits to him at home, at his own house. In cases of necessity, Christ in the Sacrament vouchsafes to come home to me. And the Court is where the King is; his blessings are with his ordinances wheresoever; but the place to which he has invited me is his house. He that made the great supper in the Gospel called in new guests, but he sent out no meat to them who had been invited and might have come and came not. Chamber prayers, single or with your family, chamber sermons, sermons read over there; and chamber Sacraments administered in necessity there are blessed assistants and supplements. They are as the alms at the gate, but the feast is within; they are as a cock of water without, but the cistern is within. He that has a handful of devotion at home shall have his devotion multiplied to a gomer here; for when he is become a part of the congregation he is joint tenant with them and the devotion of all the congregation and the blessings upon all the congregation are his blessings and his devotion.

He came to a holy place and he came by a holy motion, by the Spirit, says his evidence; without holiness no man shall see God. Not so well, without holiness of the place, but not there neither if he trust only to the holiness of the place and bring no holiness with him. Between that fearful occasion of coming to Church which St. Augustine confesses and laments, that they came to make wanton bargains with their eyes and met there because they could meet nowhere else; and that more fearful occasion of coming, when they come only to elude the Law, and proceeding in their treacherous and traitorous religion in their heart, and yet communicating with us, draw God himself into their conspiracies and to mock us make a mock of God and his religion too: between these two, this licentious coming and this treacherous coming, there are many comings to Church, comings for company, for observation, for music. And all these indispostions are ill at prayers; there they are unwholesome, but at the Sacrament, deadly. He that brings any collateral respect to prayers loses the benefit of the prayers of the congregation; and he that brings that to a sermon loses the blessings of God's ordinance in that sermon; he hears but the logic, or the rhetoric, or the ethic, or the poetry of the sermon, but the sermon of the sermon he hears not. But he that brings this disposition to the Sacrament ends not in the loss of a benefit, but he acquires and procures his own damnation.

All that we consider in Simeon and apply from Simeon to a worthy receiver of the Sacrament is how he was fitted to depart in peace. All those pieces which we have named conduce to that: but all those are collected into that one which remains yet, that his eyes had seen that salvation. For that was the accomplishment and fulfilling of God's word, "According to thy word." All that God had said should be done was done, for, as it is said, v. 26, "it was revealed unto him, by the Holy Ghost, that he should not see death before he had seen the Lord's Christ," and now his eyes had seen that salvation. Abraham saw this before, but with the eye of faith, and yet rejoiced to see it so, he was glad even of that. Simeon saw it before this time; then, when he was illustrated with that revelation, he saw it; but with the eye of hope. Of such hope Abraham had no such ground; no particular hope, no promise, that he should see the Messiah in his time. Simeon had, and yet he waited, he attended God's leisure. But hope deferred maketh the heart sick (says Solomon), but when the desire comes, it is a tree of life. His desire was come; he saw his salvation.

With his bodily eyes he saw the Lord's salvation, and his salvation; the Lord's, as it came from the Lord, and his, as it was appliable to him. He saw it according to his word, that is, so far as God had promised he should see it. He saw not how that God which was in this child, and which was this child, was the Son of God. The manner of that eternal generation he saw not. He saw not how this Son of God became man in a virgin's womb, whom no man knew. The manner of this Incarnation he saw not, for this eternal generation and this miraculous Incarnation fell not within that "according to thy word." God had promised Simeon nothing concerning those mysteries. But the Lord's salvation and his salvation, that is, the person who was all that, Simeon saw and saw with bodily eyes. Beloved, in the blessed and glorious and mysterious Sacrament of the Body and Blood of Christ Jesus, you see the Lord's salvation and your salvation, and that thus far with bodily eyes. That Bread which you see after the consecration is not the same bread which was presented before; not that it is transubstantiated to another substance, for it is bread still, but that it is severed and appropriated by God, in that ordinance, to another use. It is other Bread, so as a judge is another man upon the bench than he is at home in his own house.

And lastly, contenting himself with so much therein as was according to his word, and not inquiring farther than God had been pleased to reveal; and having reflected all these several beams upon every worthy receiver of the Sacrament, the whole choir of such worthy receivers may join with Simeon in this antiphon, "Lord now lettest thou thy servant depart in peace, etc." And so, I know not upon what grounds, Nicephorus says Simeon did wish, and had his wish; he prayed that he might die and actually he did die then. Neither can a man at any time be fitter to make and obtain this wish than when his eyes have seen his salvation in the Sacrament. At least make this an argument of your having been worthy receivers thereof, that you are in an evenness, in an indifferency, in an equanimity whether you die this night or no.

Simeon is so good a servant as that he is content to serve his old master still, in his old place, in this world, but yet he is so good a husband too as that he sees what a gainer he might be if he might be made free by death. If you desire not death (that is the case of very few, to do so in a rectified conscience and without distemper), if you be not equally disposed towards death (that should be the case of all, and yet we are far from condemning all that are not come to that equanimity), yet if you now fear death inordinately, I should fear that your eyes have not seen your salvation today. Who can fear the darkness of death that has had the light of this world and of the next too? Who can fear death this night that has had the Lord of life in his hand today? It is a question of consternation, a question that should strike him, that should answer it, dumb (as Christ's question, "Friend, how camest in hither?" did him to whom that was said), which Origen asks in this case, "When will you dare to go out of this world, if you dare not go now, when Christ Jesus has taken you by the hand to lead you out?"

This then is truly to depart in peace by the Gospel of peace to the God of peace. My body is my prison and I would be so obedient to the law as not to break prison. I would not hasten my death by starving or macerating this body. But if this prison be burnt down by continual fevers, or blown down with continual vapors, would any man be so in love with that ground upon which that prison stood as to desire rather to stay there than to go home? Our prisons are fallen, our bodies are dead to many former uses; our palate dead in a tastelessness; our stomach dead in an indigestibleness; our feet dead in a lameness, and our invention in a dullness, and our memory in a forgetfulness. And yet, as a man that should love the ground where his prison stood, we love this clay that was a body in the days of our youth, and but our prison then when it was at its best. We abhor the graves of our bodies, and the body, which in the best vigor thereof was but the grave of the soul, we over-love.

Pharaoh's butler and his baker went both out of prison in a day; and in both cases, Joseph, in the interpretation of their dreams, calls that (their very discharge out of prison) a lifting up of their heads, a kind of preferment. Death raises every man alike, so far as that it delivers every man from his prison, from the encumbrances of this body. Both baker and butler were delivered of their prison, but they passed into divers states after, one to the restitution of his place, the other to an ignominious execution.

Of your prison you shall be delivered whether you will or no. You must die. Fool, this night your soul may be taken from you; and then, what you shall be tomorrow prophesy upon yourself, by that which you have done today. If you did depart from that Table in peace you can depart from this world in peace. And the peace of that Table is to come to it with a contented mind and with an enjoying of those temporal blessings which you have, without macerating yourself, without usurping upon others, without murmuring at God; and to be at that Table in the peace of the Church, without the spirit of contradiction or inquisition, without uncharitableness towards others, without curiosity in yourself; and then to come from that Table with a bosom peace in your own conscience, in that seal of your reconciliation, in that Sacrament; that so, riding at that anchor and in that calm, whether God enlarge your voyage by enlarging your life, or put you into the harbor by the breath, by the breathlessness of death, either way, East or West, you may depart in peace, according to his word, that is, as he shall be pleased to manifest his pleasure upon you.

OF HUMAN MARRIAGE AND THE MARRIAGE OF THE SOUL WITH CHRIST; A WEDDING SERMON

7

And I will marry thee unto me forever.
HOSEA 2:19

THE WORD WHICH IS THE HINGE UPON WHICH ALL this text turns is *Erash,* and *Erash* signifies not only a betrothing, as our later translation has it, but a marriage. And so it is used by David, "Deliver me my wife Michal whom I married." And so our former translation had it, and so we accept it, and so shall handle it, "I will marry thee unto me forever."

The first marriage that was made, God made, and he made it in Paradise: and of that marriage I have had the like occasion as this to speak before, in the presence of many honorable persons in this company. The last marriage which shall be made, God shall make too, and in Paradise too; in the Kingdom of Heaven: and at that marriage, I hope in him that shall make it, to meet not some but all this company. The marriage in this text has relation to both those marriages. It is itself the spiritual and mystical marriage of Christ Jesus to the Church, and to every marriageable soul in the Church. And it has a retrospect, it looks back to the first marriage; for to that the first word carries us, because from thence God takes his metaphor and comparison, "I will marry." And then it has a prospect to the last marriage, for to that we are carried in the last word, "I will marry thee unto me forever." Be pleased therefore to

89

give me leave in this exercise to shift the scene thrice, and to present to your religious considerations three objects, three subjects: first, a secular marriage in Paradise; secondly, a spiritual marriage in the Church; and thirdly, an eternal marriage in Heaven. And in each of these three we shall present three circumstances; first the persons, *"I will marry thee";* and then the action, "I will *marry* thee"; and lastly the term, "I will marry thee to me *forever."*

In the first, the secular marriage in Paradise, the persons were Adam and Eve. Ever since, they are he and she, man and woman. They must be so much; he must be a man, she must be a woman; and they must be no more; not a brother and a sister, not an uncle and a niece. "He brought her to him," was the case between Adam and Eve; God brought them together. God will not bring me a precontracted person, he will not have me defraud another; nor God will not bring me a misbelieving, a superstitious person, he will not have me drawn from himself. But let them be persons that God has made, man and woman, and persons that God has brought together, that is, not put asunder by any law of his, and all such persons are capable of this first, this secular marriage.

Our second consideration is the action, where the active is a kind of passive. "I will marry thee" is "I will be married unto thee," for we marry not ourselves. As marriage is a civil contract, it must be done so in public as that it may have the testimony of men. As marriage is a religious contract it must be so done as that it may have the benediction of the priest. In a marriage without testimony of men they cannot claim any benefit by the law; in a marriage without the benediction of the priest they cannot claim any benefit of the Church: for how matrimonially soever such persons as have married themselves may pretend to love, and live together, yet all that love and all that life is but a regulated adultery, it is not marriage.

Now this institution of marriage had three objects: first, it was given for a remedy against burning; and then, for propagation, for children; and lastly, for mutual help. As we consider it the first way, every heating is not a burning; every natural concupiscence does not require a marriage; nay every flaming is not a burning, though a man continue under the flame of carnal temptation as long as St. Paul did, yet it needs not come presently to an "I will marry." God gave St. Paul other physic, grace to stand under that temptation; and St. Paul gave himself other physic, convenient disciplines to tame his body. These will keep a man from burning, for to be overcome by our concupiscences, that is to burn, but to quench that fire by religious ways, that is a noble, that is a perfect work.

When God at the first institution of marriage had this first use of marriage in his contemplation, that it should be a remedy against burning, God gave man the remedy before he had the disease; for marriage was instituted in the state of innocency when there was no inordinateness in the affections of man and so no burning. Let him then that takes his wife in this first and lowest sense, but as his physic, yet make her his cordial physic, take her to his heart and fill his heart with her, let her dwell there and dwell there alone, and so they will be mutual antidotes and preservatives to one another against all foreign temptations. And with this blessing, bless thou, O Lord, these whom thou hast brought hither for this blessing. Make all the days of their life like this day unto them; and as thy mercies are new every morning, make them so to one another. And if they may not die together, sustain thou the survivor of them in that sad hour with this comfort, that he that died for them both will bring them together in his everlastingness.

The second use of marriage was for children. And therefore, as St. Augustine puts the case, to contract before that they will have no children makes it no marriage but an adultery. To deny themselves to one another is as much against marriage as to give themselves to another. To hinder it by physic or any other practice; nay to hinder it so far as by a deliberate wish or prayer against children, consists not well with this second use of marriage. And yet in this second use, we do not so much consider generation as regeneration; not so much procreation as education, nor propagation as transplantation of children. For this world might be filled full enough of children though there were no marriage; but heaven could not be filled, nor the places of the fallen angels supplied, without that care of children's religious education which from parents in lawful marriage they are likeliest to receive.

How infinite and how miserable a circle of sin do we make if as we sinned in our parents' loins before we were born, so we sin in our children's actions when we are dead, by having given them either example or liberty of sinning. We have also a promise of consolation to women for children. "She shall be saved in child-bearing," says the Apostle; but as Chrysostom and others of the ancients observe and interpret that place, it is not if she, but if they, if the children continue in faith, in charity, in holiness and sobriety.

The salvation of the parents has so much relation to the children's goodness as that if they be ill by the parents' example or indulgence, the parents are as guilty as the children. Are you afraid your child should be stung with a snake, and will you let him play with the old Serpent, in opening himself to all temptations? Are you afraid to let him walk in an ill air, and are you content to let him stand in that pestilent air that is made of nothing but oaths and execrations of blasphemous mouths round about him? It is St. Chrysostom's complaint, we pay dear for our children's damnation by paying at first for all their childish vanities, and then for their sinful insolencies, at any rate; and we might have them saved, and ourselves to the bargain (which were a frugal way and a debt well hedged in), for much less than ours and their damnation stands us in. If you have a desire, says that blessed Father, to leave them certainly rich, do some such thing for God's service as you may leave God in their debt. He cannot break; his estate is inexhaustible; he will not break promise, nor break day; "He will show mercy unto thousands in them that love him and keep his commandments." And here also may another shower of his benedictions fall upon them whom he has prepared and presented here. "Let the wife be as a fruitful vine, and their children like olive plants." To thy glory, let the parents express the love of parents, and the children, to thy glory, the obedience of children, till they both lose that secular name of parents and children and meet all alike in one new name, all saints in thy Kingdom, and fellow servants there.

The third and last use in this institution of secular marriage was for mutual help. There is no state, no man in any state, that needs not the help of others. Subjects need kings, and if kings do not need their subjects, they need alliances abroad and they need counsel at home. Even in Paradise, where the earth produced all things for life without labor, and the beasts submitted themselves to man, so that he had no outward enemy; and in the state of innocency in Paradise, where in man all the affections submitted themselves to reason, so that he had no inward enemy; yet God in this abundant Paradise, and in this secure innocency of Paradise, even in the survey of his own works, saw that though all that he had made was good, yet he had not made all good; he found thus much defect in his own work, that man lacked a helper. Everybody needs the help of others; and every good body does give some kind of help to others. Even into the ark itself, where God blessed them all with a powerful and an immediate protection, God admitted only such as were fitted to help one another, couples. In the ark, which was the type of our best condition in this life, there was not a single person. Christ saved once one thief at the last gasp, to show that there may be late repentances; but in the ark he saved none but married persons, to show that he eases himself in making them helpers to one another. And therefore when we come to rely upon God primarily for our help, God comes to the "I will make thee a help" like yourself: not always like in complexion, nor like in years, nor like in fortune, nor like in birth, but like in mind, like in disposition, like in the love of God and of one another, or else there is no helper.

It was no kind of help that David's wife gave him when she spoke by way of counsel, but in truth in scorn and derision, to draw him from a religious act, as the dancing before the Ark at that time was. It is no help for any respect to slacken the husband in his religion. It was but a poor help that Nabal's wife was fain to give him by telling David, "Alas my husband is but a fool, like his name, and what will you look for at a fool's hand?" It is the worst help of all to raise a husband by dejecting herself, to help her husband forward in this world by forfeiting sinfully and dishonorably her own interest in the next.

The husband is the helper in the nature of a foundation, to sustain and uphold all; the wife in the nature of the roof, to cover imperfections and weaknesses. The husband in the nature of the head from whence all the sinews flow; the wife in the nature of the hands into which those sinews flow and enable them to do their offices. The husband helps as legs to her, she moves by his motion; the wife helps as a staff to him, he moves the better by her assistance. And let this mutual help be a part of our present benediction too. In all the ways of fortune let his industry help her, and in all the crosses of fortune let her patience help him; and in all emergent occasions and dangers spiritual or temporal, "O God make speed to save them, O Lord, make haste to help them."

There remains yet in this secular marriage the term, how long, forever, "I will marry thee forever." Now though there be properly no eternity in this secular marriage, nor in anything in this world (for eternity is only that which never had beginning, nor ever shall have end), yet we may consider a kind of eternity, a kind of circle without beginning, without end, even in this secular marriage. For first, marriage should have no beginning before marriage; no half marriage, no lending away of the mind in conditional precontracts before, no lending away of the body in unchaste wantonness before. The body is the temple of the Holy Ghost; and when two bodies by marriage are to be made one temple, the wife is not as the chancel, reserved and shut up, and the man as the walks below, indifferent and at liberty for every passenger. God in his temple looks for first fruits from both; that so on both sides marriage should have such a degree of eternity as to have had no beginning of marriage before marriage. It should have this degree of eternity too, this quality of a circle to have no interruption, no breaking in the way by unjust suspicions and jealousies. Where there is a spirit of uncleanness, there will necessarily be a spirit of jealousy.

So then this secular marriage should be eternal, forever, as to have no beginning before, and so too as to have no jealous interruption by the way; for it is so eternal as that it can have no end in this life. Those whom God has joined no man, no Devil, can separate. The Devil makes no marriages. He may have a hand in drawing conveyances; in the temporal conditions there may be practice, but the marriage is made by God in Heaven. The Devil can break no marriages neither, though he can by sin break off all

the good uses and take away all the comforts of marriage. I pronounce not now whether adultery dissolves marriage or no. It is St.
Augustine's wisdom to say, where the Scripture is silent, let me be
silent too. And I may go lower than he and say, where the Church
is silent, let me be silent too. And our Church is so far silent in
this as that it has not said that adultery dissolves marriage. Perchance then it is not the death of marriage, but surely it is a deadly
wound.

And this is the eternity of this secular marriage as far as this
world admits any eternity; that it should have no beginning before,
no interruption of jealousy in the way, no such approach towards
dissolution as that incontinency in all opinions and in all Churches
is agreed to be. And here also without any scruple of fear, or of
suspicion of the contrary, there is place for this benediction upon
this couple: Build, O Lord, upon thine own foundations in these
two and establish thy former graces with future; that no person
ever complain of either of them, nor either of them of one another,
and so he and she are married forever.

We are now come in our order proposed at first to our second
part, for all is said that I intended of the secular marriage. And of
this second, the spiritual marriage, much needs not to be said:
there is another priest that contracts that, another preacher that
celebrates that, the Spirit of God to our spirit. And for the third
marriage, the eternal marriage, it is a boldness to speak anything
of a thing so inexpressible as the joys of heaven; it is a diminution
of them to go about to heighten them; it is a shadowing of them to
go about to lay any colors or lights upon them. But yet your
patience may perchance last to a word of each of these three
circumstances, the persons, the actions, the term, both in this spiritual and in the eternal marriage.

First then, as in the former part, the secular marriage, for the
persons there we considered first Adam and Eve, and after every
man and woman, and this couple in particular. So in this spiritual
marriage we consider first Christ and his Church for the persons,
but more particularly Christ and my soul. And can these persons
meet? in such a distance, and in such a disparagement can these
persons meet? the son of God and the son of man? When I con-

sider Christ to be the bud and blossom, the fruit and offspring of
Jehovah, Jehovah himself, and myself before he took me in hand
to be not a potter's vessel of earth, but that earth of which the
potter might make a vessel if he would, and break it if he would
when he had made it; when I consider Christ to have been from
before all beginnings, and to be still the Image of the Father, the
same stamp upon the same metal, and myself a piece of rusty
copper in which those lines of the Image of God which were
imprinted in me in my creation are defaced and worn and washed
and burnt and ground away by my many and many and many sins;
when I consider Christ in his circle, in glory with his Father before
he came into the world, establishing a glorious Church when he
was in this world, and glorifying that Church with that glory which
himself had before, when he went out of this world; and then
consider myself in my circle, I came into this world washed in
mine own tears, and either out of compunction for myself or
compassion for others, I pass through this world as through a
valley of tears, where tears settle and swell, and when I pass out of
this world I leave their eyes whose hands close mine, full of tears
too, can these persons, this Image of God, this God himself, this
glorious God, and this vessel of earth, this earth itself, this inglorious worm of the earth meet without disparagement?

They do meet and make a marriage; because I am not a body
only, but a body and soul, there is a marriage and Christ marries
me. As by the law a man might marry a captive woman in the
wars, if he shaved her head and pared her nails and changed her
clothes: so my Savior having fought for my soul, fought to blood,
to death, to the death of the cross for her, having studied my soul
so much as to write all those Epistles which are in the New Testament to my soul, having presented my soul with his own picture
that I can see his face in all his temporal blessings, having shaved
her head in abating her pride and pared her nails in contracting her
greedy desires, and changed her clothes not to fashion herself after
this world, my soul being thus fitted by himself, Christ Jesus has
married my soul, married her to all the three intendments mentioned in the secular marriage. First, against burning; that whether
I burn myself in the fires of temptation by exposing myself to

occasions of temptation, or be reserved to be burnt by others in the fires of persecution and martyrdom, whether the fires of ambition, or envy, or lust, or the everlasting fires of Hell offer at me in an apprehension of the judgments of God, yet as the Spirit of God shall wipe all tears from my eyes, so the tears of Christ Jesus shall extinguish all fires in my heart, and so it is a marriage, a remedy against burning.

It is so too for children. First, woe unto that single soul that is not married to Christ; that is not come into the way of having issue by him, that is not incorporated in the Christian Church but is yet either in the wilderness of idolatry or in the labyrinth of superstition; woe unto that single man that is not married to Christ in the sacraments of the Church. And woe unto them that are barren after this spiritual marriage, for that is a great curse in the prophet Jeremiah, "write this man childless," that implied all calamities upon him. And as soon as Christ had laid that curse upon the fig tree, "Let no fruit grow upon thee forever," presently the whole tree withered; if no fruit, no leaves neither, nor body left. To be incorporated in the body of Christ Jesus and bring forth no fruits worthy of that profession is a woeful state too. First, woe unto the Gentiles not married unto Christ; and woe unto inconsiderate Christians that think not upon their calling, that conceive not by Christ. But there is a woe unto them too that are with child and are never delivered; that have sometimes good conceptions, religious dispositions, holy desires to the advancement of God's truth, but for some collateral respects dare not utter them nor bring them to their birth, to any effect. The purpose of his marriage to us is to have children by us: and this is his abundant and his present fecundity, that working now, by me in you, in one instant he has children in me and grandchildren by me.

He has married me against burning, and for children; but can he have any use of me for a helper? Surely if I be able to feed him, and clothe him, and harbor him (and Christ would not condemn men at the last day for not doing these if man could not do them), I am able to help him too. Great persons can help him over sea, convey the name of Christ where it has not been preached yet and they can help him home again; restore his name and his truth where superstition with violence has disseized him; and they can help him at home, defend his truth there against all machinations to displant and dispossess him. Great men can help him thus; and every man can help him to a better place in his own heart and his own actions than he has had there. And to be so helped in me and helped by me, to have his glory thereby advanced, Christ has married my soul. And he has married it forever, which is the third and last circumstance in this spiritual as it was in the secular marriage.

And here the eternity is enlarged. In the secular marriage it was an eternity considered only in this life; but this eternity is not begun in this world but from all eternity in the Book of Life, in God's eternal decree for my election, there Christ was married to my soul. Christ was never in minority, never under years; there was never any time when he was not as ancient as the Ancient of Days, as old as his Father. But when my soul was in a strange minority, infinite millions of millions of generations before my soul was a soul, did Christ marry my soul in his eternal decree. So it was eternal, it had no beginning. Neither does he interrupt this by giving me any occasion of jealousy by the way, but loves my soul as though there were no other soul, and would have done and suffered all that he did for me alone if there had been no name but mine in the Book of Life. And as he has married me to him forever, before all beginnings, and forever without any interruptions, so I know that "whom he loves he loves to the end," and that he has given me not a presumptuous impossibility, but a modest infallibility, that no sin of mine shall divorce or separate me from him. For that which ends the secular marriage ends not the spiritual: not death, for my death does not take me from that husband, but that husband being by his Father preferred to higher titles and greater glory in another state, I do but go by death where he is become a King, to have my part in that glory and in those additions which he has received there. And this has led us to our third and last marriage, our eternal marriage in the triumphant Church.

And in this third marriage the persons are the Lamb and my soul. "The marriage of the Lamb is come, and blessed are they that are called to the marriage supper of the Lamb," says St. John, speaking of our state in the general resurrection. That Lamb who was "brought to the slaughter and opened not his mouth," and I who have opened my mouth and poured out imprecations and curses upon men, and execrations and blasphemies against God upon every occasion; that Lamb who "was slain from the beginning"; that "Lamb which took away the sins of the world," and I who brought more sins into the world than any sacrifice but the blood of this Lamb could take away: this Lamb and I (these are the persons) shall meet and marry; there is the action.

This is not a clandestine marriage, not the private seal of Christ in the obsignation of his Spirit; and yet such a clandestine marriage is a good marriage. Nor it is not such a parish marriage as when Christ married me to himself at my baptism in a Church here; and yet that marriage of a Christian soul to Christ in that Sacrament is a blessed marriage. But this is a marriage in that great and glorious congregation, where all my sins shall be laid open to the eyes of all the world, where all the blessed virgins shall see all my uncleanness, and all the martyrs see all my tergiversations, and all the confessors see all my double dealings in God's cause; where Abraham shall see my faithlessness in God's promises; and Job my impatience in God's corrections; and Lazarus my hardness of heart in distributing God's blessings to the poor; and those virgins, and martyrs, and confessors, and Abraham, and Job, and Lazarus, and all that congregation shall look upon the Lamb and upon me, and upon one another, as though they would all forbid those banns and say to one another, Will this Lamb have anything to do with this soul? And yet there and then this Lamb shall marry me, and marry me forever, which is our last circumstance.

It is not well done to call it a circumstance, for the eternity is a great part of the essence of that marriage. Consider then how poor and needy a thing all the riches of this world, how flat and tasteless a thing all the pleasures of this world, how pallid and faint and dilute a thing all the honors of this world are, when the very treasure and joy and glory of Heaven itself were unperfect, if it were not eternal; and my marriage shall be so, forever.

The angels were not married so; they incurred an irreparable divorce from God and are separated forever, and I shall be married to him forever. The angels fell in love, when there was no object presented, before anything was created; when there was nothing but God and themselves they fell in love with themselves and neglected God and so fell forever. I shall see all the beauty and all the glory of the saints of God, and love them all, and know that the Lamb loves them too, without jealousy, on his part, or theirs, or mine, and so be married forever, without interruption or diminution, or change of affections. I shall see the sun black as sackcloth of hair, and the moon become as blood, and the stars fall as a fig tree casts her untimely figs, and the heavens rolled up together as a scroll. I shall see a divorce between princes and their prerogatives, between nature and all her elements, between the spheres and all their intelligences, between matter itself and all her forms, and my marriage shall be forever.

I shall see an end of faith, nothing to be believed that I do not know; and an end of hope, nothing to be wished that I do not enjoy, but no end of that love in which I am married to the Lamb forever. Yea, I shall see an end of some of the offices of the Lamb himself; Christ himself shall be no longer a mediator, an intercessor, an advocate, and yet shall continue a husband to my soul forever. Where I shall be rich enough without jointure, for my husband cannot die; and wise enough without experience, for no new thing can happen there; and healthy enough without physic, for no sickness can enter; and (which is by much the highest of all) safe enough without grace, for no temptation that needs particular grace can attempt me. There, where the angels, which cannot die, could not live, this very body which cannot choose but die, shall live, and live as long as that God of life that made it.

Lighten our darkness, we beseech thee, O Lord, that in thy light we may see light. Illustrate our understandings, kindle our affections, pour oil to our zeal, that we may come to the marriage of this Lamb, and that this Lamb may come quickly to this marriage. And in the meantime bless these thy servants, with making this secular marriage a type of the spiritual, and the spiritual an earnest of that eternal, which they and we, by thy mercy, shall have in the Kingdom which thy Son our Savior hath purchased with the inestimable price of his incorruptible blood.

8 OF CHRIST'S COMING TO REDEEM US,

IN THE TESTIMONY OF PAUL, I

> *This is a faithful saying, and worthy of all*
> *acceptation, that Christ Jesus came into the*
> *world to save sinners; of which I am the*
> *chiefest.*   I TIMOTHY 1:15

THE GREATEST PART OF THE BODY OF THE OLD
Testament is prophecy, and that is especially of future things.
The greatest part of the New Testament, if we number the pieces,
is epistles, relations of things past for instruction of the present.
They err not much that call the whole New Testament epistle: for
even the Gospels are good messages, and that's proper to an epistle, and the book of the Acts of the Apostles is superscribed by St.
Luke to one person, to Theophilus, and that's proper to an epistle;
and so is the last book, the book of Revelation, to the several
Churches, and of the rest there is no question. An epistle, says St.
Ambrose, though it be written far off and sent, yet it is a conference, and by this means we overcome distances, we deceive ab-
sences, and we are together even then when we are asunder. And
therefore, in this kind of conveying spiritual comfort to their
friends, have the ancient Fathers been more exercised than in any
other form; almost all of them have written epistles.

St. Paul gave them the example; he writ nothing but in this kind
and in this exceeded all his fellow Apostles. As he had asked
letters of commission of the state to persecute Christians, so by
these letters of consolation he might recompense that Church again

101

which he had so much damnified before, as the Hebrew rabbis say that Rahab did let down Joshua's spies out of her house with the same cord with which she had used formerly to draw up her adulterous lovers into her house. Now the Holy Ghost was in all the authors of all the books of the Bible, but in St. Paul's epistles there is, says Irenaeus, the vehemence, the force of the Holy Ghost. And as that vehemence is in all his epistles, so (as St. Chrysostom makes the observation) those epistles which were written in prison have most of this holy vehemence, and this (as that Father notes also) is one of them. And of all them, we may justly conceive this to be the most vehement and forcible, in which he undertakes to instruct a bishop in his episcopal function, which is to propagate the Gospel; for he is but an ill bishop that leaves Christ where he found him, in whose time the Gospel is yet no farther than it was; how much worse is he, in whose time the Gospel loses ground? who leaves not the Gospel in so good state as he found it? Now of this Gospel, here recommended by Paul to Timothy, this is the sum: "That Christ Jesus came into the world to save sinners."

The Gospel is founded and rooted in the Word; it cannot deserve all acceptation if it be not Gospel, and it is not Gospel if it be not rooted in the Word. Christ himself, as he has an eternal generation, himself is the Word of God; and as he has a human generation, he is the subject of the Word of God, of all the Scriptures, of all that was shadowed in the types and figured in the ceremonies, of all that was foretold by the prophets, of all that the soul of man rejoiced in and congratulated with the Spirit of God in the Psalms and in the canticles and in the cheerful parts of spiritual joy and exultation which we have in the Scriptures. Christ is the foundation of all those Scriptures, Christ is the burden of all those songs; Christ was in the Word. The joy of those holy persons which are noted in the Scriptures to have expressed their joy at the birth of Christ in such spiritual hymns and songs, is expressed so as that we may see their joy was in this, that that was now performed that was before in the promise, in the Word, in the Covenant of God. They rejoiced that Christ was born, but principally that all was done so, as God had spoken before, that all should be done. So then there never was, there never must be, any other Gospel than is in the written word of God in the Scriptures.

The particular comfort that a Christian conceives is principally in this, that Christ is come. His comfort is in this, that he is now saved by him; and he might have this comfort though Christ had never been prophesied, never spoken of before. But yet the proof and ground of this comfort to himself, the assurance that this was that Christ that was to save us, this is not only that, that the sun of the Gospel is risen in that Christ is come, but in this, that he is come as God had spoken of him and promised him by the mouth of his prophets from the beginning; as he was in the Word.

In the first Creation, when God made heaven and earth, that making was not in the Word, for that could not be prophesied before because there was no being before. Neither is it said that at that Creation God said anything, but only "God made heaven and earth," and no more. So that that which was made without speaking was only matter without form, heaven without light, and earth without any productive virtue or disposition to bring forth and to nourish creatures. But when God came to those specific forms, and to those creatures wherein he would be sensibly glorified after, they were made by his word. God spake, and so all things were made; light and firmament, land and sea, plants and beasts, and fishes and fowls were made all by his word. But when God came to the best of his creatures, to man, man was not only made as the rest were, by speaking a word, but by a consultation, by a conference, by a counsel: "Let us make man." There is a more express manifestation of divers persons speaking together, of a concurrence of the Trinity; and not of a saying only, but a mutual saying; not of a proposition only, but of a dialogue in the making of man. The making of matter alone was without any word at all; the making of lesser creatures was by saying, by speaking; the making of man was in a consultation.

In this first Creation thus presented there is a shadow, a representation of our second Creation, our regeneration in Christ, and of the saving knowledge of God; for first there is in man a knowledge of God without his Word, in the book of creatures. David says, "They have no language, they have no speech, and yet they declare the glory of God." The correspondence and relation of all parts of nature to one author, the dependence of every piece and joint of this frame of the world, the admirable order, the immutable succession, the lively and certain generation and birth of effects from their parents, the causes: in all these, though there be no sound, no voice, yet we may even see that it is an excellent song, an admirable piece of music and harmony; and that God does (as it were) play upon this organ in his administration and providence by natural means and instruments; and so there is some kind of creation in us, some knowledge of God imprinted without any relation to his Word. But this is a Creation as of heaven and earth, which were dark and empty, and without form, till the Spirit of God moved and till God spoke. Till there came the Spirit, the breath of God's mouth, the word of God, it is but a faint twilight, it is but an uncertain glimmering which we have of God in the creature.

But in his Word, when we come to him in his Scriptures, we find better and nobler creatures produced in us, clearer notions of God, and more evident manifestation of his power and of his goodness towards us: for if we consider him in his first Word, as he spoke from the beginning in the Old Testament, from thence we cannot only see, but feel that God hath said, "Let there be light"; and that there is a light produced in us, by which we see that this world was not made by chance, for then it could not consist in this order and regularity. And we see that it was not eternal, for if it were eternal as God, and so no creature, then it must be God too. We see it had a beginning, a beginning of nothing, and all from God. So we find in ourself that there is such a light produced. And there we may find that there is a kind of firmament produced in us, a knowledge of a difference between heaven and earth; and that there is in our constitutions an earthly part, a body, and a heavenly part, a soul, and an understanding as a firmament, to separate, distinguish and discern between these. So also may we find that God has said, "Let there be a sea," a gathering, a confluence of all such means as are necessary for the attaining of salvation; that is, that God from the beginning settled and established a Church, in which he was always careful to minister to man means of eternal happiness. The Church is that sea, and into that sea we launched in the water of baptism.

Till God spake, in his creatures only we have but a faint and uncertain and general knowledge of God. When God comes to speak at first in the Old Testament, though he come to more particulars, yet it was in dark speeches and in veils, and to them who understood best and saw clearest into God's Word, still it was but by way of promise and of a future thing. But when God comes to his last work, to make man, to make up man, that is to make man a Christian by the Gospel; when he comes not to a *fiat homo,* "Let there be a man" (as he proceeded in the rest) but to a *faciamus hominem,* "Let us make man": then he calls his Son to him and sends him into the world to suffer death, the death of the cross for our salvation: and he calls the Holy Ghost to him and sends him to teach us all truth and apply that which Christ suffered for our souls, to our souls. God leaves the nations, the Gentiles, without speaking to them; he speaks not at all to them but in the speechless creatures. He leaves the Jews under the killing letter of the Law. And he comes to us in manifesting to us that our Messiah, Christ Jesus, is come and come according to the promise of God and the foretelling of all his prophets; for that is our safe anchorage in all storms, that all things are done as God had foretold they should be done; that we have infallible marks given us before by which we may try all that is done after.

All the Word of God then conduces to the Gospel; the Old Testament is a preparation and a pedagogy to the New. All the Word belongs to the Gospel and all the Gospel is in the Word; nothing is to be obtruded to our faith as necessary to salvation except it be rooted in the Word. And as the promises that God has made to us in the Old Testament, and the accomplishing of those promises to us in the New Testament, are thus appliable to us, so is this especially, that God continues his speech and speaks to us every day. Still we must hear the Gospel in the Word, in the Word so as we may hear it, that is, the Word preached; for howsoever it be Gospel in itself, it is not Gospel to us if it be not preached in the congregation. Neither, though it be preached to the congregation, is it Gospel to me except I find it work upon my understanding and my faith and my conscience.

A man may believe that there shall be a Redeemer, and he may give an historical assent that there has been a Redeemer, and yet not hear him speak to his own soul. It cost the Apostles, and their successors, the preachers of the Gospel, more pains and more labor to persuade men that this mercy of God, and these merits of Christ Jesus, were intended to them and directed upon them in particular, than to persuade them that such things were done. They can believe the promise and the performance in the general, but they cannot find the application thereof in particular. The voice that is nearest us we least hear, not because God speaks not loud enough but because we stop our ears. Nor that neither, for we do hear, but because we do not hearken then, nor consider. No nor that neither, but because we do not answer, nor co-operate, nor assist God in doing that which he has made us able to do by his grace, towards our own salvation.

For we are Christians incorporated in Christ in his Church, and thereby, by that title, we have a new Creation and are new creatures. And as we shall have a new Jerusalem hereafter, so we have a new paradise already, which is the Christian Church. In this paradise, says St. Augustine, in the books of the Gospel, grows every tree pleasant for the sight and good for meat. And there, says that Father, Christ Jesus himself is the Tree of Life. As Christ is this Tree of Life, so the Tree of Knowledge of Good and Evil is the good use of our own will after God has enlightened us in this paradise, in the Christian Church, and so restored our dead will again by his grace precedent and subsequent and concomitant: for without such grace and such succession of grace, our will is so far unable to predispose itself to any good, as that we have no interest in ourselves, no power to do anything of or with ourselves, but to our destruction.

Miserable man! A toad is a bag of poison and a spider is a blister of poison, and yet a toad and a spider cannot poison themselves. Man has a dram of poison, original sin, in an invisible corner, we know not where, and he cannot choose but poison himself and all his actions with that. We are so far from being able to begin without grace, as then where we have the first grace we cannot proceed to the use of that without more. But yet, says St. Augustine, the will of a Christian so rectified and so assisted is the Tree of Knowledge, and he shall be the worse for knowing if he live not according to that knowledge. We were all wrapped up in the first Adam, all mankind; and we are wrapped up in the second Adam, in Christ, all mankind too; but not in both alike, for we are so in the first Adam as that we inherit death from him and incur death whether we will or no. Before any consent of ours be actually given to any sin, we are the children of wrath and of death. But we are not so in the second Adam, as that we are made possessors of eternal life without the concurrence of our own will; not that our will pays one penny towards this purchase, but our own will may forfeit it; it cannot adopt us, but it may disinherit us.

Now by being planted in this paradise and received into the Christian Church we are the adopted sons of God. And therefore, as it is in Christ, who is the natural Son of God, he was not born once and no more, but has a continual because an eternal generation, and is as much begotten today as he was one hundred, one thousand, one thousand millions of generations passed; so since we are the generation and offspring of God, since grace is our Father, that parent that begets all goodness in us conformable to the pattern Christ himself who has a continual generation; in all the acts of our understanding and in a ready concurrence of our will, let us every day, every minute feel this new generation of spiritual children. For it is a miserable short life to have been born when the glass was turned and died before it was run out; to have conceived some good motions at the beginning and to have given over all purpose of practice at the end of a sermon. Let us present our own will as a mother to the Father of light, and the Father of life, and the Father of love, that we may be willing to conceive by the overshadowing of the Holy Ghost and not resist his working upon our souls, but with the obedience of the Blessed Virgin may say, "Behold the servant of the Lord, be it done unto me according to thy Word." I will not stop mine ears to thy Word, my heart shall not doubt of thy Word, my life shall express my having heard and harkened to thy Word, that Word which is the Gospel, that Gospel which is peace to my conscience, and reconciliation to my God, and salvation to my soul; for hearing is but the conception, meditation is but the quickening, purposing is but the birth, but practicing is the growth of this blessed child.

The Gospel then, that which is the Gospel to you, that is the assurance of the peace of conscience, is grounded upon the Word; not upon imaginations of your own, not upon fancies of others, nor pretended inspirations, nor obtruded miracles, but upon the Word. And not upon a suspicious and questionable, not upon an uncertain or variable Word, but upon this, that "This is a faithful saying." It is true that this Apostle says sometimes, "This is a true saying," and "This is a faithful saying," when he does not mean that it is the Word of God, but only intends to induce a moral certitude, when he would have good credit to be given to that which follows. But in all those other places where he uses this phrase he speaks only of some particular duties, or of some particular point of religion; but here he speaks of the whole body of Divinity, of the whole Gospel, "That Christ is come to save sinners," and therefore more may be intended by this phrase here than in other places.

When he speaks of that particular point, the Resurrection, he uses this phrase, "It is a true saying; If we be dead with him we shall also live with him." When he would invite men to godliness, even by the rewards which accompany it in this life, he uses this addition, this confirmation, "For this is a true saying, and worthy to be received." When he gives a dignity to the function and office of the ministry he proposes it so, "It is a true saying; If any man desire the office of a bishop, he desireth a good work"; it is a work, not an occasion and opportunity of ease. And lastly, when he provokes men to glorify God by good works, he labors to be believed by the same phrase still, "This is a true saying, and these things I would thou shouldst affirm, That they which have believed in God, might be careful to show forth good works."

Till he have found faith and belief in God he never calls upon good works, he never calls them good; but when we have faith, he would not have us stop there, but proceed to works too. It is a phrase which the Apostle does frequently and almost proverbially use in these many places, but in all these places upon particular and lesser occasions. But here, preparing the doctrine of the whole Gospel, this phrase admits a larger extent, that as it is grounded upon the Word we must have something to show for it; so it is upon a faithful Word, upon that which is clearly and without the encumbrance of disputation the infallible Word of God; no traditional word, no apocryphal word, but the clear and faithful Word. Now of all the attributes, of all the qualities that can be ascribed to the Word of God, this is most proper to itself, and most available, and most comfortable to us, that it is a faithful Word. For this being a Word that has principally respect and relation to the fidelity of God, it implies necessarily a Covenant, a contract with us, which God has bound himself faithfully to perform unto us; and therefore God calls his Covenant with David by this name, "An everlasting Covenant, even the sure mercies of David."

Now the truth and faithfulness of the Word consists not only in this, that it is true in itself, but in this also, that it is established by good testimony to be so. It is therefore faithful because it is the Word of God, and therefore also because it may be proved to be the Word of God by human testimonies; which is that which is especially intended in this clause, "It is worthy of all acceptation"; worthy to be received by our faith, and by our reason too. Our reason tells us that God's will is revealed to man somewhere, else man could not know how God would be worshiped. And our reason tells us that this is that Word in which that will is revealed.

But the best and fullest acceptation is to prove that you have accepted it by your life and conversation; that as your faith makes no staggering at it, nor your reason no argument against it, so your actions may be arguments for it to others, to convince them that do not, and confirm them that do believe in it. For this word which signifies in our ordinary use the Gospel, *Evangelium*, was a word of civil and secular use before it was made ecclesiastical. And as it had before in civil use, so it retains still, three significations. First it signified a good and a gracious message: and so, in spiritual use, it is the message of God who sent his son; and it is the message of the Son, who sent the Holy Ghost. Secondly it signified the reward that was given to him that brought the good news: and so, in our spiritual use, it is that spiritual tenderness, that religious good nature of the soul (as we may have leave to call it) that appliableness, that ductileness, that holy credulity which you bring to the hearing of the Word, and that respect which you give to Christ, in his ministers, who brings this Gospel unto you. And then thirdly, it signifies the sacrifice which was offered to that God who sent this good message: which in our spiritual use is that which the Apostle exhorts the Romans to with the most earnestness (and so do I you): "I beseech you brethren by the mercies of God, that ye give up your bodies a living sacrifice, holy, acceptable to God, which is your reasonable serving of God."

Now a reasonable service is that which in reason we are bound to do, and which in reason we think would most glorify him, in contemplation of whom that service is done; and that is done especially when by a holy and exemplary life we draw others to the love and obedience of the same Gospel which we profess: for then have we declared this true and faithful saying, this Gospel to have been worthy of all acceptation, when we have looked upon it by our reason, embraced it by our faith, and declared it by our good works. And all these considerations arose out of the root of this Gospel, the Word, the Scripture. The Tree itself, the body of the Gospel, that is the coming of Christ and the reason of his coming, "To save sinners." And then the fruit of this Gospel, that humility, by which the Apostle confesses himself to be the greatest sinner, we reserve for another exercise.

OF CHRIST'S COMING TO REDEEM US,
IN THE TESTIMONY OF PAUL, II

9

This is a faithful saying, and worthy of all acceptation, that Christ Jesus came into the world to save sinners; of which I am the chiefest. I Timothy 1:15

WE HAVE CONSIDERED HERETOFORE THAT WHICH appertained to the root and all the circumstances thereof. That which belongs to the tree itself, what this acceptable Gospel is, "That Christ Jesus came into the world to save sinners"; and then, that which appertains to the fruit of this Gospel, the humility of the Apostle in applying it to himself, "Of which sinners I am the chiefest," were reserved for this time. In the first of these, that which we call the tree, the body of this Gospel, there are three branches: first an advent, a coming; and secondly, the person that came; and lastly, the work for which he came.

First then for the advent, this coming of Christ, we have a rule in the school: then is any person of the Trinity said to be sent, or to come, when they work in any place, or in any person, in another manner or measure than they did before. Yet that rule does not reach home to the expressing of all comings of the persons of the Trinity. The second person came more presentially than so, more than in an extraordinary work and energy and execution of his power, if it be rightly apprehended by those Fathers, who in many of those angels which appeared to the Patriarchs, and whose serv-

111

ice God used in delivering Israel out of Egypt, and in giving them the Law in Sinai, take the Son of God himself to have been present, and many things to have been attributed to the angels in those histories which were done by the Son of God, not only working but present in that place at that time. So also the Holy Ghost came more presentially than so, more than by an extraordinary extension of his power, when he came presentially and personally in the Dove to seal John's baptism upon Christ. But yet, though those presential comings of Christ as an angel in the Old Testament, and this coming of the Holy Ghost in a Dove in the New, were more than ordinary comings, and more than extraordinary workings too, yet they were all far short of this coming of the Son of God in this text: for it could never be said properly in any of those cases, that that or that angel was the Son of God, the second person, or that that Dove was the Holy Ghost, or the third person of the Trinity; but in this advent, which we have in hand here, it is truly and properly said, this man is God, this son of Mary is the Son of God, this carpenter's son is that very God that made the world. He came so to us as that he became us, not only by a new and more powerful working in us, but by assuming our nature upon himself.

It is a perplexed question in the school whether if Adam had not sinned the Son of God had come into the world and taken our nature and our flesh upon him. Out of the infinite testimonies of the abundant love of God to man many concluded that howsoever, though Adam had not sinned, God would have dignified the nature of man in the highest degree that that nature was in any ways capable of. And since it appears now (because that has been done) that the nature of man was capable of such assuming, by the Son of God, they argue that God would have done this though Adam had not sinned. Christ had not come, say they, in the nature of a physician to recover him, if man had not contracted that infectious sickness by Adam's sin. If man had not forfeited his interest and state in Heaven by Adam's sin, Christ had not come in the nature of a Redeemer, but out of a brotherly love and out of a royal favor, to exalt that nature which he did love, and to impart and convey to us a greater and nobler state than we had in our

Creation: in such a respect and to such a purpose he should have come. But since they themselves who follow that opinion come to say, that that is the more subtle opinion and the more agreeable to man's reason (because man willingly embraces and pursues anything that conduces to the dignifying of his own nature), but that the other opinion, that Christ had not come if our sins had not occasioned his coming, is more agreeable to the Scriptures, and in the way that leads to God's glory, and so say with St. Augustine, if man could have been saved otherwise the Son of God had not come in this manner: or if that may be interpreted of his coming to suffer only, we may enlarge it with, he who was Creator of the world had never become a creature in the world if our sins had not drawn him to it.

It is usefully said by Aquinas, "God has appointed all future things to be, but to be so as they are"; that is, necessary things necessarily, and contingent things contingently; absolute things absolutely, and conditional things conditionally. He has decreed my salvation, but that salvation in Christ; he had decreed Christ's coming into this world, but a coming to save sinners. And therefore it is a frivolous interrogatory, a lost question, an impertinent article, to enquire what God would have done if Adam had stood. But Adam is fallen, and we in him; and therefore though we may piously wish with St. Augustine, "I would man had not been so miserable as to put God to this way of mercy"; yet since our sins had induced this misery upon us, and this necessity (if we may so say) upon God, let us change all our disputation into thanksgiving. Blessed be the Lord God of Israel, who has visited and redeemed his people; blessed that he would come at all, which was our first, and blessed that he is come already, which is our second consideration: He came, he is come.

In that language in which God spoke to man there is such an assurance intimated, that whatsoever God promises shall be performed; that in that language ordinarily in the prophets, the times are confounded, and when God is intended to purpose or to promise anything in the future, it is very often expressed in the time past. That which God means to do he is said to have done; future and present and past is all one with God. But yet to man it is much more that Christ is come than that he would come; not but that they who apprehended faithfully his future coming had the same salvation as we, but they could not so easily apprehend it as we. God did not present so many handles to take hold of him in that promise that he would come, as in the performance that he was come. They had most of these handles that lived with him and saw him and heard him; but we that come after, have more than they which were before them, we have more in the history than they had in the prophets.

It was time for him to come in the beginning of the world, for the Devil was a murderer from the beginning. As the Devil was a murderer of himself; as he killed himself, Christ gave him over; he never came to him in that line, he never pardoned him that sin. But as he practiced upon man, Christ met with him from the beginning. He saved us from his killing by dying himself for us; for being dead and having taken us into his wounds, and being risen and having taken us into his glory; if we be dead in Christ already, the Devil cannot kill us, if we be risen in Christ the Devil cannot hold us. And so he was the Lamb slain from the beginning of the world, that is, as soon as the world had any beginning in the purpose of God. God saw from all eternity that man would need Christ, and as soon as there was conceived an "I will kill," in the Devil's mouth, then was an "I will raise from death," in God's mouth. And so there was an early coming from all eternity; for he is the ruler of Israel, says the prophet, and his goings forth have been from the beginning, and from everlasting. It is "goings" in the plural; Christ has divers goings forth, divers comings, and all from the beginning; not only from Moses' "In the beginning," which was the beginning of the Creation (for then also Christ came in the promise of a Messiah), but from St. John's "In the beginning," that beginning which was without beginning, the eternal beginning, for there Christ came in that eternal decree that he should come. Neither is this only as he is the bud of Jehovah, issuing from him as his eternal Son, but as the prophet Micah says, as he shall come out of Bethlehem, and as he shall be a ruler of Israel. So as he came in our human nature, as he came to die for us, as he came to establish a Church, so his coming is from all eternity, for all this was wrapped up in a decree of his coming. And therefore we are not carried upon the consideration of any decree, or of any means of salvation higher or precedent to the coming of Christ, for that were to antedate eternity itself.

Thus far then he has proceeded already: he came into the world and into a clean woman. It is not into so clean a woman as had no sin at all, none contracted from her parents, no original sin; for so Christ had placed his favors and his honors ill, if he had favored her most who had no need of him: to die for all the world and not for his mother, or to die for her, when she needed not that Hell, is a strange imagination. She was not without sin; for then why should she have died? For even a natural death in all that come by natural generation is of sin. But certainly as she was a vessel reserved to receive Christ Jesus, so she was preserved according to the best capacity of that nature from great and infectious sins. Mary Magdalen was a holy vessel after Christ had thrown the Devil out of her; the Virgin Mary was much more so, into whom no reigning power of the Devil ever entered.

In such an acceptation then Christ came by a clean woman into an unclean world. And he came in a purpose (as we do piously believe) to manifest himself in the Christian religion to all the nations of the world; and therefore, says David, "The Lord reigneth, let the Islands rejoice," the Islands who by reason of their situation, provision and trading, having most means of conveying Christ Jesus over the world. He has carried us up to Heaven and set us at the right hand of God, and shall not we endeavor to carry him to those nations who have not yet heard of his name? Shall we still brag that we have brought our clothes, and our hatchets, and our knives, and bread to this and this value and estimation amongst those poor ignorant souls, and shall we never glory that we have brought the name and religion of Christ Jesus in estimation amongst them? Christ is come into the world; we will do little if we will not ferry him over and propagate his name as well as our own to other nations.

At least be sure that he is so far come into the world as that he be come into you. You are but a little world, a world but of a few spans in length; and yet Christ was sooner carried from east to

west, from Jerusalem to these parts, than you can carry him over
the faculties and your soul and body. He has been in a pilgrimage
towards you long, coming towards you perchance fifty, perchance
sixty years; and how far is he got into you yet? Is he yet come to
your eyes? Have they made Job's covenant that they will not look
upon a maid; yet he is not come into your ear? Still you have an
itching ear, delighting in the libellous defamation of other men. Is
he come to your ear? Are you rectified in that sense? yet voluptuousness in your taste or inordinateness in your other senses keep
him out in those. He is come into your mouth, to your tongue; but
he is come thither as a diseased person is taken into a hospital to
have his blood drawn, to have his flesh cauterized, to have his
bones sawed.

Christ Jesus is in your mouth, but in such execrations, in such
blasphemies, as would be earthquakes to us if we were earth; but
we are all stones and rocks, obdurate in a senselessness of those
wounds which are inflicted upon our God. He may be come to the
skirts, to the borders, to an outward show in your actions, and yet
not be come into the land, into your heart. He entered into you at
baptism; he has crept farther and farther into you in catechisms
and other infusions of his doctrine into you. He has pierced into
you deeper by the powerful threatenings of his judgments in the
mouths of his messengers. He has made some survey over you in
bringing you to call yourself to an account of some sinful actions.

And yet Christ is not come into you. Either you make some new
discoveries and fall into some new ways of sin; and are loath that
Christ should come thither yet, that he should trouble your conscience in that sin, till you had made some convenient profit of it.
You have studied and must gain, you have bought and must sell,
and therefore are loath to be troubled yet. Or else you have some
land in you which you yourself have never discovered, some ways
of sin which you have never apprehended, nor considered to be
sin; and thither Christ is not come yet. He is not come into you
with that comfort which belongs to his coming in this text, except
he have overshadowed you all and be in you entirely.

We come next to the person. He was capable of this great
employment, to reconcile God to man, as he was a mixed person

of God and man. He had a commission for this service, as he was *Christus*, anointed, sealed to that office. He did actually execute this commission, as he was Jesus. Now when we consider his capacity and fitness to save the world, this capacity and fitness must have relation to that way which God had chosen; which was by justice. For God could have saved the world by his Word, as well as he had made it so. A general pardon and a light of grace had been as easy to him as a *fiat lux* at the beginning; as easy as the spreading of the light of nature. But God having purposed to himself the way of justice, then could none be capable of that employment but a mixed person; for God could not die, nor man could not satisfy by death; and both these were required in the way of justice: a satisfaction and that by death.

Now as this unexpressible mixture and union of God and man made him capable of this employment, so he had a particular commission for it implied in the same name too. For every capable person is not always employed; and this was his unction as he is *Christus,* anointed, severed, sealed for that purpose, for that office. Now whether this unction, that is, this power to satisfy God's justice for all the sins of all mankind, were infinite in itself because an infinite Godhead resided in his person, or whether this power and ability by one act to satisfy for all sins arose by the contract that had passed between the Father and him, that it was so because it was covenanted between them that it should be so, this has divided the school into that great opposition which is well known by the name of Thomists and Scotists.

The safest way is to place it in the contract, in the covenant; for if we place it absolutely in the person and cause the infiniteness of the merit from that, then any act of that person, the very Incarnation itself, had been enough to save us; but his unction, his commission was to proceed thus and thus, and no otherwise than he did in the work of our redemption. His unction was his qualification. He was anointed with the oil of gladness above his fellows, else the season of his enduring the cross could not have been joy. He was anointed liberally by that woman, when he himself was sold for thirty pieces of silver, beyond the value of three hundred pieces in ointment upon him. He was honorably embalmed by

Joseph and Nicodemus who brought an one hundred pound weight of myrrh and aloes to bury him: every way anointed more than others, by others. All his garments smell of myrrh and aloes and cassia, as it is in the Canticles; even in the garments of religion, the ceremonies of the Church, there is a sweet savor of life. Even in the outward profession of the name of Christ there is a savor of life, an assistance to salvation; for even in taking upon us this name Christ, we acknowledge both that he was able to reconcile and sent purposely to reconcile God and man.

But then the strength of our consolation lies in the other name. As he was Jesus, actually he executed that commission to which, as he was Christ, he was fitted and anointed. It was therefore upon that ground that this name was given him, "thou shalt call his name Jesus," says the angel at his conception. Why? "For he shall save his people from their sins." Not only that he shall be able to do it, nor only that he shall be sent to do it: so far he is but *Christus*, a mixed person and an anointed person; but he shall actually do it, and so he is Jesus. Names of children are not always answered in their manners and in the effects. St. Chrysostom says, "every nominal John is not a real John." Absalom's name was "his father's peace," but he was his father's affliction. But the name of Jesus had the effect; he was called a savior and he was one.

It may seem strange that when St. Matthew says that Mary was to bring forth a child and call his name Jesus, he says also that this was done that the prophecy of Isaiah might be fulfilled, who said that a virgin shall bring forth a child who shall be called Emanuel. To fulfil a prophecy of being called Emanuel he must be called Jesus. Indeed, to be Jesus is a fulfilling of his being Emanuel. Emanuel is "God with us," a mixed person, God and man. But Jesus is a Savior, the performer of that salvation which only he who was God and man could accomplish. He was Emanuel as soon as he was conceived, but not Jesus till he began to submit himself to the Law for us; which was first in his circumcision, when he took the name of Jesus and began to shed some drops of blood for us.

The name of Jesus was no new name when he took it; we find some of that name in the Scriptures, and in Josephus we find one officer that was his enemy, and another a great robber who lighted upon Josephus more than once, of that name. And yet the prophet Isaiah says of Christ (and St. Cyril interprets those words of this particular man Jesus), "thou shalt be called by a new name, which the mouth of the Lord shall name." And how was this a new name, by which so many had been called before? The newness was not in that, that none other had had that name, but that the Son of God had not that name till he began to execute the office of a Savior. He was called the bud of Jehovah before; and he was called the counsellor, and the wonderful, and the prince of peace by the same prophet. But it is the observation of Origen, and of Lactantius after (and it appears in the text itself), that Moses never calls Oshea the son of Nun, Joshua (which is the very name of Jesus), till he was made general to deliver and save his people. So what names soever were attributed to the Son of God before, the name of Jesus was a new name to him then when he began the work of salvation in his circumcision.

Take hold therefore of his name Emanuel, as God is with us, as there is a person fit to reconcile God and man; and take hold of him as he is *Christus,* a person sealed and anointed for that reconciliation. But above all, be sure of your hold upon the name Jesus your Savior. This was his name when he was carried to the altar to circumcision, and this was his name when he carried his altar, the cross; this was his style there, Jesus of Nazareth: and in the virtue of that name he shall give you a circumcised heart, and circumcised lips in the course of your life; and in the virtue of that name he shall give you a joyful "It is finished," when you come to finish all upon your last altar, your deathbed.

Now from this consideration of the person, so far as arose out of his several names, we pass to his action. He was able to redeem man, he was sent to redeem man, he did redeem man. How? We see his method in St. Matthew: "I came to call." His way is a voice now. God does but call us; he does not constrain us; he does not drive us into a pound. He calls us as birds do their young, and he would gather us as a hen does her chickens.

God draws no man against his will; no man believes in God against his will. God only excites and exalts our will, but he does not force it. Our carnal desires draw us, but this drawing is not a constraining; for then we should not be commanded to resist them nor to fight against them, for no man will bid me do so against a cannon bullet that comes with an inevitable and irresistible violence. Shall our carnal affections draw us, though they do not force us, and shall not grace do the same office too? Shall we still trust to such a power, or such a measure of that grace, at last, as that we shall not be able to resist, but shall convert us whether we will or no, and never concur willingly with God's present grace? He came to save by calling us, as an eloquent and a persuasive man draws his auditors, but yet imprints no necessity upon the faculty of the will; so works God's calling of us in his Word. God saves us by a calling and he saves us by drawing; but he calls them that hearken to him and he draws them that follow upon his drawing. He saves us who acknowledge that we could not be saved without him, and desire, and that with a faithful assurance, to be saved by him; which is that which is intended in the next word, he came to save sinners.

"He came not to call the righteous, but sinners." Is that intended of all effectually? All have sinned, and all are deprived of the glory of God. But sinners here are those sinners who acknowledge themselves to be sinners; for says he, I came to call them to repentance: and that's the meaning of that exclusion of the righteous. He came not to call the righteous; not to call them who call themselves righteous and thought themselves so, but sinners; not all whom he knew to be sinners, but all who would be brought to know themselves to be so. Them he came to call by the power of miracles when he lived upon earth, and them he stays to call by the power of his Word, now he is ascended into heaven; for as a furnace needs not the same measure and proportion of fire to keep it boiling as it did to heat it; but yet it does need the same fire, that is, fire of the same nature (for the heat of the sun will not keep it boiling how hot soever), so the Church of God needs not miracles now it is established; but still there is the same fire, the working of the same spirit to save sinners; for that was the end of miracles, and it is the end of preaching, to make men capable of salvation by acknowledging themselves to be sinners. And this has brought us to the last part of this text, the fruit of the Gospel, humility.

This brought St. Paul not only to discern and confess himself to be a sinner, but the chiefest and greatest sinner of all. "There is nothing higher than humility," it is excellently but strangely said by St. Jerome. He might rather and more credibly have used any word than that. He might have been easily believed if he had said there is no wiser thing than humility, for he that is low in his own shall be high in the eyes of others; and to have said there is not so direct a way to perfection as humility. But nothing higher must seem strangely said; there is nothing higher than lowness; no such exaltation as dejection; no such revenge as patience. And yet all this is truly and safely said, with that limitation which St. Jerome gives it, "in the sight of God," there is no such exaltation as humiliation. We must not coast and cross the nearest way, and so think to meet Christ in his end, which was glory, but we must go after him in all his steps, in the way of humiliation. For Christ's very descent was a degree of exaltation; and by that name he called his crucifying a lifting up, an exaltation.

The doctrine of this world goes for the most part otherwise. Here we say, lay hold upon something, get up one step; in all want of sufficiency, in all defection of friends, in all changes, yet the place which you hold will raise you to better. In the way to Heaven, the lower you go, the nearer the highest and best end you are. St. Augustine says, "There are but two things necessary to us to know, how ill we are, and how good we may be"; where nature has left us and whither grace would carry us. And Abraham (says that Father) expresses this twofold knowledge when he said to God, "I know I am but dust and ashes." And there is his first knowledge, how ill a condition naturally he is in; but then, for all this, though I be but dust and ashes, I have access to my God and may speak to him; there's his improvement and his dignity.

Truly every man is truly dust, for as dust is blown from one to another corner by the wind and lies dead there till another wind remove it from that corner, so are we hurried from sin to sin and have no motion in ourselves but as a new sin imprints it in us. So for our disposition to evil we are truly dust; and we are truly dry ashes, for ashes produce no seed of themselves, nor give growth to any seed that is cast into them; so we have no good in us naturally, neither can we nourish any good that is infused by God into us, except the same grace that sowed it, water it, and weed it, and cherish it. and foment it after. To know that we have no strength of ourselves, and to know that we can lack none if we ask it of God, these are St. Augustine's two arts and sciences, and this is the humility of the Gospel in general.

To come to St. Paul's more particular expressing of his humility here, "of which sinners I am the chiefest," this which St. Paul says of himself, that he was the greatest sinner, was true in his own heart, and true in a convenient sense, and so neither falsely nor inconsiderately spoken. How then was this true? Why should we or how can we charge the Apostle so heavily? Beloved, to maintain the truth of this which St. Paul says, we need not say that it was materially true, that it was indeed so; it is enough to defend it from falsehood, that it was formally true, that is, that it appeared to him to be true. First, he respected his own natural disposition and pro-clivity to great sins, and out of that evidence condemned himself; as when a man who professed an art of judging the disposition of a man by his face had pronounced of Socrates (whose virtue all the world admired), that he was the most incontinent and licentious man, the greatest thief and extortioner of any man in the world; the people despised and scorned the physiognomer and his art and were ready to offer violence unto him: Socrates himself corrected their distemper again and said, "It is true that he says, and his judgment is well grounded, for by nature no man is more inclined to these vices than I am." And this disposition to the greatest sins, St. Paul knew in himself.

He that has these natural dispositions is likely to be the greatest sinner, except he have some strong assistance to restrain him: and then, he that has the offer of such helps and abuses them is in a farther step of being the greatest sinner. And this also St. Paul had respect to now, that he had had a good and learned education, a good understanding of the Law and the prophets, a good mortifi-cation by being of the strict sect of the Pharisees; and yet he had turned all the wrong way, and was therefore in this abuse of these manifold graces the greater sinner. He looked farther than into his own nature, or into his resistance of assistances; he looked into those actions which these had produced in him, and there he saw his breathing of threatenings and slaughter against the disciples of the Lord, his hunger and thirst of Christian blood: and so says St. Augustine, "as he found himself the greatest persecutor, so he condemns himself for the greatest sinner."

But all these natural dispositions to great sins, negligences of helps offered, sinful actions produced out of these two, might be greater in many others than in St. Paul; and it is likely, and it may be certain to us that they were so; but it was not certain to him, he knew not so much ill by any other man as by himself. Consider those words in the Proverbs, "Surely I am more foolish than any man, and have not the understanding of a man in me": for though they be not the words of Solomon, yet they are the words of a prophet, and a prophet who surely was not really more foolish than any man, then in consideration of something which he found in himself, says so. He that considers himself shall find such degrees of sin as that he cannot see that any man has gone lower. Or if he have in some particular and notorious sin, yet he that is fallen lower than you in some sin yet may be above you in grace; he may have done a greater sin and yet not be the greater sinner. Another has killed a man and you have not. You may have drawn and drunk the blood of many by usury, by extortion, by oppression. Another in fury of intemperance has ravished and you have not. You may have corrupted many by your deceitful solicitations; and then in yourself are as ill as the ravisher, and you have made them worse whom you have corrupted. Cast up your own account, inventory your own goods (for sin is the wealth of the sinner and he treasures up the wrath of God); reckon your own sins and you will find yourself rich in that wealth, and find yourself of that quorum, that the highest place in that company and mystery of sinners belongs to you.

St. Paul does so here. Yes, then, when he saw his own case and saw it by the light of the spirit of God; when he took knowledge that Christ was come and had saved sinners, and had saved him; yet still he remains in his accusation of himself that he was still the greatest sinner, because he remained still in his infirmity and aptness to relapse into former sins. As long as we are, we are subject to be worse than we are; and those sins which we apprehend even with horror and amazement, when we hear that others have done them, we may come to do them with an earnestness, with a delight, with a defence, with a glory, if God leaves us to ourselves. As long as that is true of us, I am not better than the first man, than Adam was (and none of us are in any proportion so good), that is true also. I am still in a slippery state, and in an evident danger of being the greatest sinner. This is the conclusion for every humble Christian: no man is a greater sinner than I was, and I am not sure but that I may fall to be worse than ever I was, except I husband and employ the talents of God's graces better than I have done.

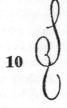

10 OF GOD AS OUR HELP IN ALL THINGS

*Because thou hast been my help, therefore
in the shadow of thy wings will I rejoice.*
PSALM 63:7

THE PSALMS ARE THE MANNA OF THE CHURCH. AS
manna tasted to every man like that that he liked best, so do the
Psalms minister instruction and satisfaction to every man in every
emergency and occasion. David was not only a clear prophet of
Christ himself, but a prophet of every particular Christian; he
foretells what I, what any, shall do and suffer and say. And as the
whole book of Psalms is (as the Spouse speaks of the name of
Christ) an ointment poured out upon all sorts of sores, a balm that
searches all wounds; so are there some certain psalms that are
imperial psalms, that command over all affections and spread
themselves over all occasions, Catholic, universal psalms that
apply themselves to all necessities. This is one of those.

Now as the spirit and soul of the whole book of Psalms is
contracted into this psalm, so is the spirit and soul of this whole
psalm contracted into this verse. The key tells us that David uttered this psalm "when he was in the wilderness of Judah." There
we see the present occasion that moved him. And we see what was
passed between God and him before, in the first clause of our text:
"Because thou hast been my help." And then we see what was to
come, by the rest; "Therefore in the shadow of thy wings will I re-

125

joice." So that we have here the whole compass of time: past, present, and future.

First, his distress in the wilderness, his present estate, carried him upon the memory of that which God had done for him before; and the remembrance of that carried him upon that of which he assured himself after. Fix upon God anywhere and you shall find him a circle. He is with you now, when you fix upon him; he was with you before, for he brought you to this fixation; and he will be with you hereafter, for, "He is yesterday, and today, and the same forever."

For David's present condition, who was now in a banishment, in a persecution in the wilderness of Judah, we shall only insist that in all those temporal calamities David was only sensible of his spiritual loss. It grieved him not that he was kept from Saul's court, but that he was kept from God's Church. For when he says, by way of lamentation, "That he was in a dry and thirsty land, where no water was," he expresses what penury, what barrenness, what drought and what thirst he meant: that spiritual losses are incomparably heavier than temporal, and that therefore the restitution to our spiritual happiness, or the continuation of it, is rather to be made the subject of our prayers to God, in all pressures and distresses, than of temporal.

In the way of this comparison, falls first the consideration of the universality of afflictions in general, and the inevitableness thereof. It is a blessed metaphor that the Holy Ghost has put into the mouth of the Apostle, that our afflictions are but light, because there is an exceeding, and an eternal weight of glory attending them. If it were not for that exceeding weight of glory, no other weight in this world could turn the scale, or weigh down those infinite weights of afflictions that oppress us here.

It is not only Job that complains that he was a burden to himself, but even Absalom's hair was a burden to him, till it was polled. It is not only Jeremiah that complains that God had made their fetters and their chains heavy to them, but the workmen in harvest complain that God had made a fair day heavy unto them ("We have borne the heat, and the burden of the day"). Sand is heavy, says Solomon. And how many suffer so, under a sandhill of crosses, daily, hourly afflictions that are heavy by their number if not by their single weight? And a stone is heavy, says he in the same place. And how many suffer so? How many, without any former preparatory cross, even in the midst of prosperity and security fall under some one stone, some grindstone, some millstone, some one insupportable cross that ruins them? But then, says Solomon there, "A fool's anger is heavier than both." And how many children, and servants, and wives suffer under the anger, and moroseness, and peevishness, and jealousy of foolish masters, and parents, and husbands, though they must not say so? David and Solomon have cried out that all this world is vanity and levity; and God knows all is weight, and burden, and heaviness, and oppression; and if there were not a weight of future glory to counterpoise it, we should all sink into nothing.

I ask not Mary Magdalen whether lightness were not a burden, for sin is certainly, sensibly a burden. But I ask Susanna whether even chaste beauty were not a burden to her; and I ask Joseph whether personal comeliness were not a burden to him. I ask not Dives, who perished in the next world, the question; but I ask them who are made examples of Solomon's rule, of that "sore evil," as he calls it, "riches kept to the owners thereof for their hurt," whether riches be not a burden.

All our life is a continual burden, yet we must not groan; a continual squeezing, yet we must not pant. And as in the tenderness of our childhood we suffer, and yet are whipped if we cry, so we are complained of it we complain, and made delinquents if we call the times ill. And that which adds weight to weight and multiplies the sadness of this consideration is this: that still the best men have had the most laid upon them. As soon as I hear God say that he hath found "an upright man, that fears God, and eschews evil," in the next lines I find a commission to Satan to bring in Sabeans and Chaldeans upon his cattle and servants, and fire and tempest upon his children, and loathsome diseases upon himself. As soon as I hear God say that he hath found "a man according to his own heart," I see his sons ravish his daughters, and then murder one another, and then rebel against the Father and put him into straits for his life. As soon as I hear God testify of Christ at his baptism, "This is my beloved Son in whom I am well pleased," I find that Son of his "led up by the Spirit to be tempted of the Devil." And after I hear God ratify the same testimony again, at his Transfiguration, I find that beloved Son of his deserted, abandoned, and given over to scribes and Pharisees, and publicans, and Herodians, and priests, and soldiers, and people, and judges, and witnesses and executioners; and he that was called the beloved Son of God and made partaker of the glory of Heaven in this world, in his Transfiguration, is made now the sewer of all the corruption, of all the sins of this world, as no Son of God but a mere man; as no man, but a contemptible worm. As though the greatest weakness in this world were man, and the greatest fault in man were to be good, man is more miserable than other creatures, and good men more miserable than any other men.

They who write of natural story, propose that plant for the greatest wonder in nature which, being no firmer than a bullrush or a reed, produces and bears for the fruit no other but an entire and very hard stone. That temporal affliction should produce spiritual stoniness and obduration is unnatural yet ordinary. Therefore does God propose it as one of those greatest blessings which he multiplies upon his people, "I will take away your stony hearts, and give you hearts of flesh." And, Lord, let me have a fleshly heart in any sense, rather than a stony heart. We find mention among the observers of rarities in nature, of hairy hearts, hearts of men that have been overgrown with hair; but of petrified hearts, hearts of men grown into stone, we read not. For this petrifaction of the heart, this stupefaction of a man, is the last blow of God's hand upon the heart of man in this world.

Let me wither and wear out my age in an uncomfortable, an unwholesome, a penurious prison, and so pay my debts with my bones and recompense the wastefulness of my youth with the beggary of my age. Let me wither under sharp and foul and infamous diseases, and so recompense the wantonness of my youth with that loathesomeness in my age. Yet if God withdraw not his spiritual blessings, his grace, his patience; if I can call my suffering his doing, my passion his action, all this that is temporal is but a caterpillar got into one corner of my garden, but a mildew fallen

upon one acre of my corn. The body of all, the substance of all, is
safe as long as the soul is safe.

But when I shall trust to that which we call a good spirit, when I
shall rely upon a moral constancy and God shall shake, and enfeeble, and enervate, destroy and demolish that constancy; when I
shall think to refresh myself in the serenity and sweet air of a good
conscience and God shall call up the damps and vapors of Hell itself and spread a cloud of diffidence and an impenetrable crust of
desperation upon my conscience; when health shall fly from me,
and I shall lay hold upon riches to succor me and comfort me in
my sickness, and riches shall fly from me and I shall snatch after
favor and good opinion to comfort me in my poverty; when even
this good opinion shall leave me and calumnies and misinformation
shall prevail against me; when I shall need peace because there is
none but thou, O Lord, that should stand for me, and then shall
find that all the wounds that I have come from thy hand, all the
arrows that stick in me from thy quiver; when I shall see that because I have given myself to my corrupt nature, thou hast changed
thine; and because I am all evil towards thee, therefore thou hast
given over being good towards me; when it comes to this height,
that the fever is not in the humors but in the spirits, that mine
enemy is not an imaginary enemy (fortune) nor a transitory enemy
(malice in great persons), but a real, and an irresistible, and an in-
exorable, and an everlasting enemy, the Lord of Hosts himself, the
Almighty God himself—the Almighty God himself only knows the
weight of this affliction. And except he put in that exceeding weight
of an eternal glory, with his own hand, into the other scale, we are
weighed down, we are swallowed up, irreparably, irrevocably, irrecoverably, irremediably.

This is the fearful depth, this is spiritual misery, to be thus fallen
from God. But was this David's case? Was he fallen thus far into
a diffidence in God? No. But the danger, the precipice, the slippery
sliding into that bottomless depth, is to be excluded from the
means of coming to God, or staying with God. And this is what
David laments here, that by being banished and driven into the
wilderness of Judah, he had not access to the sanctuary of the
Lord, to sacrifice his part in the praise and to receive his part in

the prayers of the congregation. For Angels pass not to ends but by ways and means, nor men to the glory of the Triumphant Church but by participation of the Communion of the Militant.

To this note David sets his harp in many, many psalms. Sometimes that God had suffered his enemies to possess his Tabernacle ("He forsook the Tabernacle of Shiloh, He delivered his strength into captivity, and his glory into the enemy's hands"). But most commonly he complains that God disabled him from coming to the sanctuary. In which one thing he had summed up all his desires, all his prayers ("One thing have I desired of the Lord, that will I look after; That I may dwell in the house of the Lord, all the days of my life, to behold the beauty of the Lord, and to enquire in his temple"). His vehement desire of this he expresses again ("My soul thirsteth for God, for the living God; when shall I come and appear before God?"). He expresses a holy jealousy, a religious envy, even to the sparrows and swallows ("Yea, the sparrow hath found a house, and the swallow a nest for herself, and where she may lay her young, Even thine altars, O Lord of Hosts, my King and my God"). Thou art my King and my God, and yet excludest me from that which thou affordest to sparrows, "And are not we of more value than many sparrows?"

And as though David felt some false ease, some half-temptation, some whispering, that God is in the wilderness of Judah, in every place as well as in his sanctuary, there is in the original in that place a pathetic, a vehement, a broken expression: "O thine Altars." It is true (says David) thou art here in the wilderness, and I may see thee here and serve thee here, but, "O thine Altars, O Lord of Hosts, my King and my God." When David could not come in person to that place, yet he bent towards the temple.

For, as in private prayer, when (according to Christ's command) we are shut up in our chamber, there is exercised the modesty and bashfulness of our faith, not pressing upon God in his house: so in the public prayers of the congregation there is exercised the fervor and holy courage of our faith, for it is a mustering of our forces and a besieging of God. Therefore does David so much magnify their blessedness that are in this house of God ("Blessed are they that dwell in thy house, for they will be still praising thee"). Those that look towards it may praise thee sometimes, but those men who dwell in the Church, and whose whole service lies in the Church, have certainly an advantage of all other men (who are necessarily withdrawn by worldly businesses) in making themselves acceptable to almighty God, if they do their duties and observe their Church services aright.

Man being therefore thus subject naturally to manifold calamities, and spiritual calamities being incomparably heavier than temporal, and the greatest danger of falling into such spiritual calamities being in our absence from God's Church, where only the outward means of happiness are ministered unto us, certainly there is much tenderness and deliberation to be used before the Church doors be shut against any man.

If I would not direct a prayer to God to excommunicate any man from the Triumphant Church (which were to damn him), I would not oil the key, I would not make the way too slippery for excommunications in the Militant Church; for that is to endanger him. Much circumspection is required and exercised in those cases upon earth; for, though every excommunication upon earth be not sealed in Heaven, though it damn not the man, yet it dams up that man's way by shutting him out of that Church through which he must go to the other.

Which being so great a danger, let every man take heed of excommunicating himself. The impersuasible recusant does so; the negligent libertine does so; the fantastic separatist does so; the half-present man, he whose body is here and mind away, does so; and he whose body is but half here, his limbs are here upon a cushion but his eyes, his ears are not here, does so. All these are self-excommunicators and keep themselves from hence. Only he enjoys that blessing, the want whereof David deplores, that is here entirely, and glad he is here, and glad to find this kind of service here that he does, and wishes no other.

And so we have done with David's present condition, and his danger of falling into spiritual miseries because his persecution and banishment amounted to an excommunication, an excluding of him from the service of God in the Church. And we pass to his retrospect, the consideration, what God had done for him before, "Because thou hast been my help."

From the meanest artificer through the wisest philosopher to

God himself, all that is well done or wisely undertaken, is under-taken and done according to preconceptions, designs and patterns proposed to ourselves beforehand. A carpenter builds not a house but that he first sets up a frame in his own mind, what kind of house he will build. The little great philosopher Epictetus would undertake no action but he would first propose to himself what Socrates, or Plato, what a wise man would do in that case, and according to that, he would proceed. Of God himself it is safely resolved in the School, that he never did anything in any part of time, of which he had not an eternal preconception, an eternal idea, in himself before. Of which ideas, that is preconceptions, pre-determinations in God, St. Augustine pronounces there is so much truth and so much power in these ideas, as that without acknowl-edging them no man can acknowledge God, for he does not allow God counsel and wisdom and deliberation in his actions, but sets God on work before he have thought what he will do.

Of all things in Heaven and earth, but of himself, God had an idea, a pattern in himself, before he made it. Therefore let him be our pattern for that, to work after patterns; to propose to ourselves rules and examples for all our actions; and the more, the more immediately, the more directly our actions concern the service of God. If I ask God by what idea he made me, God produces his "Let us make man in our image," that there was a concurrence of the whole Trinity to make me in Adam, according to that image which they were and according to that idea which they had predeter-mined.

If I pretend to serve God, and he ask me for my idea, how I mean to serve him, shall I be able to produce none? If he ask me an idea of my religion and my opinions, shall I not be able to say, It is that which thy word and thy Catholic Church hath imprinted in me? If he asks me an idea of my prayers, shall I not be able to say, It is that which my particular necessities, that which the form prescribed by thy Son, that which the care and piety of the Church in conceiving fit prayers hath imprinted in me? If he ask me an idea of my sermons, shall I not be able to say, It is that which the analogy of faith, the edification of the congregation, the zeal of thy work, the meditations of my heart have imprinted in me?

But if I come to pray or to preach without this kind of idea; if I come to extemporal prayer and extemporal preaching, I shall come to an extemporal faith and extemporal religion. And then I must look for an extemporal Heaven, a Heaven to be made for me; for to that Heaven which belongs to the Catholic Church I shall never come, except I go by the way of the Catholic Church, by former ideas, former examples, former patterns, to believe according to ancient beliefs, to pray according to ancient forms, to preach according to former meditations. God does nothing, man does nothing well, without these ideas, these retrospects, this recourse to preconceptions, pre-deliberations.

Something then I must propose to myself to be the rule and the reason of my present and future actions. I can propose nothing more availably than the contemplation of the history of God's former proceedings with me, which is David's way here. Because this was God's way before I will look for God in this way still. That language in which God spake to man, the Hebrew, has no present tense. They form not their verbs as our western languages do, in the present (*I hear,* or *I see,* or *I read*), but they begin at that which is past: *I have seen* and *heard* and *read.* God carries us in his language, in his speaking, upon that which is past, upon that which he has done already. I cannot have better security for present, nor future, than God's former mercies exhibited to me.

There is no state, no church, no man, that has not this tie upon God, that has not God in these bands, that God by having done much for them already has bound himself to do more. Carry it up to the first sense and apprehension that ever you had of God's working upon you, either in yourself when you came first to the use of reason, or in others in your behalf, in your baptism, yet when you think you are at the first, God had done something for you before all that. God had you before he made you. He loved you first and then created you, that you loving him, he might continue his love to you. The surest way and the nearest way to lay hold upon God is the consideration of that which he had done already. So David does. And that which he takes knowledge of in particular, in God's former proceedings towards him is, "Because thou hast been my help."

From this one word, that God has been my *help,* I make account that we have both these notions: first, that God has not left me to myself, he has come to my succor, he has helped me; and then, that God has not left out myself. He has been my help, but he has left something for me to do with him and by his help. My security for the future, in this consideration of that which is past, lies not only in that God delivered me, but that he delivered me by way of a help, and help always presumes an endeavor and cooperation in him that is helped.

God did not elect me as a helper, nor create me, nor redeem me, nor convert me, by way of helping me; for he alone did all, and he had no use at all of me. God infuses his first grace, the first way, merely as a giver, entirely, all himself; but his subsequent graces, as a helper; therefore we call them auxiliant graces, helping graces; and we always receive them when we endeavor to make use of his former grace. "Lord, I believe," says the man in the Gospel to Christ, "help mine unbelief." If there had not been unbelief, weakness, imperfectness in that faith, there had needed no help; but if there had not been a belief, a faith, it had not been capable of help and assistance.

So that if I have truly the testimony of a rectified conscience, that God has helped me, it is in both respects: first, that he has never forsaken me, and then, that he has never suffered me to forsake myself. He has blessed me with that grace, that I trust in no help but his, and with this grace too, that I cannot look for his help, except I help myself also. God did not help Heaven and earth to proceed out of nothing in the Creation, for they had no possibility of any disposition towards it, for they had no being. But God did help the earth to produce grass and herbs; for God had infused a seminal disposition into the earth which, for all that, it could not have perfected without his farther help. If I will make God's former working upon me an argument of his future gracious purposes, as I must acknowledge that God has done much for me, so I must find that I have done what I could, by the benefit of that grace with him; for God promises to be but a helper.

"Lord open thou my lips," says David: that is God's work entirely. And then, "My mouth shall shew forth thy praise": there enters David into the work with God. And then, says God to him, "Open thy mouth" (it is now made "thy mouth" and therefore do thou open it) "and I will fill it." If I pray for his help, and apprehend and husband his graces well when they come, then he is truly, properly my helper; and upon that security I can proceed to David's confidence for the future, "Because thou hast been my help, therefore in the shadow of thy wings will I rejoice."

Lest any man in his dejection of spirit should stray into a suspicion of God's power to deliver him, as God has spangled the firmament with stars, so has he his Scriptures with names, and metaphors, and denotations of power. Sometimes he shines out in the name of a sword, and of a target, and of a wall, and of a tower, and of a rock, and of a hill; and sometimes in that glorious and manifold constellation of all together: The Lord of Hosts. God, as God, is never represented to us with defensive arms; he needs them not. God is invulnerable in himself. But though God need not defensive arms for himself, yet God is to us a helmet, a breastplate, a strong tower, a rock, everything that may give us assurance and defence. And as often as he will, he can refresh that proclamation, "Our enemies shall not so much as touch us."

But here, by his metaphor "In the shadow of thy wings," we do not so much consider an absolute immunity, that we shall not be touched, as a refreshing and consolation when we are touched, though we be pinched and wounded. "Under the shadow of thy wings": that is a refreshing, a respiration, a conservation, a consolation in all afflictions that are inflicted upon me.

Yet is not this metaphor of wings without a denotation of power. No act of God's, though it seem to imply but spiritual comfort, is without a denotation of power. So that, if I have the shadow of his wings, I have the earnest of the power of them too. If I have refreshing and respiration from them, I am able to say (as those three confessors did to Nebuchadnezzar), "My God is able to deliver me," I am sure he has power; "And my God will deliver me," when it conduces to his glory, I know he will; "But, if he do not, be it known unto thee, O King, we will not serve thy gods." Be it known unto thee, O Satan, how long soever God defer my deliverance, I will not seek false comforts, the miserable comforts of this world. I will not, for I need not; for I can subsist under this shadow of these wings, though I have no more.

Though God do not actually deliver us, nor actually destroy our enemies, yet if he refresh us in the shadow of his wings, if he maintain our subsistence (which is a religious constancy) in him, this should not only establish our patience (for that is but half the work), but it should also produce a joy, and rise to an exultation: "Therefore in the shadow of thy wings, I will rejoice."

I would always raise your hearts and dilate your hearts to a holy joy, to a joy in the Holy Ghost. There may be a just fear that men do not grieve enough for their sins. But there may be a just suspicion, too, that they may fall into inordinate griefs and diffidence of God's mercy. God has accompanied and complicated almost all our bodily diseases of these times, with an extraordinary sadness, a predominant melancholy, a faintness of heart, a cheerlessness, a joylessness of spirit. And therefore I return often to this endeavor of raising your hearts, dilating your hearts with a holy joy, joy in the Holy Ghost, for "under the shadow of his wings" you may, you should, "rejoice."

If you look upon this world in a map you find two hemispheres, two half worlds. If you crush Heaven into a map you may find two hemispheres too, two half heavens; half will be joy and half will be glory, for in these two, the joy of Heaven and the glory of Heaven, is all Heaven often represented unto us. And as of those two hemispheres of the world, the first has been known long before but the other (that of America, which is the richer in treasure), God reserved for later discoveries; so though he reserve that hemisphere of Heaven which is the glory thereof, to the Resurrection, yet the other hemisphere, the joy of Heaven, God opens to our discovery and delivers for our habitation even while we dwell in this world. As God has cast upon the unrepentant sinner two deaths, a temporal and a spiritual death, so he has breathed into us two lives. As the word for death is doubled, "Thou shalt die the death," so is the word for life expressed in the plural, "God breathed into his nostrils the breath of lives," of divers lives.

Though our natural life were no life, but rather a continual dying, yet we have two lives besides that; an eternal life reserved for Heaven, but yet a heavenly life too, a spiritual life, even in this world. And as God thus inflicts two deaths and infuses two lives, so does he also pass two judgments upon man, or rather repeats the same judgment twice. For that which Christ shall say to your soul at the last judgment, "Enter into thy Master's joy," he says to your conscience now. The everlastingness of the joy is the blessedness of the next life, but the entering is afforded here. For that which Christ shall say then to us, "Come ye blessed," are words intended to persons that are coming, that are upon the way, though not at home. Here in this world he bids us, "Come"; there in the next he shall bid us, "Welcome."

The Angels of Heaven have joy in your conversion, and can you be without that joy in yourself? If you desire revenge upon your enemies, as they are God's enemies, that God would be pleased to remove and root out all such as oppose him, that affection appertains to glory. Let that alone till you come to the hemisphere of glory. There join with those martyrs under the altar, "How long O Lord, dost thou defer judgment?" and you shall have your answer there for that. While you are here, join with David and the other saints of God in that holy increpation of a dangerous sadness, "Why art thou cast down O my soul? why art thou disquieted in me?"

That soul that is dissected and anatomized to God, in a sincere confession, washed in the tears of true contrition, embalmed in the blood of reconciliation, the blood of Christ Jesus, can assign no reason, can give no just answer to that interrogatory, "Why art thou cast down O my soul? why art thou disquieted in me?" No man is so little as that he can be lost under these wings; no man so great as that they cannot reach to him. To what temporal, to what spiritual greatness soever we grow, still pray we him to shadow us under his wings; for the poor need those wings against oppression, and the rich against envy.

The Holy Ghost, who is a Dove, shadowed the whole world under his wings. He hovered over the waters, he sat upon the waters, and he hatched all that was produced; and all that was produced so, was good. Be you a mother where the Holy Ghost would be a father; conceive by him and be content that he produce joy in your heart here. First think that as a man must have some land, or else he cannot be in a wardship, so a man must have some of the love of God, or else he could not fall under God's correction. God would not give him his physic, God would not study his cure, if he cared not for him. And then think also, that if God afford you the shadow of his wings, that is, consolation, respiration, refreshing, though not a present and plenary deliverance in thy afflictions, not to thank God is a murmuring, and not to rejoice in God's ways is an unthankfulness.

Howling is the noise of Hell, singing the voice of Heaven; sadness the damp of Hell, rejoicing the serenity of Heaven. He that has not this joy here lacks one of the best pieces of evidence for the joys of Heaven, and has neglected or refused that earnest which God uses to bind his bargain, that true joy in this world shall flow into the joy of Heaven, as a river flows into the sea. This joy shall not be put out in death and a new joy kindled in me in Heaven; but as my soul, as soon as it is out of my body, is in Heaven, so the true joy of a good soul in this world is the very joy of Heaven.

We go thither, not that being without joy we might have joy infused into us, but that as Christ says, "Our joy might be full," perfected, sealed with an everlastingness. For as he promises "that no man shall take our joy from us," so neither shall death itself take it away, nor so much as interrupt it, or discontinue it. But as in the face of death when he lays hold upon me, and in the face of the Devil when he attempts me, I shall see the face of God (for everything shall be a glass to reflect God upon me), so in the agonies of death, in the anguish of that dissolution, in the sorrows of that valediction, in the irreversibleness of that transmigration, I shall have a joy which shall no more evaporate than my soul shall evaporate; a joy that shall pass up and put on a more glorious garment above, and be joy super-invested in glory. *Amen.*

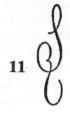

11 OF PRAYER, OF IGNORANCE, AND THE MERCY OF GOD

Father, forgive them, for they know not
what they do. LUKE 23:24

THE WORD OF GOD IS EITHER THE CO-ETERNAL AND co-essential Son, our Savior, which took flesh, or it is the spirit of his mouth, by which we live, and not by bread only. And so, in a large acceptation, every truth is the Word of God; for truth is uniform, and irrepugnant, and indivisible, as God. More strictly the Word of God is that which God has uttered, either in writing, as twice in the Tables to Moses; or by ministry of Angels, or prophets, in words; or by the unborn, in action, as in John the Baptist's exultation within his mother; or by new-born, from the mouths of babes and sucklings; or by things unreasonable, as in Balaam's Ass; or insensible, as in the whole book of such creatures, "The heavens declare the glory of God, etc." But nothing is more properly the Word of God to us than that which God himself speaks in those organs and instruments which himself has assumed for his chief work, our redemption. For in creation God spoke, but in redemption he did; and more, he suffered. And of that kind are these words. God in his chosen manhood says, "Father forgive them, for they know not what they do."

These words shall be fitliest considered, like a goodly palace, if we rest a little, as in an outward court, upon consideration of prayer in general; and then draw near the view of the palace, in a

139

second court, considering this special prayer in general as the face of the whole palace. Thirdly, we will pass through the chief rooms of the palace itself; and then insist upon four steps: *1.* Of whom he begs (Father). *2.* What he asks (forgive them). *3.* That he prays upon reason (for). *4.* What the reason is (they know not). And lastly, going into the backside of all, we will cast the objections: as why only Luke remembers this prayer: and why this prayer (as it seems by the punishment continuing upon the Jews to this day) was not obtained at God's hand.

So therefore prayer is our first entry, for when it is said, "Ask and it shall be given," it is also said, "Knock and it shall be opened," showing that by prayer our entrance is. And not the entry only, but the whole house: "My house is the house of prayer." Of all the conduits and conveyances of God's graces to us, none has been so little subject to cavillations as this of prayer. The sacraments have fallen into the hands of flatterers and robbers. Some have attributed too much to them, some detracted. Some have painted them, some have withdrawn their natural complexion. It has been disputed whether they be, how many they be, what they be, and what they do. The preaching of the Word has been made a servant of ambitions and a shop of many men's new-fangled wares. Almost every means between God and man suffers some adulteratings and disguises; but prayer least; and it has most ways and addresses. It may be mental, for we may think prayers. It may be vocal, for we may speak prayers. It may be actual, for we do prayers. For deeds have voice; the vices of Sodom did cry, and the alms of Tobit. And if it were proper for St. John in the first of the revelations to turn back and to see a voice, it is more likely God will look down to hear a work. So then to do the office of your vocation sincerely is to pray. How much the favorites of princes and great personages labor that they may be thought to have been in private conference with the prince. And though they be forced to wait upon his purposes, and talk of what he will, how fain they would be thought to have solicited their own, or their dependent's business. With the Prince of Princes, this every man may do truly; and the sooner, the more beggar he is: for no man is heard here but as a beggar.

Here we may talk long, welcomely, of our own affairs, and be
sure to speed. You cannot whisper so low alone in your chamber
but he hears you, nor sing so loud in the congregation but he
distinguishes you. He grudges not to be chidden and disputed with,
by Job. "The arrows of the Almighty are in me, and the venom
thereof hath drunk up my spirit. Is my strength the strength of
stones, or is my flesh of brass, etc." Not to be directed and counselled by Jonah, who was angry and said, "Did not I say, when I
was in my country, thou wouldest deal thus?" And when the Lord
said, "Doest thou well to be angry?" he replied, "I do well to be
angry to the death." Nor almost to be threatened and neglected by
Moses: "Do this, or blot my name out of thy book." It is an honor
to be able to say to servants, "Do this": but to say to God, "Lord,
do this," and prevail, is more; and yet more easy.

God is replenishingly everywhere; but most contractedly and
workingly in the temple. Since then every rectified man is the
temple of the Holy Ghost, when he prays; it is the Holy Ghost
itself that prays; and what can be denied where the asker gives? He
plays with us, as children, shows us pleasing things, that we may
cry for them, and have them. "Before we call, he answers, and
when we speak, he hears." Physicians observe some symptoms so
violent that they must neglect the disease for a time and labor to
cure the accident; as burning fevers, in dysenteries. So in the sinful
consumption of the soul, a stupidity and indisposition to prayer
must first be cured. For "Ye lust, and have not, because ye ask
not." The adulterous mother of the three great brothers, Gratian,
Lombard, and Comestor, being warned by her confessor to be
sorry for her fact, said she could not, because her fault had so
much profited the Church. "At least," said he, "be sorry that you
cannot be sorry." So whosoever you be, that cannot readily pray,
at least pray that you may pray. For, as in bodily, so in spiritual
diseases, it is a desperate state to be speechless.

It were unmannerliness to hold you longer in the entry. One turn
in the inner court, of this special prayer in general, and so enter the
palace. This is not a prayer for his own ease, as that in his agony
seems. It has none of those infirmities which curious schismatics
find in that. No suspicion of ignorance, as there ("if it be pos-

sible"). No tergiversation nor abandoning the noble work which he had begun, as there ("let this cup pass"). It is not an exemplar, or form, for us to imitate precisely (otherwise than in the doctrine), as that prayer which we call the Lord's Prayer, not because he said it, for he could never say "forgive us our trespasses," but because he commanded us to say it. For though by Matthew, which says, "After this manner pray," we seem not bound to the words, yet Luke says, "When you pray, say, Our Father which art, etc." But this is a prayer of God, to God; as when foreign merchandise is misported, the prince may permit or inhibit his subjects to buy it, or not to buy it. Our blessed Savior arriving in this world freighted with salvation, a thing which this world never had power to have without him, except in that short time between man's Creation and fall, he by this prayer begs that even to these despisers of it, it may be communicable, and that their ignorance of the value of it may not deprive them of it. Teaching that by example here, which he gave in precept before, "Pray for them which persecute you, that you may be the children of your Father which is in heaven." Therefore, doing so now, he might well say, "Father, forgive them," which is the first room in this glorious palace.

And in this contemplation, O my unworthy soul, you are presently in the presence. No passing of guards, nor ushers. No examination of your degree or habit. The Prince is not asleep, nor private, nor weary of giving, nor refers to others. He puts you not to prevail by Angels nor Archangels. But lest anything might hinder you from coming into his presence, his presence comes into you. And lest majesty should dazzle you, you are to speak but to your Father. Of which word, *Abba,* the root is "to will"; from which root, the fruit also must be willingness and propenseness to grant. God is the Father of Christ, by that mystical and eternal unexpressible generation, which never began nor ended. Of which incomprehensible mystery, Moses and the ancient prophets spake so little, and so indirectly, that till the dawning of the day of Christ, after Esdras' time, those places seem not to be intended of the Trinity. Nay, a good while after Christ they were but tenderly applied to that sense. And at this day, the most of the writers in the reformed Churches, considering that we need not such far-fetched and such forced helps, and withal weighing how well the Jews of these times are provided with other expositions of those places, are very sparing in using them, but content themselves modestly herein with the testimonies of the New Testament.

Truly, this mystery is rather the object of faith than reason; and it is enough that we believe Christ to have ever been the Son of God, by such generation, and ourselves his sons by adoption. So that God is Father to all; but yet so, that though Christ say, "My Father is greater than all," he adds, "I and my Father are all one," to show his eternal interest; and he seems to put a difference, "I go to my Father, and your Father, my God, and your God." The Roman stories have that when Claudius saw it conduce to his ends to get the tribuneship, of which he was incapable because a patrician, he suffered himself to be adopted. But against this adoption two exceptions were found; one, that he was adopted by a man of lower rank, a plebeian; which was unnatural; and by a younger man than himself, which took away the presentation of a father. But our adoption is regular. For first, we are made the sons of the Most High, and thus also by the Ancient of Days. There was no one word, by which he could so nobly have maintained his dignity, kept his station, justified his cause, and withal expressed his humility and charity, as this, "Father." They crucified him for saying himself to be the Son of God. And in the midst of torments, he both professes the same still, and lets them see that they have no other way of forgiveness, but that he is the Son of that Father, "For no man cometh to the Father but by the Son."

And at this voice (Father) O most blessed Savior, your Father, which is so fully yours that for your sake he is ours too; which is so wholly yours that he is yourself; which is all mercy, yet will not spare you; all justice, yet will not destroy us. And that glorious army of Angels, which hitherto by their own integrity maintained their first and pure condition, and by this work of yours, now near the "it is finished," attend a confirmation and infallibility of ever remaining so. And that faithful company of departed saints, to whom your merit must open a more inward and familiar room in your Father's Kingdom, stand all attentive to hear what you will ask of this Father. And what shall they hear? What do you ask?

"Forgive them," forgive them? Must murderers be forgiven? Must the offended ask it? And must a Father grant it? And must he be solicited and remembered by the name of Father to do it? Was not your passion enough, but you must have compassion? And is your mercy so violent, that you will have a fellow feeling of their imminent afflictions, before they have any feeling? The Angels might expect a present employment for their destruction: the Saints might be out of fear, that they should be assumed or mingled in their fellowship. But you will have them pardoned.

And yet dost not out of your own fulness pardon them, as you did the thief upon the cross, because he did already confess you; but you tell them, that they may be forgiven but at your request, and if they acknowledge their adovcate to be the Son of God. "Father, forgive them." I that cannot revenge your quarrel cannot forgive them. I that could not be saved, but by their offence, cannot forgive them. And must a Father, Almighty, and well pleased in you, forgive them? You are more charitable towards them, that by your direction we may be to ourselves. We must pray for ourselves limitedly: forgive us, as we forgive. But you will have their forgiveness illimited and unconditioned. You seem not so much as to presume a repentance; which is so essential and necessary in all transgressions, as where by man's fault the actions of God are diverted from his appointed ends, God himself is content to repent the doing of them. As he repented first the making of man, and then the making of a king. But God will have them within the arms of his general pardon. And we are all delivered from our debts; for God has given his word, his co-essential word, for us all. And though (as in other prodigal debts, the interest exceed the principal) our actual sins exceed our original, yet God by giving his word for us has acquitted all.

But the affections of our Savior are not inordinate, nor irregular. He has a "for" for his prayer: "Forgive them, for, etc." And where he has not this "for," as in his prayer in his agony, he quickly interrupts the violence of his request, with a but, "Father, let this cup pass, but not my will." In that form of prayer which himself taught us, he has appointed a "for," on God's part, which is ever the same unchangeable: "For thine is the Kingdom." Therefore supplications belong to you: the power, "Thou openest thy hand and fillest every living thing": the glory, "for thy Name is glorified in thy grants." But because on our part the occasions are variable, he has left our "for" to our religious discretion. For when it is said, "You lust and have not, because you ask not," it follows presently, "You ask and miss, because you ask amiss." It is not a fit "for," for every private man to ask much means for he would do much good. I must not pray, Lord put into my hands the strength of Christian Kings, for out of my zeal I will employ your benefits to your advantage, your soldiers against your enemies, and be a bank against that deluge wherewith your enemy the Turk threatens to overflow your people. I must not pray, "Lord fill my heart with knowledge and understanding," for I would compose the schisms in your Church, and reduce your garment to the first continual and seamless integrity; and redress the deafnesses and oppressions of judges, and officers. But he gave us a convenient scantling for our "fors," who prayed, "Give me enough, for I may else despair, give me not too much, for so I may presume."

Of schoolmen, some affirm prayer to be an act of our will; for we would have that which we ask. Others, of our understanding; for by it we ascend to God, and better our knowledge, which is the proper aliment and food of our understanding; so that is a perplexed case. But all agree that it is an act of our reason, and therefore must be reasonable. For only reasonable things can pray; for the beasts and ravens are not said to pray for food, but "to cry."

Two things are required to make a prayer: good effect, which was not in the Devil's request, "Let us go into the swine"; nor "Stretch out thy hand, and touch all he hath"; and "Stretch out thy hand, and touch his bones"; and therefore these were not prayers. And it must be of things which are good: for our government in that point, this may inform us. Things absolutely good, as remission of sins, we may absolutely beg: and to escape things absolutely ill, as sin. But mean and indifferent things, qualified by the circumstances, we must ask conditionally and referringly to the giver's will. For when Paul begged the thorn in the flesh to be taken from him, it was not granted, but he had this answer, "My grace is sufficient for thee."

Let us now (not in curiosity but for instruction) consider the reason: "They know not what they do." First, if ignorance excuse: and then, if they were ignorant.

Have you, O God, filled all your Scriptures, both of your recorders and notaries, which have penned the history of your love to your people; and of your secretaries the prophets, admitted to the foreknowledge of your purposes, and instructed in your cabinet; have you filled these with phrases and persuasions of wisdom and knowledge, and must these persecutors be pardoned for their ignorance? Have you bid Isaiah to say, "It is a people of no understanding, therefore he that made them, shall not have compassion of them." And Hosea, "My people are destroyed for lack of knowledge"; and now do you say, "Forgive them because they know not?" Shall ignorance, which is often the cause of sin, often a sin itself, often the punishment of sin, and ever an infirmity and disease contracted by the first great sin, advantage them? "Who can understand his faults?" said the man according to your heart, "Lord cleanse me from my secret faults." He durst not make his ignorance the reason of his prayer, but prayed against ignorance.

But your mercy is as the sea: both before it was the sea, for it overspreads the whole world: and since it was called into limits: for it is not the less infinite for that. And as by the sea the most remote and distant nations enjoy one another by traffic and commerce, East and West becoming neighbors: so by mercy the most different things are united and reconciled: sinners have Heaven; traitors are in the prince's bosom: and ignorant persons are in the spring of wisdom, being forgiven, not only though they be ignorant, but because they are ignorant. But all ignorance is not excusable; nor any less excusable than not to know what ignorance is not to be excused. Therefore, there is an ignorance which they call a not knowing of things not appertaining to us. This we had had, though Adam had stood: and the Angels have it, for they know not the latter day, and therefore for this we are not chargeable. They call the other privation, which if it proceed merely from our own sluggishness, in not searching the means made for our instruction, is ever inexcusable. If from God, who for his own just ends has cast clouds over those lights which should guide us, it is often excusable. For Paul says, "I was a blasphemer, and a persecutor, and an oppressor, but I was received to mercy, for I did it ignorantly, through unbelief." So though we are all bound to believe, and therefore faults done by unbelief cannot escape the name and nature of sin, yet since belief is the immediate gift of God, faults done by unbelief, without malicious concurrences and circumstances, obtain mercy and pardon from that abundant fountain of grace, Christ Jesus.

And therefore it was a just reason, "Forgive them, for they know not." If they knew not, which is evident both by this speech from truth itself, and by, "Had they known it, they would not have crucified the Lord of glory"; and "I know that through ignorance ye did it." And though after so many powerful miracles, this ignorance were vincible, God having revealed enough to convert them, yet there seems to be enough on their parts to make it a perplexed case, and to excuse, though not a malicious persecuting, yet a not consenting to his doctrine. For they had a law, "Whosoever shall make himself the son of God, let him die." And they spoke out of their laws, when they said, "We have no other King but Caesar." There were therefore some among them reasonable and zealously ignorant. And for those, the Son ever welcome and well heard, begged of his Father, ever accessible and exorable, a pardon ever ready and natural.

We have now passed through all those rooms which we unlocked and opened at first. And now may that point, why this prayer is remembered only by one evangelist, and why by Luke, be modestly inquired. For we are all admitted and welcomed into the acquaintance of the Scriptures, upon such conditions as travellers are into other countries: if we come as praisers and admirers of their commodities and government, not as spies into the mysteries of their state, nor searchers, nor calumniators of their weaknesses. For though the Scriptures, like a strong rectified state, be not endangered by such a curious malice of any, yet he which brings that, deserves no admittance. When those great commissioners which are called the Septuagint, sent from Jerusalem to translate the Hebrew Scriptures into Greek, had perfected their work, it was and is an argument of divine assistance, that writing severally, they differed not. The same may prove even to weak and faithless men that the Holy Ghost superintended the four evangelists, because they differ not; as they which have written their harmonies make it evident.

But to us, faith teaches the other way. And we conclude not, because they agree, the Holy Ghost directed; for heathen writers and malefactors in examinations do so; but because the Holy Ghost directed, we know they agree and differ not. For as an honest man, ever of the same thoughts, differs not from himself, though he do not ever say the same things, if he say not contraries; so the four evangelists observe the uniformity and sameness of their guide, though all did not say all the same things, since none contradicts any. And as, when my soul, which enables all my limbs to their functions, disposes my legs to go, my whole body is truly said to go, because none stays behind; so when the Holy Spirit, which had made himself as a common soul to their four souls, directed one of them to say anything, all are well understood to have said it. St. Augustine teaches that it is more wonderful that all the prophets spake one by Spirit, and so agreed, than if any one of them had spoken all those things; and therefore he adds, "All say what any of them say." And in this sense most congruously is that of St. Jerome appliable, that as the four chariot wheels, though they look to the four corners of the world, yet they move to one end and one way, so the evangelists have both one scope and one way.

Other singularities of Luke, of form or matter, I omit and end with one like this in our text. As in the apprehending of our blessed Savior, all the evangelists record that Peter cut off Malchus' ear, but only Luke remembers the healing of it again: (I think) because that act of curing was most present and obvious to his consideration, who was a physician: so he was therefore most apt to remember this prayer of Christ, which is the physic and *Balsamum* of our soul, and must be applied to us all (for we do all crucify him, and we know not what we do). And therefore St. Jerome gave a right character of him, in his Epistle to Paulinus, "As he was a physician, so all his words are physic for a languishing soul."

Now let us dispatch the last consideration of the effect of this

prayer. Did Christ intend the forgiveness of the Jews, whose utter
ruin God (that is, himself) had foredecreed? And which he foresaw and bewailed even then hanging upon the cross? For those
divines which reverently forbear to interpret the words, "Lord,
Lord, why hast thou forsaken me?" of a suffering hell in his soul,
or of a departing of the Father from him; offer no exposition of
those words more convenient than that the foresight of the Jews'
imminent calamities expressed and drew those words from him:
"In their affliction, were all kinds, and all degrees of misery." So
that as one writer of the Roman story says elegantly, "He that
considers the acts of Rome, considers not the acts of one people,
but of mankind": I may truly say of the Jews' afflictions, he that
knows them is ignorant of nothing that this world can threaten. For
to that which the present authority of the Romans inflicted upon
them, our schools have added upon their posterity; that they are
as slaves to Christians, and their goods subject to spoil, if the laws
of the princes where they live did not out of indulgency defend
them. Did he then ask, and was not heard? God forbid. A man is
heard, when that is given which his will desired; and our will is
ever understood to be a will rectified, and concurrent with God.
This is *Voluntas*, a discoursed and examined will. That which is
upon the first sight of the object, is *Velleitas,* a willingness, which
we resist not only because we thought not of it. And such a willingness had Christ, when suddenly he wished that the cup might
pass: but quickly conformed his will to his Father's. But in this
prayer his will was present, therefore fulfilled. Briefly then, in this
prayer he commended not all the Jews, for he knew the chief to sin
knowingly, and so out of the reach of his reason ("for they know
not"). Nor any, except they repented after: for it is not ignorance,
but repentance, which derives to us the benefit of God's pardon.
For he that sins of ignorance may be pardoned if he repent; but he
that sins against his conscience, and is thereby impenitible, cannot
be pardoned. And this is all which I will say of these words,
"Father forgive them, for they know not what they do."

O eternal God, look down from thy Throne to thy footstool:
from thy blessed company of Angels and saints, to us, by our own

faults made more wretched and contemptible than the worms which shall eat us, or the dust which we were, and shall be. O Lord, under the weight of thy justice we cannot stand. Nor had any other title to thy mercy, but the name of Father, and that we have forfeited. That name of sons of God, thou gavest to us, all at once in Adam; and he gave it away from us all by his sin. And thou hast given it again to every one of us, in our regeneration by baptism, and we have lost it again by our transgressions. And yet thou wert not weary of being merciful, but didest choose one of us, to be a fit and worthy ransom for us all; and by the death of thy Christ, our Jesus, gavest us again the title and privilege of thy Sons; but with conditions, which though easy, we have broke, and with a yoke, which though light, and sweet, we have cast off. How shall we then dare to call thee Father? Or to beg that thou wilt make one trial more of us? These hearts are accustomed to rebellions, and hopeless. But, O God, create in us new hearts, hearts capable of the love and fear due to a Father. And then we shall dare to say, "Father," and to say, "Father forgive us." Forgive us, O Father, and all which are engaged, and accountable to thee for us: forgive our parents, and those which undertook for us in baptism. Forgive the civil magistrate, and the minister. Forgive them their negligences, and us our stubbornnesses. And give us the grace that we may ever sincerely say, both this prayer of example and counsel, "Forgive our enemies," and that other of precept, "Our Father which art in Heaven, etc."

12 ON PRAYER, REPENTANCE, AND THE MERCY OF GOD; A LENTEN SERMON

Not for any injustice in my hands: Also my prayer is pure. O Earth cover not thou my blood; and let my cry have no place. Also now behold, my witness is in Heaven, and my record is on high JOB 16:17-19

JOB'S FRIENDS (AS IN CIVILITY WE ARE FAIN TO call them, because they came upon a civil pretense, to visit him and to comfort him) had now done speaking. It was long before they would have done. "I have often heard such things as you say," says Job to them, they are not new to me; and therefore, "miserable comforters, troublesome comforters are ye all," old and new. But, says he, "Shall your windy words," your empty, your airy, your frothy words "have any end?" Now they have an end. Eliphas ends his charge in the last, and in this chapter Job begins to answer for himself. But how? By a middle way. Job does not justify himself; but yet he does not prevaricate, he does not betray his innocence neither. For there may be a pusillanimity even towards God. A man may overclog his own conscience, and belie himself in his confessions, out of a distempered jealousy and suspicion of God's purposes upon him. Job does not so. Many men have troubled themselves more, how the soul comes into man, than how it goes out. They wrangle whether it comes in by infusion from God, or by propagation from parents, and never consider

151

whether it shall return to him that made it, or to him that marred it; to him that gave it, or to him that corrupted it. So many of our expositors upon this book of Job have spent themselves upon the person, and the place, and the time, who Job was, when Job was, where Job was, and whether there were ever any such person as Job or no, and have passed over too slightly the senses and doctrines of the book.

In this chapter and before this text, we have Job's anatomy, Job's skeleton, the ruins to which he was reduced. In the eighth verse he takes knowledge, that God had filled him with leanness and wrinkles, and that those wrinkles and that leanness were witnesses against him; and that they that hated him had torn him in pieces, in the ninth verse. In the eleventh verse, that God had delivered him over to the ungodly; and that God himself had shaked him in pieces, and set him up as a mark to shoot at, in the twelfth verse. That God had cleft his reins and poured out his gall upon the ground, in the thirteenth verse, and in the fourteenth, that he broke him, breach after breach, and ran over him as a giant, and at last, in the sixteenth verse, that foulness was upon his face, and the shadow of death upon his eyelids. Now let me ask in Job's behalf God's question to Ezekiel, "Dost thou believe that these bones can live?" Can this anatomy, this skeleton, these ruins, this rubbish of Job speak? It can, it does in this text, "Not for any injustice in my hands, etc."

And in these words it delivers us, first, the confidence of a godly man. Do God what he will, say you what you will, that because I am more afflicted than other men, therefore I am guilty of more heinous sins than other men, yet I know that whatsoever God's end be in this proceeding, it is not for any injustice in my hands. "Also my prayer is pure." Secondly, it delivers us that kind of infirm anguish and indignation, that half-distemper, that expostulation with God, which sometimes comes to an excess even in good and godly men, "O earth cover not thou my blood, and let my cry have no place"; I desire not that anything should be concealed or disguised, let all that ever I have done be written in my forehead and read by all men. And then thirdly and lastly, it delivers us the foundation of his confidence, and the recovery from this his in-

firmity, and from his excess in the manner of expressing it, if he
have been over bold therein, "My witness is in heaven, and my
record is on high." God is his witness that that which they charge
him with is false, that that which he says in his own discharge (in
that sense that he says it) is true. And in these three, Job's protestation, not guilty; Job's manifest, I would all the world knew all;
Job's establishment and consolidation, "My witness is in heaven";
in these three branches, and in some fruits which in passing we
shall gather from them, we shall determine all that appertains to
these words.

I remember St. Gregory, in handling one text, professes that he
will endeavor to handle it so as that the weakest understanding
might comprehend the highest points, and the highest understanding not be weary to hear ordinary doctrines so delivered. Indeed it
is a good art to deliver deep points in a holy plainness, and plain
points in a holy delightfulness: for many times one part of our
auditory understands us not, when we have done, and so they are
weary; and another part understands us before we begun, and so
they are weary. Today my humble petition must be that you will be
content to hear plain things plainly delivered. Of which, be this the
first, that Job found himself under the oppression and calumny of
that misinterpretation, that kings themselves, and states have not
escaped.

The tower of Siloe [Siloam] fell and slew them, therefore they
were the greater sinners in Jerusalem; this man prospers not in the
world, therefore he proceeds not in the fear of God; the heir wastes
the estate, therefore the estate was ill gotten, are hasty conclusions
in private affairs. Treasures are empty, therefore there are unnecessary wastes; discontented persons murmur, therefore things are
ill carried; our neighbors prosper by action, therefore we perish by
not appearing, are hasty conclusions in state affairs. This man is
affected when he hears a blasphemous oath, and when he looks
upon the general liberty of sinning; therefore he is a Puritan; that
man loves the ancient forms, and doctrines, and disciplines of the
Church, and retains and delights in the reverend names of priest,
and altar, and sacrifice, therefore he is a Papist, are hasty conclusions in Church affairs. When we do fall under these misinter-

pretations and ill applications of God's proceedings, we may say with Job, "I also could speak, as you do; if your soul were in my soul's stead, I could heap up words against you, and shake my head at you," conclude desperarely, speak scornfully of you. But I will not; yet I will not betray myself, I will make my protestation, what end soever God propose to himself in this his proceeding. "It is not for any injustice in my hands, Also my prayer is pure."

In these two, cleanness of hands, pureness of prayer, are all religious duties comprehended: for clean hands denote justice and righteousness towards men, and pure prayer devotion, and the service and worship of God. Job protests for both. Therefore does Origen say of Job, "I do verily believe, and therefore may be bold to say, that for constancy and fidelity towards God, Job did exceed not only men, but Angels themselves." For, says Origen, Job did not only suffer without being guilty of those things to which his afflictions were imputed, but he said grace when he had no meat, when God gave him stones for bread, and scorpions for fish; he praised God as much for the affliction itself as for his former or his subsequent benefits and blessings. Not that Job was merely innocent, but that he was guilty of no such things as might confer those conclusions which, from his afflictions, his enemies raised. "If I justify myself," says Job, "mine own mouth shall condemn me." Every self-justification is a self-condemnation; when I give judgment for myself, I am therein a witness against myself. "If I say I am perfect," says he in the same place, "even that proves me perverse." If I say I never go out of the way, I am out then, and therefore, because I say so. "I have sinned," says he, "what shall I do unto thee, O thou preserver of men?" Job felt the hand of destruction upon him, and he felt the hand of preservation too; and it was all one hand. This is God's method, and his alone, to preserve by destroying. Men of this world do sometimes repair and recompense those men whom they have oppressed before, but this is an after recompense. God's first intention even when he destroys is to preserve, as a physician's first intention, in the most distasteful physic, is health. Even God's demolitions are super-edifications, his anatomies, his dissections are so many recompactings, so many resurrections. God winds us off the skein, that he may weave

us up into the whole piece, and he cuts us out of the whole piece
into pieces, that he may make us up into a whole garment.

But for all these humiliations and confessions, Job does not
waive his protestation; "My righteousness I hold fast, and my
heart shall not reproach me as long as I live." Not that I shall
never sin, but never leave any sin unrepented; and then, my heart
cannot reproach me of a repented sin, without reproaching God
himself. "The sun must not set upon my anger"; much less will I
let the sun set upon the anger of God towards me, or sleep in an
unrepented sin. Every night's sleep is a *Nunc dimittis;* then the Lord
lets his servant depart in peace. Your lying down is a valediction, a
parting, a taking leave (shall I say so?), a shaking hands with
God; and when you shake hands with God, let those hands be
clean. Enter into your grave, your metaphorical, your quotidian
grave, your bed, as you entered into the Church at first, by water,
by baptism. Rebaptize yourself every night, in Job's snow water, in
holy tears that may cool the inordinate lusts of your heart, and
withhold unclean abuses of those hands even in that your grave,
your bed. And ever more remember Job's fear and jealousy in that
place, that when he had washed himself in snow water, "mine own
clothes will make me foul again." Your flesh is your clothes; and
to this mischievous purpose of fouling your hands with your own
clothes, you have most clothes on when you are naked; then in that
nakedness you are in most danger of fouling your hands with your
own clothes. Miserable man! that could have no use of hands nor
any other organ of sense, if there were no other creature but
yourself, and yet if there were no other creature but yourself, could
sin upon yourself and foul your hands with your own hands. How
much more then, if you strike with those hands, by oppression in
your office, or shut up those hands and that which is due to another in them? Sleep with clean hands, either kept clean all day, by
integrity; or washed clean at night by repentance; and whensoever
you wake, though all Job's messengers thunder about you, and all
Job's friends multiply misinterpretations against you, yet Job's
protestation shall be your protestation, what end soever God have
in this proceeding, "It is not for any injustice in my hands," and
the other part of his protestation too, "Also my prayer is pure."

As clean hands denote all righteousness towards man, so do pure prayers all devotion, and worship, and service of God. For we are of the household of the faithful, and the service which we are to do, as his household servants, is prayer; for his house is the house of prayer. And therein only is it possible to us to fulfil that commandment, "Pray continually," that continually, in all our familiar actions, we may serve God, glorify God (whether we eat or drink, we may do it to his glory), and every glorifying, every thanksgiving, is prayer. There cannot be a more effectual prayer for future, than a thankful acknowledgment of former benefits. How often is that repeated in the Gospel, and in the epistles? "Ask, and it shall be given ye"; no grant without prayer, no denial upon prayer.

It must be prayer, and my prayer; "Also my prayer is pure." I must not rely upon the prayers of others; not of Angels; though they be ministerial spirits, and not only to God himself, but between God and man, and so, as they present our prayers, no doubt pour out their own for us too, yet we must not rely upon the prayers of Angels. Nor of saints; though they have a more personal and experimental sense of our miseries than Angels have, we must not rely upon the prayers of saints. No, nor upon the prayers of the congregation, though we see and hear them pray, except we make ourselves parts of the congregation, by true devotion, as well as by personal presence.

It must be my own prayer, and no prayer is so truly, or so properly mine, as that that the Church has delivered and recommended to me. In sudden and unpremeditated prayer, I am not always I; and when I am not myself, my prayer is not my prayer. Passions and affections sometimes, sometimes bodily infirmities, and sometimes a vain desire of being eloquent in prayer, aliens me, withdraws me from myself, and then that prayer is not my prayer.

In that African Council, in which St. Augustine was present, to remedy the abuse of various forms of prayers which divers Churches assumed, it was decreed that no prayers should be received in the Church but such as were composed or approved by the Council. We have proceeded so too. No prayers received for public use but those that are delivered by public authority; and so,

they become my prayers. As the law of the land is my law, and I
have an inheritance in it, so the prayers of the Church are my
prayers, and I have an interest in them, because I am a son of that
family. My baptism is mine, and my absolution is mine, because
the Church has given them to me, and so are her prayers mine.
You would scarce thank a man for an extemporal elegy, or epi-
gram, or panegyric in your praise, if it cost the poet, or the orator
no pains. God will scarce harken to sudden, inconsidered irrev-
erent prayers. Men will study even for compliments; and princes
and ambassadors will not speak to one another without thinking
what they will say. Let not us put God to speak to us so (preaching is God's speaking to us). Let us not speak to God so (praying
is our speaking to God), not extemporally, unadvisedly, inconsiderately. Prayer must be my prayer; and even in this kind, what
have I that I have not received? I have received my prayer altogether, as a bundle of myrrh, in that prayer which I have received
from my Savior, and then I have received it appropriated to me
and apportioned to my particular necessities, and sacrifices, by the
piety and wisdom of the Church; so it is my prayer, and as Job's
prayer was pure prayer, also my prayer is pure.

The Holy Ghost has so marshaled and disposed the qualifications of prayer in this place, as that there is no pure prayer without
clean hands. The lifting up of hands was the gesture of prayer,
even among the heathen. Amongst the Jews, prayer and the lifting
up of hands was one and the same thing, "Let the lifting up of my
hands be an evening sacrifice"; and longer than Moses' hands were
lifted up, his prayer had no effect. All this, perchance therefore
especially, that this lifting up of my hands brings them into my
sight; then I can see them, and see whether they be clean or no,
and consider that if I see impurity in my hands, God sees impurity
in my prayer. Can I think to receive ease from God with that hand
that oppresses another? Mercy from God with that hand that exercises cruelty upon another? Or bounty from God with that hand
that withholds right from another? Prayer is our hand, but it must
be a clean hand, pure prayer.

The Emperor whom no religion would lose, Constantine (for
the heathen deified him and the Christians canonized him; they

made him a god, and we came as near as we could, we made him a saint), that Emperor was coined praying. Other emperors were coined triumphing, in chariots, or preparing for triumphs, in battles and victories, but he, Constantine, in that posture, kneeling, praying. He knew his coin would pass through every family; and to every family he desired to be an example of piety. Every piece of single money was a catechism, and testified to every subject all this, surely he will graciously receive my petition, and look graciously upon me when I kneel, for behold he kneels too, and he exhibits petitions to that God, from whom he acknowledges that he needs as much as I can from him. And yet this symbolical and catechistical coin of Constantine's was not so convincing, nor so irrefragable a testimony of his piety (for Constantine might be coined praying and yet never pray) as when we see as great a prince as he, actually, really, personally, daily, duly at prayer with us.

To end this branch, let not your prayer be lucrative, nor vindicative, pray not for temporal superfluities, pray not for the confusion of them that differ from you in opinion, or in manners, but condition your prayer, inanimate your prayer with the glory of God, and your own everlasting happiness, and the edification of others, and this prayer is Job's prayer, pure prayer. And farther we enlarge not his protestation, "My hands are clean," I do no man wrong; my prayer is pure, I mock not God. But because continuing under so great afflictions, men would not believe this, he proceeds perchance to some excess and inconsiderateness, in desiring a manifestation of all his actions, "O earth, cover not thou my blood, and let my cry have no place."

Blood in this text is the blood of the soul, exhausted by sin (for every sin is an incision of the soul, a lancination, a phlebotomy, a letting of the soul blood, and then a delight in sin is a going with open veins into a warm bath and bleeding to death). This will be the force of Job's admiration, or imprecation, "O earth cover not thou my blood," I am content to stand as naked now as I shall do at the day of judgment, when all men shall see all men's actions. I desire no disguise, I deny, I excuse, I extenuate nothing that ever I did, I would mine enemies knew my worst, that they might study some other reason of God's thus proceeding with me than those heinous sins which, from these afflictions, they will necessarily conclude against me.

But had Job been able to have stood out this trial? Was Job so innocent as that he need not care, though all the world knew all? Perchance there may have been some excess, some inordinateness in his manner of his expressing it; we cannot excuse the vehemence of some holy men, in such expressions. We cannot say that there was no excess in Moses', "Pardon this people or blot my name out of thy book"; or that there was no excess in St. Paul's saying that he wished to be accursed, to be separated from Christ for his brethren. But for Job we shall not need this excuse; for either we may restrain his words to those sins which they imputed to him, and then they have but the nature of that protestation which David made so often to God, "Judge me, O Lord, according to my right-eousness, according to mine innocency, according to the cleanness of my hands"; which was not spoken by David simply, but respec-tively; not of all his sins, but of those which Saul pursued him for. Or if we enlarge Job's words generally to all his sins, we must consider them to be spoken after his repentance and reconciliation to God thereupon. If they knew (may Job have said) how it stood between God and my soul, how earnestly I have repented, how fully he has forgiven, they would never say these afflictions pro-ceeded from those sins.

And truly, so may I, so may every soul say that is rectified, refreshed, restored, re-established by the seals of God's pardon, and his mercy, so the world would take knowledge of the conse-quences of my sins, as well as of the sins themselves, and read my leaves on both sides, and hear the second part of my story as well as the first; so the world would look upon my temporal calamities, the bodily sicknesses, and the penuriousness of my fortune con-tracted by my sins, and upon my spiritual calamities, dejections of spirit, sadness of heart, declinations towards a diffidence and dis-trust in the mercy of God, and then when the world sees me in this agony and bloody sweat, in this agony and bloody sweat would also see the Angels of heaven ministering comforts unto me; so they would consider me in my earnest confessions, God in his powerful absolutions, me drawn out of one sea of blood, the blood of mine own soul, and cast into another sea, the bottomless sea of the blood of Christ Jesus; so they would know as well what God has done for my soul, as what my soul and body have done against my God. So they would read me throughout, and look upon me altogether, I would join with Job in his confident adjuration, "O earth cover not thou my blood"; let all the world know all the sins of my youth, and of mine age too, and I would not doubt but God should receive more glory, and the world more benefit, than if I had never sinned. This is that that exalts Job's confidence, he was guilty of nothing, that is, no such thing as they concluded upon, of nothing absolutely, because he had repented all. And from this, his confidence rises to a higher pitch than this, "O earth cover not thou my blood, and let my cry have no place."

What means Job in this? In the former part (Job's protestation) he considered God and man; righteousness towards man in clean hands, and in pure prayers, devotion towards God. In this part (his manifest) he pursues the same method, he considers man and God. Though men knew all my sins, that should not trouble me, says he (and that we have considered) yes, though my cry find no place, no place with God, that should not trouble me. I should be content that God should seem not to hear my prayers, but that he laid me open to that ill interpretation of wicked men, "Tush, he prays, but the Lord hears him not; he cries, but God relieves him not." And yet, when will you relieve me, O thou reliever of men, if not upon my cries, upon my prayers? Yet, St. Augustine has repeated more than once, more than twice, be not overjoyed when God grants you your prayer. The Devil had his prayer granted, says that Father, when he had leave to enter into the herd of swine; and so he had when he obtained power from God against Job. But all this aggravated the Devil's punishment; so may it do yours, to have some prayers granted. And as that must not overjoy you, if it be, so if your prayer be not granted, it must not deject you. God suffered St. Paul to pray and pray and pray, yet, after his thrice praying, granted him not that he prayed for. God suffered that "if it be possible," and that "let this cup pass," to pass from Christ himself, yet he granted it not.

But in many of these cases a man does easilier satisfy his own mind than other men. If God grant me not my prayer, I recover quickly, and I lay hold upon the horns of that altar, and ride safely at that anchor: God saw that that which I prayed for was not so good for him, nor so good for me. But yet because God may propose further glory to himself, more benefit to me, and more edification even to them, at last, who at first made ill constructions of his proceedings, I admit, as Job admits, "O earth cover not thou my blood" (let all the world see all my faults) "and let my cry have no place" (let them imagine that God has forsaken me and does not hear my prayers). My satisfaction, my acquiescence arises not out of their opinion and interpretation, that must not be my trial, but "my witness is in heaven, and my record is on high," which is our third and last consideration.

All that we are to consider is but this, "My witness is in heaven." And truly, that is enough. I care not though all the world knew all my faults, I care not what they conclude of God's not granting my prayers, "my witness is in heaven." To be condemned unjustly amongst men, to be ill interpreted in the acts of my religion is a heavy case; but yet I have a relief in all this, "my witness is in heaven."

The first comfort is, he whom I rely upon is in Heaven. For that is the foundation and basis upon which our Savior erects that prayer which he has recommended unto us, "Our Father, which art in heaven." When I lay hold upon him there, in Heaven, I pursue cheerfully and confidently all the other petitions, for daily bread, for forgiveness of sins, for deliverance from temptations, from, and for all. He is in Heaven, and he sits in Heaven; that as I see him in that posture that Stephen saw him, standing at the right hand of the Father, and so in a readiness, in a willingness to come to my succor, so I might contemplate him in a judiciary posture, a sovereign posture, sitting, and consider him as able, as willing to relieve me. He is in Heaven, and he sits in Heaven, and then he dwells in Heaven, he is, and he is always, there. Baal's priests could not always find him at home; Job's God, and our God is never abroad. He dwells in the heavens, and he dwells on high; so high that God humbles himself to behold the things that are in Heaven. With

what amazedness must we consider the humiliation of God in
descending to the earth, lower than so, to Hell, when even his
descending unto Heaven is a humiliation? God humbles himself
when he beholds anything lower than himself, though Cherubim,
though Seraphim, though the human nature, the body of his own
and only eternal Son; and yet he beholds, considers, studies us,
worms of the earth, and no men.

This then is Job's and our first comfort, because he is in
Heaven, and sits in Heaven, and dwells in Heaven, in the highest
Heaven, and so sees all things. But then if God see and say nothing, David apprehends that for a most dangerous condition; and
therefore he says, "Be not silent, O Lord, lest if thou be silent, I
perish." And again, "Hold not thy peace, O God of my praise, for
the mouth of the wicked is opened against me." And, Lord, let
your mercy be as forward as their malice. And therefore, as God
from that height sees all (and the strictest examination that we put
upon any witness is, that if he pretend to testify anything upon his
knowledge, we ask how he came by that knowledge, and if he be a
witness that saw it, this is good evidence), as God is to this purpose, all eye, and sees all, so for our farther comfort, he descends
to the office of being a witness, there is a witness in Heaven.

But then, God may be a witness and yet not my witness, and in
that there is small comfort, if God be a witness on my adversaries'
side, a witness against me. "Even I know, and am a witness," says
the Lord; that is, a witness of the sins, which I know by you. Now
if our own heart, our own conscience condemn us, this is shrewd
evidence, says St. John; for my own conscience, single, is a thousand witnesses against me. But then (says the Apostle) God is
greater than the heart, for he knows all things. He knows circumstances of sin, as well as substance; and that we seldom know,
seldom take knowledge of. If then my own heart be a thousand,
God, that is greater, is ten thousand witnesses, if he witness against
me. But if he be my witness, a witness for me, as he always
multiplies in his ways of mercy, he is thousands of thousands,
millions of millions of witnesses in my behalf, for "there is no
condemnation," no possible condemnation, "to them that are in
him."

But will all this come home to Job's end and purpose; that he need not care though all men knew all his faults, he need not care though God passed over his prayers, because God is his witness? What declarations soever he had in himself, would the world believe that God testified in his behalf, when they saw his calamities multiplied upon him, and his prayers neglected? If they will not, herein lies his and our final comfort, that he that is my witness is in the highest Heaven, there is no person above him, and therefore he that is my witness is my judge too. I shall not be tried by an arbitrary court, where it may be wisdom enough to follow a wise leader, and think as he thinks. I shall not be tried by a jury, that had rather I suffered than they fasted, rather I lost my life than they lost a meal. Nor tried by peers, where honor shall be the Bible. But I shall be tried by the King himself, than which no man can propose a nobler trial, and that King shall be the King of Kings too; for he who in the first of the Revelation is called "the faithful Witness," is in the same place called "the Prince of the Kings of the earth," and as he is there produced as a witness, so he is ordained to be the judge of the quick and the dead, and so all judgment is committed to him. He that is my witness is my judge, and the same person is my Jesus, my Savior, my Redeemer; he that has taken my nature, he that has given me his blood. So that he is my witness, in his own cause, and my judge, but of his own title, and will, in me, preserve himself. He will not let that nature that he has invested, perish, nor that treasure, which he has poured out for me, his blood, be ineffectual. My witness is in Heaven, my Judge is in Heaven, my Redeemer is in Heaven, and in them, who are but One, I have not only a constant hope that I shall be there too, but an evident assurance that I am there already, in his Person.

Go then in this peace, that you always study to preserve this testification of the Spirit of God, by outward evidences of sanctification. You are naturally composed of four elements, and three of those four are evident and unquestioned. The fourth element, the element of fire, is a more litigious element, more problematical, more disputable. Every good man, every true Christian, in his metaphysics (for, in a regenerate man, all is metaphysical, supernatural), has four elements also; and three of those four are de-

clared in this text. First, a good name, the good opinion of good
men, for honest dealing in the world, and religious discharge of
duties towards God, that there be no injustice in our hands, also
that our prayer be pure. A second element is a good conscience in
myself, that either a holy wariness before, or a holy repentance
after, settle me so in God as that I care not though all the world
knew all my faults. And a third element is, my hope in God, that
my witness which is in Heaven, will testify for me, as a witness in
my behalf, here, or acquit me, as a merciful judge, hereafter. Now
there may be a fourth element, an infallibility of final perseverance, grounded upon the eternal knowledge of God; but this is, as
the element of fire, which may be, but is not so discernible, so
demonstrable as the rest.

And therefore, as men argue of the element of fire, that whereas
the other elements produce creatures in such abundance, the earth
such herds of cattle, the waters such shoals of fish, the air such
flocks of birds, it is no unreasonable thing to stop upon this consideration, whether there should be an element of fire, more spa-
cious and comprehensive than all the rest, and yet produce no
creatures; so if your pretended element of infallibility produce no
creatures, no good works, no holy actions, you may justly doubt
there is no such element in you. In all doubts that arise in you, still
it will be a good rule to choose that now which you would choose
upon your deathbed. If a temptation to beauty, to riches, to honor,
be proposed to you, upon such and such conditions, consider
whether you would accept that, upon those conditions, upon your
deathbed, when you must part with them in a few minutes. So,
when you doubt in what you should place your assurance in God,
think seriously, whether you shall not have more comfort then,
upon your deathbed, in being able to say, "I have finished my
course, I have fought a good fight, I have fulfilled the sufferings of
Christ in my flesh," I have clothed him when he was naked, and
fed him when he was poor, than in any other thing that you may
conceive God to have done for you. And do all the way as you
would do then; prove your element of fire by the creatures it
produces, prove your election by your sanctification; for that is the
right method, and shall deliver you over, infallibly, to everlasting
glory at last, *Amen*.

13 ON THE CONVERSION OF ST. PAUL. HOW GOD MAY STRIKE DOWN A MAN TO RAISE HIM UP

And he fell to the earth, and heard a voice,
saying, Saul, Saul, why persecutest thou me?
ACTS 9:4

"LET US NOW PRAISE FAMOUS MEN, AND OUR FA-thers that begat us" (says the Wiseman), that is, that assisted our second generation, our spiritual regeneration. Let us praise them, commemorate them. "The Lord hath wrought great glory by them, through his power from the beginning," says he there, that is it has always been the Lord's way to glorify himself in the conversion of men, by the ministry of men. For he adds, "They were leaders of the people by their counsel, and by their knowledge and learning meet for the people, wise and eloquent men in their instructions." And that is, that God who gives these gifts for this purpose, looks for the employment of these gifts, to the edification of others, to his glory. "There be of them, that have left a name behind them" (as it is also added in that place), that is, that though God can amply reward his servants in the next world, yet he does it sometimes in this world; and though not with temporal happinesses, in their life, yet with honor, and commemorations, and celebrations of them after they have gone out of this life; they leave a name behind them. And amongst them, in a high place, shines our blessed and glorious Apostle St. Paul, whose conversion the Church celebrates now, and for the celebration thereof, has appointed this part of Scripture from whence this text arises, to be the Epistle of the day,

165

"And he fell to the earth, and heard a voice, saying, Saul, Saul, why persecutest thou me?"

There are words in the text that will reach to all the story of St. Paul's conversion, embrace all, involve and enwrap all. We must contract them. Into less than three parts, we cannot well. Those will be these: first, the person, Saul, he, "He fell to the earth"; and then, his humiliation, his exinanition of himself, his divesting, putting off of himself, "He fell to the earth"; and lastly, his investing of Christ, his putting on of Christ, his rising again by the power of a new inanimation, a new soul breathed into him from Christ, "He heard a voice, saying, Saul, Saul, why persecutest thou me?" Now a redistribution, a subdivision of these parts into their branches we shall present to you anon, more opportunely, as we shall come in due order to the handling of the parts themselves. In the first, the branches will be but these: Saul's indisposition when Christ took him in hand, and Christ's work upon him; what he found him, what he left him, will determine our first part, the person.

First then, what he was at that time, the Holy Ghost gives evidence enough against him, and he gives enough against himself. Of that which the Holy Ghost gives, you may see a great many heavy pieces, a great many appliable circumstances, if at any time, at home, you do but paraphrase, and spread to yourself the former part of this chapter, to this text. Take a little preparation from me: "Saul yet breathing threatenings and slaughter," says the first verse. Then when he was in the height of his fury, Christ laid hold upon him. It was, for the most part, Christ's method of curing. Then when the sea was in a tempestuous rage, when the waters covered the ship, and the storm shaked even that which could remove mountains, the faith of the Disciples, then Christ rebukes the wind, and commands a calm. Then when the sun was gone out to run his race as a giant (as David speaks), then God by the mouth of another, of Joshua, bids the sun stand still. Then when that unclean spirit foamed, and fumed, and tore, and rent the possessed persons, then Christ commanded them to go out. Let the fever alone, say our physicians, till some fits be passed, and then we shall see farther and discern better. The note is St. Chrysostom's, and he applies it to Christ's proceeding with Saul; Christ staid not till Saul being made drunk with blood were cast into a slumber, as satisfied with the blood of Christians; but in the midst of his fit he gave him physic, in the midst of his madness he reclaims him.

So is it also part of the evidence that the Holy Ghost gives against him, that he sued to the state for a commission to persecute Christians. When the state will put men to some kind of necessity of concurring to the endamaging or endangering of the cause of Christ, and will be displeased with them if they do not, men make to themselves and to their consciences some faint color of excuses. But when they themselves set actions on foot which are not required at their hands, where is their evasion? Then when Saul sued out this commission, "That if he found any of that way" (that is, Christians, for he had so scattered them before that he was not sure to find any; they did not appear in any whole body, dangerous, or suspicious to the state), but, if he found any, "any man or woman," that he might have the power of the state so as that he need not fear men; that he might have the impartiality and the inflexibility of the state, so as that he need not pity women; then when his glory was "to bring them bound to Jerusalem," that he might magnify his triumph and greatness in the eye of the world, then, then says Christ to this tempest, "Be calm," to this unclean spirit, "Come out," to this sun, in his own estimation, "Go no farther."

Thus much evidence the Holy Ghost gives against him; and thus much more himself, "I persecuted this way unto the death; I bound and delivered into prison, both men and women." And after, more than this, "I punished them, and that oft, and in every Synagogue, and compelled them to blaspheme, and was exceedingly mad against them, and persecuted them even unto strange cities." What could he say more against himself? And then, says Christ, to this tempest, Be still; to this glaring sun, Stand still; to this unclean spirit, Come forth. In this sense especially does St. Paul call himself a person born out of season, that whereas Christ's other Disciples and Apostles had a breeding under him, and came first to be Disciples, and after to be Apostles; St. Paul was born a man, an

Apostle, not carved out, as the rest in time; but a fusil Apostle, an Apostle poured out and cast in a mold. As Adam was a perfect man in an instant, so was St. Paul an Apostle as soon as Christ took him in hand.

Now, beloved, will you make this perverse use of this proceeding, God is rich in mercy, therefore I cannot miss mercy? Would you say, and not be thought mad for saying so, God has created a West Indies, therefore I cannot want gold? Will you be so ill a logician to yourself and to your own damnation as to conclude so, God is always the same in himself, therefore he must be always the same to me? So ill a musician as to say, God is all concord, therefore he and I can never disagree? So ill a historian as to say, God has called Saul, a persecutor, then when he breathed threatenings and slaughter, then when he sued to the state for a commission to persecute Christ; God has called a thief, then when he was at the last gasp; and therefore if he have a mind to me, he will deal so with me too, and if he have no such mind, no man can imprint, or infuse a new mind in God? God forbid. It is not safe concluding out of single instances.

It is true that if a sour, and heavy, and severe man will add to the discomforts of a disconsolate soul, and in that soul's sadness and dejection of spirit, will heap up examples, that God has still suffered high-minded sinners to proceed and to perish in their irreligious ways, and tell that poor soul (as Job's company did him), "It is true, you take God aright, God never pardons such as you"; in these cases, these singular, these individual examples that God has done otherwise once, have their use. One instance to the contrary destroys any peremptory rule. No man must say, "God never does it." He did it to Saul here; he did it to the thief upon the cross. But to that presumptuous sinner who sins on because God showed mercy to one at last, we must say, a miserable comforter is that rule that affords but one example.

Nay, is there one example? The conversion of Saul, a persecutor, and of the thief upon the cross, is become the sinner's proverb, and serves him, and satisfies him in all cases. But is there any such thing? Such a story there is, and it is as true as Gospel, it is the truth of Gospel itself. But was this a late repentance?

Answer St. Cyril: Tell me beloved, you that defer your repentance, do you do it upon confidence of these examples? You delude your own soul. The thief was not converted at last, but at first; as soon as God afforded him any call, he came; and at how many lights have you winked? And to how many calls have you stopped your ears, that defer your repentance? Christ said to him, "This day thou shalt be with me in Paradise." When you can find such another day, look for such another mercy; a day that cleft the gravestones of dead men; a day that cleft the temple itself; a day that the sun durst not see; a day that saw the soul of God (may we not say so, since that Man was God too) depart from Man. There shall be no more such days; and therefore presume not of that voice, "This day thou shalt be with me," if you make your last minute that day, though Christ, to magnify his mercy and his glory, and to take away all occasion of absolute desperation, did here, under so many disadvantages call and draw St. Paul to him.

But we say no more of that, of the danger of sinning by precedent, and presuming of mercy by example; we pass from our first consideration, *from* what, to the other, *to* what, Christ brought this persecutor, this Saul. He brought him to that remarkable height, as that the Church celebrates the conversion of no man but this. Many bloody executioners were converted to Christ, even in the act of that bloody execution; then when they took a delight in tearing the bowels of Christians, they were received into the bowels of Christ Jesus, and became Christians. Men that rode to market, and saw an execution upon the way; men that opened a window to take air, and saw an execution in the street; the ecclesiastical story abounds with examples of occasional conversions, and upon strange occasions; but yet the Church celebrates no conversion but this. The Church does not consider the martyrs as born till they die; till the world see how they persevered to the end, she takes no knowledge of them. Therefore she calls the days of the deaths, their birthdays. Then she makes account they are born, when they die. But of St. Paul the Church makes herself assured the first minute; and therefore celebrates his conversion, and none but his. Here was a true transubstantiation, and a new Sacrament. These few words, "Saul, Saul, why persecutest thou me," are words of consecration. After these words, Saul was no longer Saul, but he was Christ: "It is not I that live," not I that do anything, "but Christ in me."

It is but a little way that St. Chrysostom goes, when he speaks of an inferior transubstantiation, of a change of affections, and says that here is another manner of lycanthropy, than when a man is made a wolf; for here a wolf is made a lamb, says that Father. A bramble is made a vine; cockle and tares become wheat; a pirate becomes a safe pilot; the lees are come to swim on the top, and the last is grown first; and he that was born out of time has not only the perfection but the excellency of all his lineaments. St. Chrysostom goes farther than this; he that was the mouth of blasphemy is become the mouth of Christ; he that was the instrument of Satan is now the organ of the Holy Ghost. He goes very far when he says, being yet but upon earth, he is an angel, and being yet but a man, he is already in Heaven. Yet St. Paul was another manner of Sacrament, and had another manner of transubstantiation, than all this; as he was made the same spirit with the Lord, so in his very body he had *Stigmata,* the very marks of the Lord Jesus. From such a lowness, raised to such a height, as that Origen says, many did believe that St. Paul had been that Holy Ghost which Christ had promised to the world after his departing from it.

It is but a little way that St. Jerome has carried his commendation neither, when he calls him the roaring of a lion, if we consider in how little a forest the roaring of a lion is determined; but that he calls him the roaring of our lion, of the lion of the tribe of Judah, that as far as Christ is heard, St. Paul is heard too; wheresoever I open St. Paul's epistles, I meet not words but thunder, and universal thunder, thunder that passes through all the world. For that that was done upon him wrought upon all the world; he was struck blind and all the world saw the better for that. So universal a priest (says St. Chrysostom, who loves to be speaking of St. Paul) as that he sacrificed not sheep and goats, but himself; and not only that, he prepared the whole world as a sacrifice to God. He built an Ark, that is, established a Church; and to this day, received, not eight, but all into that Ark; and whereas in Noah's Ark, if he came in a raven, he went out a raven; St. Paul, in his Ark, as himself was, so he transubstantiates all them, and makes them doves of ravens. Nay, so over absolutely did he sacrifice himself, and his state in this world, for this world, as that he sacrificed his reversion, his future state, the glory and joy of Heaven, for his brethren, and chose rather to be *Anathema,* separated from Christ, than they should.

I love thee, says St. Chrysostom to Rome, for many excellencies, many greatnesses; but I love thee so well, says he, therefore because St. Paul loved thee so well. What a fragrant rose shall Rome present Christ with, when he comes to judgment, in redelivering to him the body of St. Paul? And though he join them both together, that St. Peter and St. Paul were that yoke of oxen that ploughed the whole Church; though he say of both, how many prisons have you two consecrated, and made prisons Churches? How many fetters and chains of iron have you two changed into chains of gold? Yet we may observe a difference in St. Chrysostom's expressing of persons so equal to one another: What can exceed Peter, or what can equal Paul? Still be all this far from occasioning any man to presume upon God, because he afforded so abundant mercy to a persecutor: but still from this, let every faint soul establish itself in a confidence in God; God that would find nothing to except, nothing to quarrel at, in St. Paul, will not lie heavy upon your soul, though you must say, as he did, that you are a greater sinner than you know any other man to be.

We are, in our order proposed at first, devolved now to our second part; from the person, and in that, what he was found, a vehement persecutor, and then, what he was made, a laborious Apostle, to the manner, to his humiliation; he fell, and he fell to the ground and he fell blind, as by the history and context appears. We use to call every declination, of any kind, and in any subject, a falling; for, for our bodies, we say a man is fallen sick, and for his state, fallen poor, and for his mind, fallen mad, and for his conscience, fallen desperate; we are born low, and yet we fall every way lower, so universal is our falling sickness. Sin itself is but a falling. The irremediable sin of the Angels, the undeterminable sin of Adam, is called but so, the fall of Adam, the fall of Angels. And therefore the effectual visitation of the Holy Ghost to man is called a falling too; we are fallen so low, as that when the Holy Ghost is pleased to fetch us again, and to infuse his grace, he is still said to fall upon us. But the fall which we consider in the text is not a figurative falling, not into a decay of estate, nor decay of health, nor a spiritual falling into sin, a decay of grace; but it is a medicinal falling, a falling under God's hand, but such a falling under his hand as that he takes not off his hand from him that is fallen, but throws him down therefore that he may raise him. To this posture he brings Paul, now, when he was to reinanimate him with his spirit; rather, to preinanimate him; for, indeed, no man has a soul till he have grace.

Christ, who in his human nature has received from the Father all judgment, and power, and dominion over this world, has received all this upon that condition that he shall govern in this manner, "Ask of me, and I shall give thee the heathen for thine inheritance," says the Father. How is he to use them, when he has them? Thus, "Thou shalt break them with a rod of iron, and dash them in pieces like a potter's vessel." Now, God meant well to the nations, in this bruising and breaking of them. God intended not an annihilation of the nations, but a reformation. For Christ asks the nations for an inheritance, not for a triumph; therefore it is intended of his way of governing them; and his way is to bruise and beat them; that is, first to cast them down, before he can raise them up, first to break them before he can make them in his fashion. The Lord, and only the Lord knows how to wound us, out of love; more than that, how to wound us into love; more than all that, to wound us into love, not only with him that wounds us, but into love with the wound itself, with the very affliction that he inflicts upon us. The Lord knows how to strike us so as that we shall lay hold upon that hand that strikes us, and kiss that hand that wounds us. No man kills his enemy therefore, that his enemy might have a better life in Heaven; that is not his end in killing him. It is God's end. Therefore he brings us to death, that by that gate he might lead us into life everlasting. And he has not discovered, but made that northern passage, to pass by the frozen sea of calamity and tribulation to Paradise, to the heavenly Jerusalem. There are fruits that ripen not, but by frost. There are natures (there are scarce any other) that dispose not themselves to God, but by affliction. And as nature looks for the season for ripening and does not perfect the whole work till that come. It is nature that brings the season, and it is grace that brings the assent; but till the season for the fruit, till the assent of the soul come, all is not done.

Therefore God began in this way with Saul, and in this way he led him all his life. He died as many deaths as he lived days; for so himself says, "I die daily." God gave him suck in blood, and his own blood was his daily drink. He catechized him with calamities at first, and calamities were his daily sermons, and meditations after; and to authorize the hands of others upon him, and to accustom him to submit himself to the hands of others without murmuring, Christ himself strikes the first blow, and with that, he fell (which was our first consideration, in his humiliation), and then, "He fell to the ground," which is our next.

I take no farther occasion from the circumstance, but to arm you with consolation, how low soever God be pleased to cast you, though it be to the earth, yet he docs not so much cast you down, in doing that, as bring you home. Death is not a banishing of you out of this world; but it is a visitation of your kindred that lie in the earth; neither are any nearer of kin to you than the earth itself, and the worms of the earth. You heap earth upon your souls, and encumber them with more and more flesh, by a superfluous and luxuriant diet. You add earth to earth in new purchases, and measure not by acres, but by manors, nor by manors, but by shires; and there is a little quillet, a little close, worth all these, a quiet grave. And therefore, when you read that God makes your bed in your sickness, rejoice in this, not only that he makes that bed, where you lie, but that bed where you shall lie. That that God, that made the whole earth, is now making your bed in the earth, a quiet grave, where you shall sleep in peace till the Angel's trumpet wake you at the Resurrection, to that judgment where your peace shall be made before you come, and writ, and sealed, in the blood of the Lamb.

Saul falls to the earth; so far; but he falls no lower. God brings his servants to a great lowness here; but he brings upon no man a perverse sense, or a distrustful suspicion of falling lower hereafter.

His hand strikes us to the earth, by way of humiliation. But it is not his hand that strikes us into Hell by way of desperation. Will you tell me that you have observed and studied God's way upon you all your life, and out of that can conclude what God means to do with you after this life? That God took away your parents in your infancy, and left you orphans then; that he has crossed you in all your labors in your calling ever since; that he has opened you to dishonors, and calumnies, and misinterpretations, in things well intended by you; that he has multiplied sicknesses upon you, and given you thereby an assurance of a miserable and a short life, of few and evil days; nay, that he has suffered you to fall into sins that you yourselves have hated; to continue in sins that you yourselves have been weary of; to relapse into sins that you yourselves have repented; and will you conclude out of this that God had no good purpose upon you, that if ever he had meant to do you good he would never have gone thus far, in heaping of evils upon you? Upon what do you ground this? Upon yourself? Because you should not deal thus with any man, whom you meant well to? How poor, how narrow, how impious a measure of God is this, that he must do as you would do if you were God! God has not made a week without a sabbath; no temptation without an issue; God inflicts no calamity, no cloud, no eclipse, without light, to see ease in it, if the patient will look upon that which God has done to him, in other cases, or to that which God has done to others, at other times. Saul fell to the ground, but he fell no lower; God brings us to humiliation, but not to desperation.

He fell; he fell to the ground, and he fell blind; for so it is evident in the story. Christ had said to the Pharisees, "I came into the world, that they which see, might be made blind." And the Pharisees ask him, "Have you been able to do so upon us? Are we blind?" Here Christ gives them an example; a real, a literal, an actual example: Saul, a Pharisee, is made blind. He that will fill a vessel with wine must take out the water. He that will fill a covetous man's hand with gold, must take out the silver that was there before, says St. Chrysostom. Christ, who is about to infuse new light into Saul, withdraws that light that was in him before; that light by which Saul thought he saw all before, and thought himself a competent judge, which was the only true religion, and that all others were to be persecuted, even to death, that were not of his way.

"Every man that trusts in his own wit is a fool," says God in the prophet. But "Let him become a fool, that he may be wise," says the Apostle. Let him be so, in his own eyes, and God will give him better eyes, better light, better understanding. Saul was struck blind, but it was a blindness contracted from light. It was a light that struck him blind, as you see in his story. This blindness which we speak of, which is a sober and temperate abstinence from the immoderate study, and curious knowledges of this world, this holy simplicity of the soul, is not a darkness, a dimness, a stupidity in the understanding, contracted by living in a corner; it is not an idle retiring into a monastery, or into a village, or a country solitude; it is not a lazy affectation of ignorance; not a darkness, but a greater light, must make us blind.

The sight and the contemplation of God, and our present benefits by him, and our future interest in him, must make us blind to the world so as that we look upon no face, no pleasure, no knowledge, with such an affection, such an ambition, such a devotion, as upon God and the ways to him. Saul had such a blindness as came from light; we must affect no other simplicity than arises from the knowledge of God and his religion. And then, Saul had such a blindness as that he fell with it. There are birds, that when their eyes are sealed, still soar up and up till they have spent all their strength. Men blinded with the lights of this world, soar still into higher places, or higher knowledges, or higher opinions; but the light of Heaven humbles us, and lays flat that soul which the leaven of this world had puffed and swelled up. That powerful light felled Saul; but after he was fallen, his own sight was restored to him again. Ananias says to him, "Brother Saul, receive thy sight." To those men who employ their natural faculties to the glory of God, and their own and others' edification, God shall afford an exaltation of those natural faculties. In those who use their learning, or their wealth, or their power well, God shall increase that power, and that wealth, and that learning, even in this world.

You have seen Saul's sickness, and the exaltation of the disease, then when he breathed threatenings and slaughter, then when he went in his triumph. And you have seen his death, the death of the righteous, his humiliation, "He fell to the earth." And there remains yet his resurrection; the Angel of the great counsel, Christ Jesus, with the trumpet of his own mouth, raises him with that "Saul, Saul, why persecutest thou me?"

First then, God speaks. For, beloved, we are to consider God, not as he is in himself, but as he works upon us. The first thing that we can consider in our way to God, is his Word. Our regeneration is by his Word; that is, by faith, which comes by hearing. "The seed is the word of God," says Christ himself; even the seed of faith. Carry it higher, the Creation was by the Word of God; God spoke, and all things were made. Carry it to the highest of all, to eternity, the eternal generation, the eternal production, the eternal procession of the second Person in the Trinity, was so much by the Word, as that he is the Word; it was that Word that was made Flesh. So that God, who cannot enter into bands to us, has given us security enough. He has given us his Word; his written Word, his Scriptures; his essential Word, his Son. Our principal, and radical, and fundamental security is his essential Word, his Son Christ Jesus. But how many millions of generations was this Word in Heaven, and never spoke? The Word, Christ himself, has been as long as God has been. But the uttering of this Word, speaking has been but since the Creation. Peter says to Christ "To whom shall we go? Thou hast the words of eternal life." It is not only, you are the word of eternal life (Christ is so), but you have it. You have it, where we may come to you for it, in your treasury, in your ordinance, in your Church. You have it, to derive it, to convey it upon us. Here then is the first step of Saul's cure and of ours, that there was not only a word, the Word, Christ himself, a Son of God in Heaven, but a voice, the Word uttered, and preached; Christ manifested in his ordinance: "He heard a voice."

He heard it. How often does God speak and nobody hears the voice? He speaks in his cannon, in thunder, and he speaks in our cannon, in the rumor of wars. He speaks in his music, in the harmonious promises of the Gospel, and in our music, in the temporal blessings of peace and plenty. And we hear a noise in his judgments, and we hear a sound in his mercies; but we hear no voice, we do not discern that this noise, or this sound comes from any certain person; we do not feel them to be mercies, nor to be judgments uttered from God, but natural accidents, casual occurrences, emergent contingencies, which as an atheist might think, would fall out though there were no God, or no commerce, no dealing, no speaking between God and man. Though Saul came not instantly to a perfect discerning who spoke, yet he saw instantly it was a Person above nature, and therefore speaks to him in that phrase of submission, "Lord who art thou?" And after, with trembling and astonishment (as the text says) "Lord what wilt thou have me to do?" Then we are truliest said to hear, when we know from whence the voice comes.

Princes are God's trumpet, and the Church is God's organ, but Christ Jesus is his voice. When he speaks in the prince, when he speaks in the Church, there we are bound to hear, and happy if we do hear. Man has a natural way to come to God, by the eye, by the creature. So visible things show the invisible God. But then, God has superinduced a supernatural way, by the ear. For, though hearing be natural, yet that faith in God should come by hearing a man preach, is supernatural. God shut up the natural way in Saul: seeing. He struck him blind. But he opened the supernatural way; he enabled him to hear, and to hear him. God would have us beholden to grace, and not to nature, and to come for our salvation to his ordinances, to the preaching of his Word, and not to any other means. Though he were blind, even that blindness, as it was a humiliation, and a diverting of his former glaring lights, was a degree of mercy, of preparative mercy. Yet there was a voice, which was another degree; and a voice that he heard, which was a degree above that; and so far we are gone. And he heard it, *saying,* that is distinctly and intelligibly, which is our next circumstance.

He hears him saying, that is, he hears him so as that he knows what he says, so as that he understands him; for he that hears the word and understands it not, is subject to that which Christ says, "That the wicked one comes, and catches away that that was sown." St. Augustine puts himself earnestly upon the contemplation of the Creation, as Moses has delivered it. He finds it hard to conceive, and he says, "If Moses who writ this were here, I would hold him fast, and beg of him, for thy sake, O my God, that he would declare this work of the Creation more plainly unto me. But then," says that blessed Father, "if Moses should speak Hebrew to me, mine ears might hear the sound, but my mind would not hear the voice; I might hear him, but I should not hear what he said." This was that that distinguished between St. Paul, and those who were in his company at this time. St. Luke says in this chapter, "That they heard the voice," and St. Paul relating the story again, after says, "They heard not the voice of him that spoke to me." They heard a confused sound, but they distinguished it not to be the voice of God, nor discerned God's purpose in it.

In the twelfth of John, "there came a voice from heaven," from God himself, "and the people said, it thundered." So apt is natural man to ascribe even God's immediate and miraculous actions to natural causes; apt to rest and determine in nature, and leave out God. The Poet chides that weakness (as he calls it) to be afraid of God's judgments, or to call natural accidents judgments. He says the conscience may be over tender, and that such timorous men are sick of the fear of God. But it is a blessed disease, the fear of God, and the true way to true health. And though there be a moral constancy that becomes a Christian well, not to be easily shaken with the variations and revolutions of this world, yet it becomes him to establish his constancy in this, that God has a good purpose in that action, not that God has no hand in that action. That God will produce good out of it, not that God has nothing to do in it. The magicians themselves were forced to confess the finger of God, in a small matter. Never think it a weakness to call that a judgment of God which others determine in nature. Do so, so far as works to your edification, who sees that judgment, though not so far as to argue and conclude the final condemnation of that man upon whom that judgment is fallen.

Certainly we were better call twenty natural accidents judgments of God, than frustrate God's purpose in any of his powerful deliverances, by calling it a natural accident, and suffer the thing to vanish so, and God be left unglorified in it, or his Church unedified by it. Then we hear God when we understand what he says. And therefore, as we are bound to bless God, that he speaks to us, and hears us speak to him, in a language which we understand, and not in such a strange language as that a stranger who should come in and hear it would think the congregation mad; so also let us bless him for that holy tenderness, to be apt to feel his hand in every accident, and to discern his presence in every thing that befalls us. "Saul heard the voice, saying"; he understood what it said, and by that, found that it was directed to him, which is also another step in this last part.

This is an impropriation without sacrilege, and an enclosure of a common without damage, to make God mine own, to find that all that God says is spoken to me, and all that Christ suffered was suffered for me. And as Saul found this voice at first to be directed to him, so ever after he bends his eye the same way, and observes the working of God especially upon himself. As at the beginning, so in the way too; particularly there, "By the grace of God I am that I am"; and then, "His grace was bestowed on me, and not in vain." And again, "I have labored more abundantly than all." And after all, still he considers himself, and finds himself to be the greatest sinner. It is called a greatness of spirit, or constancy, but it is indeed an incorrigible height of pride, when a man will not believe that he is meant in a libel, if he be not named in that libel. It is a fearful obduration, to be sermon-proof, or not to take knowledge that a judgment is denounced against him, because he is not named in the denouncing of that judgment. Is not your name Simon Magus if you buy and sell spiritual things yourself? And is not your servant's name Gehazi, if he exact after? Is not your name Cain, if you rise up against your brother? And is not your name Zaccheus, if you multiply your wealth by oppression? Is not your name Dinah, if you gad abroad, to see who will solicit you? And is not the name of Potiphar's wife upon you, if you stay at home and solicit your servants? Postdate the whole Bible, and whatsoever you hear spoken of such as you are, before, believe all that to be spoken but now, and spoken to you. This was one happiness here, that Saul found this voice to be directed to him. And another (which is our last consideration) is what this voice said; it said, "Saul, Saul, why persecutest thou me?"

Here, to make sure of him, God calls him by his name, that he should not be able to transfer the summons upon any other, or say it was not he. They say that men that walk in their sleep will wake if they be called by their names. To wake Saul out of this dream (for to think to oppose Christ and his cause is, in the highest person of the world, of what power or of what counsel soever, but a vertiginous dream and a giddy vapor), to wake him, he calls him by his name, to let him know he means him. And to wake him thoroughly, he calls him twice, Saul, and Saul again. The great desolation which was to fall upon that land, God intimates, God interminates, God intonates with such a vehemency, "Earth, earth, earth hear the Word of the Lord." God should be heard at first, believed at first; but such is his abundant goodness as that he ingeminates, multiplies his warnings. And to this whole land he has said, "Earth, earth, earth hear the Word of the Lord." Once in an invasion, once in a powder-treason; and again and again in pestilential contagions. And to every one of us, he has said oftener than so, Dust, dust, dust why do you lift up yourself against your Maker? "Saul, Saul why persecutest thou me?"

Here Christ calls the afflictions of those that are his, in his purpose, his afflictions. Christ will not absolutely verify his own words, to his own ease. He had said before this, upon the cross, "All is finished"; but though all were finished in his Person, he has a daily passion in his saints still. This language which the Apostle learned of Christ here, himself practiced, and spake after, "Who is weak, and I am not weak? who is offended, and I burn not?" Since Christ does suffer in our sufferings, be this our consolation, till he be weary, we should not be weary, nor faint, nor murmur under our burdens; and this too, that when he is weary, he will deliver us even for his own sake; for he, though he cannot suffer pain, may suffer dishonor in our sufferings; therefore attend his leisure.

We end all in this, "Why dost Thou persecute Me?" Why *Saul* Christ? Put it upon a nation, (what is any Saul, any one man to a nation?) Put it upon all the nations of the world, and you shall hear God ask with an indignation, "Why do the heathen rage, why do the people imagine a vain thing?" Why will they do it? What can they get? "He that sitteth in the heavens shall laugh; the Lord shall have them in derision." Christ came into the temple and disputed with the doctors; but he did not despise them, he did not laugh at them. When all the Midianites, and all the Amalekites, and all the children of the East were in a body against Israel, God did not laugh at them. Gideon, his general, mustered two and thirty thousand against them. God would not employ so many in the day of battle, yet he did not laugh at them, he did not whip them out of the field, he made the face of an army, though it were but three hundred. But when God can choose his way, he can call in nation against nation, he can cast a damp upon any nation, and make them afraid of one another, he can do an execution upon them by themselves (I presume you remember those stories in the Bible, where God did proceed by such ways), or he can sit still in a scorn, and let them melt away of themselves. When he can cast down Saul to the earth, and never appear in the cause; benight his noon, frustrate his purposes, evacuate his hopes, annihilate him in the height of his glory, why will any Saul, any nation, any world of Sauls persecute Christ, any sinner tempt him, who is so much too hard for him?

Why do you offer this to me, who being thus much too hard for you, would yet fain be friends with you? and therefore come to a parley, to a treaty? For, says St. Chrysostom, these are not so much offensive as defensive words. He would not confound Saul, but he would not betray his own honor. To many nations God has never spoken. To the Jews he spoke, but suffered them to mistake him. To some whole Christian Churches he speaks, but he lets them speak too; he lets them make their word equal to his. To many of us he has spoken and chidden, but given over before we are cured. As he says of Israel, in a manner, that she is not worth his anger, not worth his punishing, "A people laden with sins, why should they any more be smitten?" Why should I go about to recover them? But if God speak to you still, and speak in a mixed voice of correction and consolation too, "Saul, Saul, why persecutest thou me?" Him that receives so little benefit by you, and yet is so loath to lose you; him that can so easily spare you, and yet makes your soul more precious than his own life; him that can resolve you, scatter you, annihilate you with a word, and yet afford so many words, so many hours' conferences, so many sermons to reclaim you, why persecute you him? Answer this question, with Saul's answer to this question, by another question, "Lord, what wilt thou have me do?" Deliver yourself over to the will of God, and God shall deliver you over, as he did Saul to Ananias; provide you by his ministry in his ordinance, means to rectify you in all dejection of spirit, light to clear you in all perplexities of conscience, in the ways of your pilgrimage, and more and more effectual seals thereof, at the hour of your transmigration into his joy, and your eternal rest.

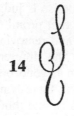

OF PATIENCE IN ADVERSITY,

14 AWAITING THE WILL OF GOD

Lord all my desire is before thee, and my groaning is not hid from thee.

PSALM 38:9

OUT OF THE SITE AND PLACE OF THESE WORDS, AS they stand between the narration of miseries of two kinds, some before it, some after it, we collected that God does not always put an end to our miseries as soon as we take knowledge of his purpose upon us by those miseries. We pray and yet are not delivered. It is true, when God's corrections have brought us to a religious desire of being delivered, then not to be delivered is a new and the greatest correction, yea the most dangerous temptation of all. When I pray to be delivered, and begin to think that God has bound himself by his promise to give me the issue with the temptation, that he makes the wound and binds up, he smites and his hand makes whole, that he will deliver me in six troubles but in the seventh the evil shall not touch me, that he will preserve me from despair in all the afflictions of my life, but in the seventh, that is when I am come to my sabbath, to my rest and confidence in his mercy, that then it shall not touch me, it shall pass away presently; when I begin to come to these meditations, though God deliver me sooner than I deserve, yet it seems long in doing, if it be not as soon as I have conceived that which appears to me to be so religious a desire.

But "the Lord is not slack concerning his promise as some men

183

count slackness." In that place of the Apostle his promise is judgment, punishment for sin; and if God be not slack in that promise, much less is he slack in the dispensing of his mercies and removing those judgments again. The mistaking rises out of the different computations between God and us. We never reckon beyond one hundred years, because that is the longest life; we think there is no more, no other life but that. But with God one day is as one thousand years, and one thousand years as one day. Whensoever he comes to judgment, he comes soon to you if he come before you be prepared; and whensoever he comes in mercy, he comes soon to you too, considering how far you were run away from him. It is all one when that fire begins that shall never go out. If the torments of Hell must take hold of you, they begin soon if they begin in your desperation upon your deathbed, and if your tribulations end upon your deathbed they end soon, considering how much rust and dross there was to be burned off of your soul.

It was long in the Roman state before they came to a distinction of hours; all their reckoning for some hundreds of years was, this was done after the rising, and this after the setting of the sun; but the distinction of hours in the degrees of the ascending or descending of the sun they had not. We reckon all things so too. We reckon from the rising of the sun when any great fortune fell upon us, when we came to years, when the father dies and leaves the estate, when the mother dies and leaves the jointure, when the predecessor dies and leaves the office. And we reckon from the setting of the sun when any great calamity falls upon us, when a decree passed against us and swept away such a manor; when a shipwreck impoverished us; when a fire, a rot, a murrain, a fever overthrew our bodies or our estates. The rising and setting of the sun, height of prosperity, depth of adversity we observe, but we observe not the degrees of the ascending of this sun, how God has led us every step and preserved us in many particular dangers in our rising.

Nor the degrees of the descending of this sun we observe not. We observe not that God would show us in the loss of our children the sinful wantonness in which they were begotten and conceived; in the loss of health, the sinful voluptuousness in which the body was pampered; in the loss of goods, the sinful extortion in which they were gathered. We consider sometimes in general Job's "Naked came I," that we came naked out of our mother's womb, that we rose of nothing, and in general Job's "Naked shall I return," that we shall return naked again, that we shall carry away no more than we brought. But we consider not in particular that it is the Lord that gave and the Lord that takes away, and thereupon bless the name of the Lord for it in all his steps and degrees of our rising and falling.

God has not only given you a natural day, from period to period to consider your birth and your death, this you were born to and this you die worth, but he has given you an artificial day, and a day which he has distinguished into hours by continual benefits, and a day which you have distinguished into hours by continual sins. And he would have you remember those hours when and how and by what degrees, by what means he raised you and humbled you again, and at what time and place with what actions you have provoked his anger; and then you will find that it was in the cool of the evening, it was late before God came to correct Adam, but he has filled us with mercy in the morning that we might be glad and rejoice all the day.

God is not slack in his promises says the Apostle. It is not only the Lord is not slack of his promise, but the Lord of his promise is not slack. He is Lord of his promise and in that case we are sure that he can, and may be sure that he will, perform his promise. Delays in courts of princes and in courts of justice proceed out of this, that men are not lords of their promises, masters of their words. There are afflictions within and fear of offending without; letters from above, kindred from within, money from both sides, which keeps them from being lords of their promises, masters of their words. Either they think that if they dispatch a suitor too soon there's an end of his observance, of his attendance, of his respect, he undervalues the favor if it be so soon showed, and so there's a delay out of state, to give a dignity, a majesty to the business; or else they see that when there is an end, a dispatch of the cause, there is an end of the profit too, and here's a delay to keep a way open to extortion and bribery. Perchance abundance of wealth (or else of honor and command if not of wealth) may make them overindulgent to their own ease, and here's a delay out of laziness. Perchance corrupt means have brought an insufficient man to the place, and then he must put off business till he be better informed, till he have consulted with more sufficient men, and here's a delay out of ignorance. Every man has made a promise to God and to the state to do the duties of his place, and either for fear, or love, or money, for state, for ease, or ignorance he is not lord of that promise, master of that word; he is not able to perform it. God only is so. And therefore whatsoever you count slackness, that's the time for your deliverance which God has appointed. If you pray for deliverance and be not delivered, do not think that you are not heard, nay do not think that you are not delivered for God delivers you by continuing you in that calamity from some greater.

Limit not God therefore in his ways or times, but if you would be heard by him, hear him; if you would have him grant your prayers, do his will. We pray you in Christ's stead that you would be reconciled to God; and are you reconciled? durst you hear the trumpet now? Christ Jesus prays for you now to his Father in Heaven that you might be converted, and are you converted? If the prayers of the Church Militant and the Church Triumphant and the head of both Churches, Christ Jesus, be not yet heard effectually on your behalf, yet they shall be in his time, his eternal election shall infallibly work upon you. So if your own prayers for your deliverance in any temporal or spiritual affliction be not presently heard, persevere for yourselves as the Churches and the head of them persevere in your behalf, and God will certainly deliver you in his time and strengthen you to fight out his battle all the way.

Since he made all things he has a care of all things, a providence which (in such perfection as becomes us to ascribe to God) he could not have except he saw all things. Our seeing of God hereafter is the blessedness we hope for, and our comfort in the way to that is that he sees us, for so we never are, never shall be out of sight of one another. If any sinner can conceit that wish that God did not see him, he should lose more by it than he should get. Though he would be glad not to be seen by him in his sinful pleasures, yet he would be sorry not to be seen by him in his miseries and afflictions, and the miseries, the afflictions of this life are more than the pleasures in the most habitual sinner. A man that would be glad that God saw not his extortions, his oppressions, his grinding of the poor by color of an office, would yet be sorry that God saw not those privy whisperings, those machinations and plots and practices above in high places to traduce him, to defame him, to supplant him and wring his office from him, perchance for things he never did, though he has done as ill. And then we make ourselves supervisors, overseers of God, if we will appoint what he should see and what not.

You know how certain and how speedy a conviction it is if a man be taken in the manner, and you know how heavily the fault is aggravated which is done in the face of the court. All our actions are so, in the face of the court, and there needs no evidence. We are deprehended in the manner; in corners where nothing sees us, God sees us, and in Hell where we shall see nothing, he shall see us too. He sees as God and therefore he always saw all. "He calls those things which be not, as though they were," says the Apostle. "He looks upon all things after they be brought to pass," says the Wiseman, "and he knew them ere ever they were made." You would think him a weak lawyer that could not foresee what would be the issue of a cause which depended wholly upon the law, without relation to the opinion of the judge or to the affection of the jury; and a weak astrologer that could not foresee eclipses and positions of the heavens; and a weak counsel that could not foresee the good or ill of such a war, or such a peace, or such a marriage; and shall the sight and knowledge of God depend upon our actions?

Omniscience is an attribute of his, as well as omnipotence. God can be no more ignorant of a thing than impotent in it. And whatsoever is his attribute was always so. Was not God omnipotent, had he not all power till I was made, upon whom he exercises part of that power which he did not before I was? Was he not omniscient, did he not know all things before those things were produced into action and execution? God ever knew all things that were, that are, and that shall be, and that may be, and that may not be, because he will not have them be, for if he would, they should be. He knows them otherwise than they are, for he knows future things as present, and he knows contingent things as certain and necessary.

It is true he shall say at the last day to hypocrites, "I do not know you, I never did know you." But this is that knowledge of which St. Gregory speaks, so God never knew the hypocrites, nor ever shall, as to accept them, to allow them, to approve them. And so also it is said of Christ, "he who knew no sin was made sin for us." Experimentally, actually, personally he knew no sin, but in his eternal knowledge he ever knew all our particular sins, and he knew the general root of all, the sin of Adam, before that sin was, or before that man was.

But was this knowledge or foreknowledge the cause of it? God forbid! The opinion is detestable, abominable. Therefore let us be afraid of coming so near this detestable and abominable opinion as to express ourselves in misinterpretable terms, and phrases too bold and too different from the modest and sober use of the ancient doctors and fathers, that there is in God an effectual and an actual, and a positive and a consulted and a deliberate reprobation of certain men, before their sins, yea before their creation was considered, or that there is in man a necessary damnation which he was made for and created to.

God's foreknowledge of sin prints not a necessity of sin. An astrologer's foreknowledge of an eclipse causes not that eclipse. My knowledge that he that will fall from a steeple will break his bones did not thrust him down, nor precipitate him to that ruin. But God might have preserved him from sin, and so cannot an astrologer work upon an eclipse, nor I upon a desperate man that will cast himself down. It is true, God might have preserved him by making him an angel in a confirmed estate, and he might have preserved him by making him a beast without a reasonable soul, for then he could not have sinned and he had been the better for it. But God's will was to make him a man, and as a man he finds the reason of his sin to be the perverseness of his own will. Who perverts that? Did God? Abominate, detest the opinion. But God might have prevented this perverseness, he might have made him so strong as that he could not have perverted himself. But then God had not made him man. God did abundantly enough in making him good, and able to continue so; and he does abundantly enough in giving us those general declarations of his desire that we should all return to that goodness, that he would have no man to perish, but that all men should come to repentance. He sees all things, even sins, and foresees them, but yet his foresight is no cause of them.

God sees and foresees all desires, for David does not speak this by way of discomfort, as though God did only watch our ill desires to punish them, and not our obedience to cherish and reward that. It is true as the prophet Jeremiah testifies, "Our iniquity is marked before the Lord," but it is also true which David says, that our tears are put into his bottle and into his register. Consider the desire of the blessed saints in heaven, who though they be in full possession of happiness, have yet a further desire of a consummation and a reunion of body and soul. Consider the desire of the righteous: "The desire of the righteous is only good," says Solomon. It is good as it is a desire to know God. "My heart breaketh for the desire to thy judgments always." And it is good as it is a desire to propagate this their knowledge of God to others by instruction or at least by good example. For God has given every man a commandment concerning his neighbor. And it is good, as it is a desire to be united to God; as Simeon expressed it in his "Lord now lettest thou thy servant depart in peace," and St. Paul in his "I desire to be dissolved and to be with Christ." Consider it lastly as the divers and contrary desires of sinners, every way, every desire; David's desire to live in the Church, the Apostles' desire to be satisfied with things necessary in the Church, the desire of the saints in Heaven for the consummation, the desire of the saints in earth to know God, to make him known to others and to be united to him, and the desire of sinful men too, all these meet in the center, in the eye of God. All our desires are before him.

But principally this is intended of corrupt and sinful desires, for though it be all desires, yet all the imaginations of the thoughts of our hearts are only evil continually; the imaginations, before it come to be a formal and debated thought; and then the thoughts themselves, when I have discovered them, debated them, and in my heart at home seriously, not only in temptations presented to my fancy or senses. These imaginations and all these imaginations, they are evil. If any good be mingled with them, yet it is so little, as that they are evil, because they are evil for the most part. But it is worse than so, for they are only evil, no dram, no tincture of good in them; all evil and only evil and this continually, evil in the root, in the first concupiscence, and evil in the fruit, in the growth and in the perseverance. So that desires here are most properly imaginations, the first imaginations, and they are evil and their sinful affection is in the sight of God. But so are our groanings too; he sees them, and what is good or evil in them, as well as in our desires.

First then, as David had expressed it before in the verse precedent, it is the groaning of the heart; a hearty groaning and not merely sensual. It must be a groaning, not a roaring; the voice of a turtle not of a lion. If we take it here for the voice of sorrow in worldly crosses, we must not presently roar out in petitions, in suits, in complaints for every such cross. "There is a fault amongst you," says the Apostle, "because you go to law with one another. Why rather suffer ye not wrong, why rather sustain ye not harm?" The Apostle would not call it expressly a sin but he calls it a fault, and in a word which signifies weakness and imperfection. The stream of the Fathers runs somewhat vehemently in this point, for they scarce excuse any suit at law from sin, or occasion of sin, and they will not depart from the literal understanding of those words of our Savior, "If any man will sue thee at law for thy coat, Let him have thy cloak too, for if thine adversary have it not, thine advocate will." Howsoever, every man feels in his own conscience whether he be not the less disposed to charity, the less fit to come worthily to the Sacrament, and the more apt to corrupt and bribe an officer, and to delude and circumvent a judge, by having suits in law than otherwise.

So then if we consider this groaning to be the voice of sorrow for worldly losses, it must not be a vociferation, a crying out as though we were undone, as though we could not be happy except we were rich, and as though we could not be rich except we had just so much. It is not an immoderate complaining for worldly losses to the magistrate for remedy for every petty injury; it must be groaning both these ways. And take it, as it is most properly to be taken, for the voice of spiritual sorrow, a sorrow for our sins. It must not be an immoderate sorrow that terrifies, or argues a distrust in God's goodness. Drown that body of sin which you have built up in you, drown that world of sin which you have created; for we have a creation as well as God: man is God's creature and the sinner is man's creature. Spare your world no more than God spared his, who drowned it with the flood. Drown yours too with repentant tears. But when that work is religiously done, be as merciful to your soul as he was to mankind, drown it no more, suffer it not to lie under the water of distrustful diffidence, for so you may fall too low to be able to tug up against the tide again, so you may be swallowed in Cain's whirlpool, to think your sins greater than can be forgiven.

God sees every tear, our first tear, and is affected with that. When the child was dead, David arose from the ground and ate bread; when the sin is dead by your true repentance, raise yourself from this sad dejection and come and eat the bread of life, the body of your Savior, for the seal of your pardon. For there in this repentance and this seal you levy a fine upon your sins which cuts off and concludes all titles. And when God has provided that your sins shall rise no more to your condemnation at the last day, if you raise them up here to the vexation of your conscience, you are a litigious man to your own destruction. This was then David's comfort and is ours; the beginning of our sinful concupiscences and the beginning of our repentance are seen by God. And God of his mercy stops those desires at the beginning; either he keeps away the Devil or the woman, he takes away either my lust to that sin or the occasion and opportunity for the sin. In his mercy he stops me at the beginning of my desire, and in his mercy he perfits the beginnings of my repentance, he sees desires and groans.

The study of our conversion to God is in this like the study of your profession, it requires a whole man for it. It is for the most part loss of time in you to divert upon other studies, and it is for the most part loss of charity in us all to divert from ourselves unto the consideration of other men; to prognosticate ill for the future upon any man: I see his covetous desires, I see his carnal desires, I see his sinful courses, this man can never repent. Or to collect ill from that which is past: I see his repentance, his sadness, his dejection of countenance and spirit, his approach towards desperation; surely this man is a more grievous sinner than we took him for. To prognosticate thus, to collect thus upon others is an intrusion, an usurpation upon them and a dangerous dereliction and abandoning of ourselves. When the disciples of Christ would needs call into question the sins of that man which was born blind, rather than let them go on in that, although no punishment be inflicted without sin preceding, yet Christ says there, "Neither this man nor his parents have sinned." Not that he or they were simply without sin, but he would draw his disciples from that which concerned not them, the sins of another, to that which concerned them more, the contemplation of his omnipotence who would recover that man of his blindness in their sight.

"Think you," says Christ, "that those eighteen upon whom the tower in Siloam fell, were the greatest sinners in Jerusalem?" No; Christ had a care to deliver them from that misinterpretation then, and the Holy Ghost has not suffered the names nor the sins of those men so slain to come to our knowledge. In all the evangelists, in all the other histories of the Jewish nation and affairs there is no mention, no word, no record of the death of those men nor of the fall of this tower. God would not have posterity know their names nor their sins so particularly, after he had inflicted that extraordinary punishment upon them. Be your own text then, and be your own comment, watch your own desires and God shall stop them, and your own groans, and God shall perfit them with his unexpressible comfort.

But all this must be before God, in his presence, and so before him that nothing be hid from him. Now is that your desire, that your enemies might come to confusion? And is that a fit desire for the presence of God? Is this a writing after your copy, after your master Christ? His copy is, "Father forgive them, for they know not what they do." Or is it after his usher, his disciple Stephen? His copy is, "O Lord lay not this sin to their charge." If you will needs pray for your enemies' death, the same Father teaches you a good way, pray for their amendment, and the enemy is dead when the enmity is dead. But this phrase of David here, that all this is before him, imports not only God's seeing of it, but it implies our bringing of our desires and groanings into his sight.

"Lord thou hast heard the desires of the poor," says David. But how? "Thou preparest their heart, and thou bendest thine ear to hear them." First God's preventing grace prepares, enables us, and then he bends down with a farther supply of concurring grace, but that is to hear us. For if we do nothing then, if we speak not then, he departs from us. "He hath looked down from the height of his sanctuary," says he in another place. Here's his first grace, that he looks towards us, and then he hears the mourning of the prisoner and he delivers the child of death. But first the prisoner must know himself to be in prison and send forth a voice of mourning. He saw and succored Hezekiah, but not till he saw his tears. He looks for outward demonstrations of our sorrow, for confession and amendment of life.

It is one thing in a judge to know, another to know so as he may take knowledge and judge upon it. God knows your desires and your groans, but he will not take knowledge of them to your comfort to stop your desires, to perfect your repentance, except you bring them judicially before him; your desires by way of confession, and your groans by way of thankfulness. It is nothing for a rich man to say in general, Lord all I have is from thee, and if you will have it again I am ready to part with it. This is a hypocritical compliment to say to God or man, all's at your service. But give God some part of that, house Christ Jesus where he is harborless, help to beautify and build that house where his name may be glorified and his sabbath sanctified, clothe him where he is naked, feed him in his hunger, deliver him in his imprisonment, when he suffers this in his afflicted members. All your recognitions to God without subsidies, without benevolences, without relieving him in his distressed children, are but ceremonial, but hypocritical compliments. So your telling to God that he knows all your desires and all your groans, this is an easy matter for any man, it is a word soon said. But bring all these before him, show him where and how when by neglecting his grace you have strayed into these and these desires, and where and how and when you have taken light at his visitation to return towards him, and then he shall overthrow your work and build up his own, extinguish your desires and perfect your repentance.

This David intends in that word "before thee," and more fully in the next, "not hid." For I may be content to bring some things before God and yet hide others, or hide circumstances that may aggravate, yea that may alter the very nature of the fact. We must not hide our desires under our groans, nor hide our groans under our desires; not our desires under our groans, by wrapping up all our sins in a sadness, in a dejection, in a stupidity, so that I never see my sins in a true proportion as they lie upon Christ's shoulders and not upon my soul, nor in their true apparel as they are clothed with Christ's righteousness and not with my corruption, nor with their true weight as they are weighed down with Christ's merits, but as they weight down my soul into desperation. This is a hiding of our desires in our groanings, our sins in our dejection. And the hiding of our groanings in our desires is to wrap up all sorrow for sin in a verbal confession and enumeration of our sins without any particular contrition for the sin or detestation of it. We must hide neither, but anatomize our soul in both, and find every sinew and fiber, every lineament and ligament of this body of sin, and then every breath of that new spirit, every drop of that new blood that must restore and repair us.

Study all the history and write all the progress of the Holy Ghost in yourself. Take not the grace of God, or the mercy of God, as a medal, or a wedge of gold to be laid up, but change your medal or your wedge into current money, find this grace and this mercy applied to this end, this action. For though the merit of Christ be a sea, yet be you content to take it in drop after drop and to acknowledge in the presence of God that at such a particular time the memory of his fasting rescued you from a voluptuous and riotous meeting, and the memory of his proceeding and behavior in his temptations brought you also to deliver yourself by applying his word and the promises of the Gospel from those dangerous attempts of the tempter. Hide nothing from God, neither the diseases you were in, nor the degrees of health that you are come to, nor the ways of your falling or rising. If I mistake not the measure of your conscience, you will find an infinite comfort in this particular tracing of the Holy Ghost and his working in your soul.

Now the conclusion of all shall be a short application of some of the most important passages to the person of Christ of whom many ancient expositors have understood this Psalm to have been principally intended. First then, he "in the days of his flesh offered up prayers and supplications with strong cryings and tears unto him that was able to save him from death; and was also heard in that which he feared." He was heard, but when? First, when prayed he that vehement prayer? All agree that that place of the Apostle has relation to Christ's prayer in his agony in the garden, when besides his tears of water he opened as many eyes as he had pores in his body and wept out blood at every one of those eyes. And they agree that that place of the Apostle has relation to his vehement prayer upon the cross, *"Eli, Eli . . .* My God, my God . . ." So that Christ prayed in his affliction, and yet prayed again. That which was David's case and is ours, was his case too. He was heard, but not at the first praying. After his first prayer of "Let this cup pass," he was put to his expostulation, "Why hast thou forsaken me?" The Father was always with him, and is with us, but our deliverance is in his time and not in ours, which was the doctrine raised out of the first part of the text.

For the second, the knowledge and foreknowledge of God, it is true that God who sees all, and foresees all, foresaw all the malignity of the Jews in crucifying of Christ, but yet he was no cause of it. As Matthew expresses it, "How else should the Scriptures be fulfilled, which say that it must be so?" But were these prophecies the cause of it? No; the prophecies were long before the execution, but the foreknowledge of God was long before the prophecies. This foreknowledge was the cause of this prophecy, but neither the foreknowledge nor the prophecy was any cause of the sinful part of their fact. And that's as much as is appliable to Christ in the second part.

In the third part, to pass speedily through some of the principal words: first, for desires, himself tells us what his desire was: "With

desire I have desired to eat this passover with you before I suffer."
Other Passovers he had eaten with them before, but this Passover
(which was to be a memorial not of their departing out of Egypt,
but of his departing out of this world by a bitter and ignominious
death for their salvation), he had a desire to institute and celebrate, and to commend to their desires in imitation and com-
memoration of him.

When we consider the next, his mournings, they were vehement,
but yet still they ended in a calm. At first in "My soul is sorrowful"
and in "If it be possible," there appear some gusts, some beginning
of a storm, but all becalmed presently in "Yet not my will, but thy
will be done." So at first in the "Why hast thou forsaken me?"
there appears a gust, but in "Into thy hands" a calm again. We do
not call that an immoderate nor overpassionate sorrow for sin,
which sees day, and apprehends the presence of God, in that dejection of spirit. But exclamations upon destiny, imputations upon
necessity, aspersions upon the decrees of God himself (as if anything but the perverseness of my will were the cause of my sin),
those are the roarings of that lion that seeks whom he may devour,
and not the voice of that dove that comes to the ark with an olive
branch, settles in the Church with the testimonies of peace and
reconciliation which are there. Moreover Christ was to be glorified
with the glory which he had before, and now he longed till that was
accomplished, but yet his meat was to do his Father's will, and till
his time was come, says Christ, "My hour is not yet come."

To end all; he proposed all to his Father, so as his Father had a
Church upon earth, and therefore, though there were a new
Church to be erected by him, yet he yielded all obedience to that
which was formerly erected. In that he was circumcized and
presented; and in that his Mother was purified according to the
Law, and in that he sent his own disciples to be instructed by the
scribes and Pharisees. And to conclude, all refractory persons, by
his example: in that Church he honored with his presence the feast
of the dedication, which was an anniversary feast, and a feast not
of divine institution, but ordained by the Church.

15 OF CHRIST AS FOUNDATION AND CORNERSTONE

Whosoever shall fall on this stone shall be broken; but on whomsoever it shall fall, it will grind him to powder.

MATTHEW 21:44

ALMIGHTY GOD MADE US FOR HIS GLORY, AND HIS glory is not the glory of a tyrant, to destroy us, but his glory is in our happiness. He put us in a fair way towards that happiness in nature, in our creation. That way would have brought us to Heaven, but then we fell, and (if we consider ourselves only) irrecoverably. He put us after into another way, over thorny hedges and ploughed lands, through the difficulties and incumbrances of all the ceremonial law. There was no way to Heaven then, but that. After that, he brought us a cross way, by the cross of Jesus Christ and the application of his Gospel, and that is our way now.

Here God takes all into his own hands, and he comes to dwell upon us himself, to which purpose he ploughs up our hearts and he builds upon us: "Ye are God's husbandry and God's building." Now of this husbandry God speaks familiarly and parabolically many times in Scriptures: of this building, particularly and principally in this place, where, having intimated unto us the several benefits we have received from Christ Jesus in that appellation, as he is a stone, he tells us also our dangers in misbehaving ourselves

197

toward it: "Whosoever shall fall on this stone, shall be broken."

Christ then is a stone, and we may run into two dangers: first, we may fall upon this stone, and then this stone may fall upon us. But yet we have a great deal of comfort presented to us, in that Christ is presented to us as a stone, for there we shall find him, first, to be the foundation stone, nothing can stand which is not built upon Christ; secondly, to be a cornerstone, that unites things most disunited; and then to be the stone that Jacob slept upon; fourthly, to be the stone that David slew Goliath withal; and lastly to be such a stone as is a rock, and such a rock as no waters nor storms can remove or shake. These are benefits: Christ Jesus is a stone, no firmness but in him; a fundamental stone, no building but on him; a cornerstone, no piecing nor reconciliation but in him; and Jacob's stone, no rest, no tranquility but in him; and David's stone, no anger, no revenge but in him; and a rocky stone, no defence against troubles and tribulations but in him. And upon this stone we fall and are broken, and this stone may fall on us and grind us to powder.

First in the metaphor, that Christ is called a stone, the firmness is expressed: forasmuch as he loved his own which were in the world, says St. John, "He loved them to the end." He loved not only them who were in a confirmed estate of mutual loving him too, but even them who were themselves conceived in sin and then conceived all their purposes in sin too; them who could have no cleansing but in his blood; them who by nature are not able to love him at all, and when by grace they are brought to love him, can express their love no other way but to be glad that he was betrayed, and scourged, and scorned, and nailed, and crucified; and to be glad, that if all this were not already done, it might be done yet, to long, and wish, that if Christ were not crucified he might be crucified now (which is a strange manner of expressing love). Those men he loved, and loved unto the end.

He leaves them not uncalled at first, he leaves them not unaccompanied in the way, he leaves them not unrecompensed at the last, that God who is Almighty, Alpha and Omega, first and last. That God is also love itself, and therefore this love is Alpha and Omega, first and last, too. Consider Christ's proceeding with Peter in the ship, in the storm. First he suffered him to be in some danger, but then he visits him with that strong assurance, "Be not afraid, it is I." Any testimony of his presence rectifies all. This puts Peter into that spiritual knowledge and confidence, "Lord, bid me come to thee." He hath a desire to be with Christ, but yet stays his bidding. He puts not himself into an unnecessary danger without a commandment. Christ bids him, and Peter comes, but yet, though Christ were in his sight, and even in the actual exercise of his love to him, yet as soon as he saw a gust, a storm, he was afraid, and Christ lets him fear, and lets him sink, and lets him cry. But he directs his fear and his cry to the right end, "Lord save me," and thereupon he stretches out his hand and saves him.

God does not raise his children to honor, and great estates, and then leave them, and expose them to be subjects and exercises of the malice of others, nor he does not make them mighty and then leave them, and expose them to be subjects and exercises of the malice of others, nor he does not make them mighty and then leave them, that he should think it a glory to be able to do harm. He does not impoverish and dishonor his children and then leave them; leave them insensible of that doctrine that patience is as great a blessing as abundance. God gives not his children health and then leaves them to a boldness in surfeiting; nor beauty, and leaves them to a confidence and opening themselves to all solicitations; nor valor and then leaves them to a spirit of quarrelsomeness. God makes no patterns of his works, no models of his houses. He makes whole pieces, he makes perfect houses, he puts his children into good ways, and he directs and protects them in those ways. For this is the constancy and the perseverance of the love of Christ Jesus, as he is called in this text a stone. To come to the particular benefits; the first is that he is a foundation stone; for other foundation can no man lay than that which is laid, which is Christ Jesus.

If any man therefore have laid any other foundation to his faith, or any other foundation to his actions, possession of great places, alliance in great families, strong practice in courts, obligation upon dependents, acclamations of people; if he have laid any other foundations for pleasure, and contentment, care of health, and complexion, appliableness in conversation, delightfulness in discourses, cheerfulness in disportings, interchanging of secrets, and other such small wares of courts and cities as these are: whosoever has laid such foundations as these must proceed as that general did, who when he received a besieged town to mercy, upon condition that in sign of subjection they should suffer him to take off one row of stones from their walls, he took away the lowest row, the foundation, and so ruined and demolished the whole walls of the city. So must he that has these false foundations (that is, these habits), divest the habit, root out the lowest stone, that is, the general and radical inclination to these disorders.

And then after we have considered him first in the foundation, he grows to be the cornerstone, to unite those Christians which seem to be of diverse ways, diverse aspects, diverse professions, together. As we consider him in the foundation, there he is the root of faith. As we consider him in the corner, there he is the root of charity.

Consider first, what diverse things he unites in his own person: that he should be the son of a woman and yet no son of man, that the son of a woman should be the son of God, that man's sinful nature and innocency should meet together, a man that should not sin, that God's nature and mortality should meet together, a God that must die; briefly, that he should do and suffer so many things impossible as man, impossible as God. Thus he was a cornerstone that brought together natures naturally incompatible. Thus he was a cornerstone in his person. Consider him in his offices, as a redeemer, as a mediator, and so he has united God to man; yes, rebellious man to jealous God. He is such a cornerstone as has united Heaven and earth, Jerusalem and Babylon, together.

Thus in his person, and thus in his offices, consider him in his power, and he is such a cornerstone as that he is the God of peace and love, and union, and concord. Such a cornerstone as is able to unite and reconcile (as it did in Abraham's house) a wife and a concubine in one bed, a covetous father and a wasteful son in one family, a severe magistrate and a licentious people in one city, an absolute prince and a jealous people in one kingdom, law and conscience in one government, Scripture and tradition in one

Church. If we would but make Christ Jesus and his peace the life and soul of all our actions and all our purposes; if we would mingle that sweetness and suppleness which he loves and which he is in all our undertakings; if in all controversies, book controversies and sword controversies, we would fit them to him and see how near they would meet in him, that is how near we might come to be friends and yet both sides be good Christians, then we placed this stone in his second right place, who as he is a cornerstone reconciling God and man in his own person, and a cornerstone in reconciling God and mankind in his office, so he desires to be a cornerstone in reconciling man and man, and settling peace among ourselves. Not for worldly ends, but that we might all meet in him to love one another. Not because we made a stronger party by that love, not because we made a sweeter conversation by that love, but because we met closer in the bosom of Christ Jesus, where we must at last either rest altogether eternally, or be altogether eternally thrown out, or be eternally separated and divorced from one another.

Having then received Christ for the foundation stone (we believe aright), and for the cornerstone (we interpret charitably the opinions and actions of other men), the next is that he be the stone of Jacob, a stone of rest and security to ourselves. When Jacob was in his journey, he took a stone, and that stone was his pillow. Upon that he slept all night, and resting upon that stone, he saw the ladder that reached from Heaven to earth. It is much to have this egress and regress to God, to have a sense of being gone from him, and a desire and means of returning to him. When we do fall into particular sins, it is well if we can take hold of the first step of this ladder, if we can remember God of his Covenant to his people and to their seed. It is more if we can clamber a step higher on this ladder, if we come to open our lips in a true confession of our wretched condition and of those sins by which we have forfeited our interest in that Covenant. And more than that, too, if we overflow and make ourselves drunk with tears, in a true sense, and sorrow for those sins. And more than all this, if we can expostulate with God in an "How long, O Lord, shall I take counsel in myself, having weariness in my heart?" These steps, these gradations towards God, do well. These wrestlings with God bring a man to peace with him. But then is a man upon this stone of Jacob, when in a fair, and even, and constant religious course of life, he enters into his sheets every night, as though his neighbors next day were to shroud and wind him in those sheets; he shuts up his eyes every night, as though his executors had closed them; and lies down every night, not as though his man were to call him up next morning to hunt, or to the next day's sport, or business, but as though the Angels were to call him to the Resurrection. And this is our third benefit: as Christ is a stone, we have security and peace of conscience in him.

The next is, that he is the stone with which David slew Goliath, and with which we may overcome all our enemies. David's sling was a type of the cross, and the stone was a type of Christ. We will choose to insist upon spiritual enemies, sins, and this is that stone that enables the weakest man to overthrow the strongest sin, if he proceed as David did. David says to Goliath, "Thou comest to me with a sword, with a spear, and with a shield, but I come to thee in the name of the God of the hosts of Israel, whom thou hast railed upon." If you watch the approach of any sin, any giant sin that transports you most; if you apprehend it to rail against the Lord of Hosts (that is, that there is a loud and active blasphemy against God in every sin), if you discern it to come with a sword or a spear (that is, persuasions of advancement if you do it, or threatenings of dishonor if you do it not), if it come with a shield (that is, with promises to cover and palliate it, though you do it); if then this David (your attempted soul) can put his hand into his bag as David did (for a man's heart is that bag in which God lays up all good directions), if he can but take into his consideration his Jesus, his Christ, and sling one of his works, his words, his commandments, his merits, this Goliath, this giant sin, will fall to the ground. And then, as it is said of David that he slew him when he had no sword in his hand, and yet in the next verse, that he took his sword and slew him with that: so even by the consideration of what my Lord has done for me, I shall give that sin the first death's wound. And then I shall kill him with his own sword; that is, his own abomination, his own foulness shall make me detest him. If I dare but look my sin in the face, if I dare tell him, "I come in the name of the Lord," I shall triumph over it. That God that gave me courage to fight, will give me strength to overcome.

The last benefit which we consider in Christ, as he is a stone, is that he is a Rock. The Rock gave water to the Israelites in the wilderness, and he gave them honey out of the stone, and oil out of the hard rock. Now when St. Paul says, "That our Fathers drank of the same Rock as we," he adds that the same Rock was Christ; so that all temporal and all spiritual blessings to us, and to the Fathers, were all conferred upon us in Christ. But we consider not now any miraculous production from the Rock, but that which is natural to the Rock; that it is a firm defence to us in all tempests, in all afflictions, in all tribulations.

For as Christ is our foundation, we believe in him, and as he is our cornerstone, we are at peace with the world in him; as he is Jacob's stone, giving us peace in ourselves, and David's stone, giving us victory over our enemies, so he is a Rock of stone (no affliction, no tribulation, shall shake us). And so we have passed through all the benefits proposed to be considered in this first part, as Christ is a stone.

It is some degree of thankfulness to stand long in the contemplation of the benefit which we have received, and therefore we have insisted thus long upon the first part. But it is a degree of spiritual wisdom, too, to make haste to the consideration of our dangers, and therefore we come now to them. We may fall upon this stone and be broken. This stone may fall upon us and grind us to powder. And in the first of these, we may consider what the falling of this stone is; and secondly, what it is to be broken upon it; and then thirdly, the latitude of this, that whosoever falls so, is so broken.

As the Wiseman said of manna, that it had abundance of all pleasure in it, and was meat for all tastes, so this stone, Christ Jesus, hath abundance of all qualities of stone in it, and is such a stone to every man as he desires it should be. "Unto you that believe," says St. Peter, "it is a precious stone, but unto the disobedient, a stone to stumble at." For if a man walk in a gallery, where windows, and tables, and statues, are all of marble, yet if he walk in the dark, or blindfold, or carelessly, he may break his face as dangerously against that rich stone as if it were but brick. So though a man walk in the true Church of God, in that Jerusalem which is described in the Revelation, the foundation, the gates, the walls, all precious stone, yet if a man bring a misbelief, a misconcept, that all this religion is but a part of civil government and order; if a man be scandalized at that humility, that patience, that poverty, that lowliness of spirit which the Christian religion inclines us unto; if he will say, If Christ will be kind, let him come down from the cross, and then we will believe in him, let him deliver his Church from all crosses, first, of doctrine, and then of persecution, and then we will believe him to be King; if we will say, We will admit Christ, but we will not admit him to reign over us, to be King; if he will be content with a consulship, with a colleagueship, that he and the world may join in the government, that we may give the week to the world and the sabbath to him, that we may give the day of the sabbath to him and the night to our licentiousness, that of the day we may give the forenoon to him, and the afternoon to our pleasures; if this will serve Christ, we are content to admit him. But we will none of that absolute power, that whether we eat or drink, or whatsoever we do, we must be troubled to think on him and respect his glory in everything.

If he will say, God has given us in charge to his Angels, and therefore we need not to look to our own ways, he has locked us up safely, and lodged us softly under an eternal election, and therefore we are sure of salvation; if he will walk thus blindly, violently, wilfully, negligently in the true Church, though he walk among the sapphires, and pearls, and chrysolites, which are mentioned there (that is, in the outward communion and fellowship of God's saints), yet he may bruise and break, and batter himself as much against these stones as against the stone gods of the heathen. For first, the place of this falling upon this stone is the true Church. He that is already upon the ground, in no church, can fall no lower, till he fall to Hell; but he whom God has brought into his true Church, if he come to a confident security that he is safe enough in these outward acts of religion, he falls, though it be upon this stone; he errs, though in the true Church.

This is the place, then, the true Church; the falling itself is a falling into some particular sin, but not such as quenches our faith; we fall so, as we may rise again. St. Hierome expresses it so, He that falls, but yet believes, that falls and has a sense of his fall, that man is reserved by God's purpose, to come by repentance to salvation. For this man that falls there, falls not so desperately, as that he feels nothing between Hell and him, nothing to stop at, nothing to check him by the way; he falls upon something. Nor he falls not upon flowers, to wallow and tumble in his sin, nor upon feathers, to rest and sleep in his sin, nor into a cooling river, to disport, and refresh, and strengthen himself in his sin; but he falls upon a stone, where he may receive a bruise, a pain upon his fall, a remorse of that sin that he is fallen into.

And in this fall our infirmity appears three ways: the first is to stumble, for though he be upon the right stone in the true religion, and have light enough, yet as the prophet says, "Even at noon we stumble." We have much more light, by Christ being come, than the Jews had, but we are sorry we have it. When Christ has said to us for our better understanding of the Law, "He that looketh and lusteth hath committed adultery, he that coveteth hath stolen, he that is angry hath murdered," we stumble at this, and we are scandalized with it; and we think that other religions are gentler, and that Christ has dealt hardly with us, and that we had rather Christ had not said so, we had rather he had left us to our liberty and discretion, to look, and court, and to give a way to our passions, as we should find it most conduce to our ease and to our ends. And this is to stumble, not to go on in an equal and even pace, not to do the will of God cheerfully. And a second degree is to kick, to spurn at this stone; that is, to bring some particular sin, and some particular law into comparison: to debate thus, "If I do not this now, I shall never have such a time; if I slip this, I shall never have the like opportunity; if I will be a fool now, I shall be a beggar all my life: and for the law of God that is against it, there is but a little evil for a great deal of good; and there is a great deal of time to recover and repent that little evil."

Now to remove a stone which was a landmark, and to hide and cover that stone, was all one fault in the Law. To hide the will of God from our own consciences with excuses and extenuations, this is as much as we can to spurn the stone, the landmark, out of the way. But the fullness and accomplishment of this is in the third word of the text, to fall. He falls as a piece of money falls into a river. We hear it fall, and we see it sink, and by and by we see it deeper, and at last we see it not at all. So no man falls at first into any sin but he hears his own fall. There is a tenderness in every conscience at the beginning, at the entrance into a sin, and he discerns a while the degrees of sinking, too. But at last he is out of his own sight, till he meet this stone (this stone is Christ); that is, till he meet some hard reprehension, some hard passage of a sermon, some hard judgment in a prophet, some cross in the world, something from the mouth or something from the hand of God, that breaks him. He falls upon the stone and is broken.

To be broken upon this stone is to come to this sense, that though our integrity be lost, that we be no more whole and entire vessels, yet there are means of piecing us again. Though we be not vessels of innocency, yet we may be vessels of repentance acceptable to God, and useful to his service. For when anything falls upon a stone, the harm that it suffers is not always (or not only) according to the proportion of the hardness of that which it fell upon, but according to the height that it falls from, and according to that violence that it is thrown with. If their fall who fall by sins of infirmity should refer only to the stones they fall upon, every sinner would be broken to pieces, and ground to powder. But if they fall not from too far a distance, if they have lived within any nearness, any consideration of God, if they have not fallen with violence, taken heart and force in the way, grown perfect in the practice of their sin; if they fall upon this stone, that is, sin, and yet stop at Christ after the sin, this stone shall break them; that is, break their force and confidence, break their presumption and security, but yet it shall leave enough in them for the Holy Ghost to unite to his service. Yes, even the sin itself, the very fall itself, shall be an occasion of his rising. And therefore though St. Augustine seem to venture far, it is not too far, when he says a sinner falls to his advantage that falls into some such sin as, by being manifested to the world, manifests his own sinful state to his own sinful conscience, too. It is well for that man that falls so, as that he may thereby look the better to his footing ever after. St. Bernard says, all creatures can say, Lord thou art my creator; all living creatures can say, Thou art my shepherd, Thou givest me meat in due season; all men can say, Thou art my Redeemer; but only he which is fallen, and fallen upon this stone, only he which has been overcome by a temptation and is restored, can say, Lord, thou hast supported me, thou hast collected my shivers, and reunited me; only to him has this stone expressed both abilities of stone: first to break him with a sense of his sin and then to give him peace and rest upon it.

Now there is in this part this circumstance more—"whosoever falls": that is, whosoever he be, he falls. Since the Father of man, Adam, could not, how shall the sons of him, that inherit his weakness and contract more and contribute their temptations to one another, hope to stand? Adam fell, and he fell far off, for he could see no stone to fall upon, for when he fell, there was no such Messiah, no such means of reparation proposed nor promised when he fell, as now to us. The Blessed Virgin, and the forerunner of Christ, John the Baptist, fell too, but they fell nearer hand, they fell but a little way, for they had this stone (Christ Jesus) in a personal presence, and their faith was always awake in them, but yet he, and she, and they all fell into some sin. "Whosoever falls," is whosoever he be, he falls, and whosoever falls (as we said before), is broken. If he fall upon something and fall not to an infinite depth; if he fall not upon a soft place, to a delight in sin, but upon a stone, and this stone (no harder, sharper, ruggeder than this, not into a diffidence or distrust in God's mercy), he that falls so, and is broken so, that comes to a remorseful, to a broken and a contrite heart, he is broken to his advantage, left to a possibility, yes brought to a nearness of being pieced again by the Word, by the sacraments, and other medicinal institutions of Christ in his Church.

We must end only with touching upon the third part, "upon whom this stone falls, it will grind him to powder," where we shall only tell you first what this grinding is, and then what the falling of this stone is. And briefly, this grinding to powder is to be brought to that desperate and irrecoverable estate in sin as that no medicinal correction from God, no breaking, no bowing, no melting, no molding can bring him to any good fashion.

"I will break them as a potter's vessel," says God in Jeremiah. There shall be no possible means (of those means which God has ordained in his Church) to recompact them again, no voice of God's word to draw them, no threatenings of God's judgments shall drive them, no censures of God's Church shall fit them, no Sacrament shall cement and glue them to Christ's body again. In temporal blessings he shall be unthankful, in temporal afflictions he shall be obdurate. And these two shall serve as the upper and nether stone of a mill to grind this reprobate sinner to powder.

Lastly, this is to be done by Christ's falling upon him, and what is that? I know some expositors take this to be but the falling of God's judgments upon him in this world. But in this world there is no grinding to powder, all God's judgments here (for anything that we can know), have the nature of physic in them, and may, and are wont to cure; and no man is here so absolutely broken in pieces but that he may be reunited. We choose therefore to follow the ancients in this, that the falling of this stone upon this reprobate is Christ's last and irrecoverable falling upon him in his last judgment; that when he shall wish that the hills might fall and cover him, this stone shall fall and grind him to powder. He shall be broken and be no more found, says the prophet. Yes, he shall be broken and no more sought. No man shall consider him what he is now, nor remember him what he was before. For that stone which in Daniel was cut out without hands (which was a figure of Christ who came without ordinary generation), when that great image was to be overthrown, broke not an arm or a leg but brake the whole image in pieces, and it wrought not only upon the weak parts, but it brake all: the clay, the iron, the brass, the silver, the gold. So when this stone falls thus, when Christ comes to judgment, he shall not only condemn him for his clay, his earthly and covetous sins; nor for his iron, his revengeful oppressing, and rusty sins; nor for his brass, his shining and glittering sins which he has filed and polished, but he shall fall upon his silver and gold, his religious and precious sins, his hypocritical hearing of sermons, his singular observing of sabbaths, his pharisaical giving of alms, and as well his subtle counterfeiting of religion as his atheistical opposing of religion; this stone, Christ himself, shall fall upon him and a shower of other stones shall oppress him too.

There shall fall upon him the natural law which was written in his heart and did rebuke him when he prepared for a sin. There shall fall upon him the written Law which cried out from the mouths of the prophets to avert him from sin. There shall fall upon him those sins which he has done and those sins which he has not done, if nothing but want of means and opportunity hindered him from doing them. There shall fall upon him those sins which he has done after another's dehortation, and those which others have done after his provocation. There the stones of Nineveh shall fall upon him and of as many cities as have repented with less proportions of mercy and grace than God afforded him. There the rubbage of Sodom and Gomorrah shall fall upon him, and as many cities as in their ruin might have been examples to him. All these stones shall fall upon him and to add weight to all these Christ Jesus himself shall fall upon his conscience with unanswerable questions and grind his soul to powder. But he that overcomes shall not be hurt by the second death. He that feels his own fall upon this stone shall never feel this stone fall upon him. He that comes to a remorse early and earnestly after a sin and seeks by ordinary means his reconciliation to God in his Church, is in the best state that man can be in now. For howsoever we cannot say that repentance is as happy an estate as innocency, yet certainly every particular man feels more comfort and spiritual joy after a true repentance for a sin than he had in that degree of innocence which he had before he committed that sin; and therefore in this case also we may safely repeat those words of Augustine, "I dare be bold to say that many a man has been the better for some sin."

Almighty God, who gives that civil wisdom to make use of other men's infirmities, give us also this heavenly wisdom to make use of our own particular sins, that thereby our own wretched conditions in ourselves and our means of reparation in Jesus Christ may be the more manifested unto us.

16 DEATH'S DUEL OR, A CONSOLATION TO THE SOUL, AGAINST THE DYING LIFE, AND LIVING DEATH OF THE BODY

And unto God the Lord belong the issues of death [i.e., from death].

PSALM 68:20

BUILDINGS STAND BY THE BENEFIT OF THEIR foundations that sustain and support them, and of their buttresses that comprehend and embrace them, and of their contignations that knit and unite them. The foundations suffer them not to sink, the buttresses suffer them not to swerve, and the contignation and knitting suffers them not to cleave. The body of our building is in the former part of this verse. It is this: "He that is our God is the God of salvation"; *ad salutes,* of salvations in the plural, so it is in the original; the God that gives us spiritual and temporal salvation too.

But of this building, the foundation, the buttresses, the contignations are in this part of the verse, which constitutes our text, and in the three divers acceptations of the words amongst our expositors. "Unto God the Lord belong the issues from death." For first the foundation of this building (that our God is the God of all salvations) is laid in this; that unto this "God the Lord belong the issues of death," that is, it is in his power to give us an issue and deliverance, even then when we are brought to the jaws and teeth of death, and to the lips of that whirlpool, the grave. And so in this

210

acceptation of these words, and that upon which our translation lays hold, "the issues from death."

And then secondly the buttresses that comprehend and settle this building, that he that is our God, is the God of all salvations, are thus raised. "Unto God the Lord belong the issues of death," that is, the disposition and manner of our death: what kind of issue and transmigration we shall have out of this world, whether prepared or sudden, whether violent or natural, whether in our perfect senses or shaken and disordered by sickness. There is no condemnation to be argued out of that, no judgment to be made upon that, for howsoever they die, "precious in his sight is the death of his saints," and with him are "the issues of death," the ways of our departing out of this life are in his hands. And so in this sense of the words, this issue of death is a deliverance in death. Not that God will deliver us from dying, but that he will have a care of us in the hour of death, of what kind soever our passage be.

And then lastly the contignation and knitting of this building, that he that is our God is the God of all salvations, consists in this, "Unto this God the Lord belong the issues of death," that is, that this God the Lord having united and knit both natures in one, and being God, having also come into this world, in our flesh, he could have no other means to save us, he could have no other issue out of this world, nor return to his former glory, but by death. And so in this sense, this issue of death is a deliverance by death, by the death of this God, our Lord Christ Jesus. And this is St. Augustine's acceptation of the words, and those many and great persons that have adhered to him.

In all these three lines then, we shall look upon these words. First, as the God of power, the Almighty Father rescues his servants from the jaws of death. And then as the God of mercy, the glorious Son rescued us, by taking upon himself this issue of death. And then between these two, as the God of comfort, the Holy Ghost rescues us from all discomfort by his blessed impressions beforehand, that what manner of death soever be ordained for us, yet our issue in death shall be an entrance into everlasting life.

The Showing Forth of Christ

And these three considerations, our deliverance from death, in death, and by death, will abundantly do all the offices of the foundations, of the buttresses, of the contignation of this our building: that "He that is our God is the God of all salvations" because "unto this God the Lord belong the issues of death."

First, then, we consider that with God the Lord are the issues of death, and therefore in all our deaths, and deadly calamities of this life, we may justly hope of a good issue from him. And all our periods and transitions in this life are so many passages from death to death. Our very birth and entrance into this life is an issue from death, for in our mother's womb we are dead so, as that we do not know we live, not so much as we do in our sleep. Neither is there any grave so close, or so putrid a prison, as the womb would be unto us if we stayed in it beyond our time, or died there before our time. In the grave the worms do not kill us, we breed and feed, and then kill those worms which we ourselves produced. In the womb the dead child kills the mother that conceived it, even after it is dead. And if we be not dead so in the womb, so as that being dead we kill her that gave us our first life, our life of vegetation, yet we are dead so, as David's idols are dead. In the womb we have "eyes and see not, ears and hear not." There in the womb we are fitted for works of darkness, all the while deprived of light. And there in the womb we are taught cruelty, by being fed with blood, and may be damned, though we be never born.

Of our very making in the womb, David says, "I am wonderfully and fearfully made," and "Such knowledge is too excellent for me," for even that is the Lord's doing, and it is wonderful in our eyes. It is "he that hath made us, and not we ourselves," nor our parents neither. "Thy hands have made me and fashioned me round about," says Job, and (as the original word is) "thou hast taken pains about me," and yet, says he, "thou dost destroy me." Though I be the masterpiece of the greatest Master (man is so), yet if you do no more for me, if you leave me where you made me, destruction will follow. The womb which should be the house of life becomes death itself if God leaves us there. That which God threatens so often, the shutting of the womb, is not so heavy, nor so discomfortable a curse in the first, as in the latter shutting, nor in the shutting of barrenness, as in the shutting of weakness, when children are come to the birth and there is not strength to bring forth.

It is the exaltation of misery to fall from a near hope of happiness. And in that vehement imprecation, the prophet expresses the highest of God's anger, "Give them O Lord, what wilt thou give them? give them a miscarrying womb." Therefore as soon as we are men (that is, inanimated, quickened in the womb), though we cannot ourselves, our parents have reason to say in our behalf, "Wretched man that he is, who shall deliver him from this body of death?" for even the womb is a body of death if there be no deliverer. It must be he that said to Jeremiah, "Before I formed thee I knew thee, and before thou camest out of the womb I sanctified thee."

We are not sure that there was no kind of ship nor boat to fish in, nor to pass by, till God prescribed Noah that absolute form of the Ark. That word which the Holy Ghost, by Moses, uses for the Ark is common to all kinds of boats, *Thebah*, and is the same word that Moses uses for the boat that he was exposed in, that his mother laid him in an ark of bulrushes. But we are sure that Eve had no midwife when she was delivered of Cain, therefore she might well say, "I have gotten a man from the Lord," wholly, entirely from the Lord. It is the Lord that enabled me to conceive, the Lord that infused a quickening soul into that conception, the Lord that brought into the world that which himself had quickened. Without all this might Eve say, My body had been but the house of death, and to "God the Lord belong the issues of death."

But then this issue, this deliverance from that death, the death of the womb, is an entrance, a delivering over to another death, the manifold deaths of this world. We have a winding sheet in our mother's womb, which grows with us from our conception, and we come into the world, wound up in that winding sheet, for we come to seek a grave. And as prisoners discharged of actions may lie for fees, so when the womb has discharged us, yet we are bound to it by cords of flesh by such a string, as that we cannot go thence, nor stay there. We celebrate our own funerals with cries, even at our birth; as though our three score and ten years life were spent in our mother's labor, and our circle made up in the first point thereof; we beg our baptism, with another Sacrament, with tears. And we come into a world that lasts many ages, but we last not.

"In my Father's house," says our Savior, speaking of Heaven, "there are many mansions," divers and durable, so that if a man cannot possess a martyr's house (he has shed no blood for Christ), yet he may have a Confessor's, he has been ready to glorify God in the shedding of his blood. And if a woman cannot possess a virgin's house (she has embraced the holy state of marriage), yet she may have a matron's house, she has brought forth and brought up children in the fear of God. "In my Father's house," in Heaven, "there are many mansions," but here upon earth, "the son of man hath not where to lay his head," says he himself. How then has God given this earth to the sons of men? He has given them earth for their materials, to be made of earth, and he has given them earth for their grave and sepulture, to return and resolve to earth, but not for their possession. Here we have no continuing city, nay no cottage that continues, nay no persons, no bodies that continue.

Even the Israel of God has no mansions, but journeys, pilgrimages in this life. By that measure did Jacob measure his life to Pharaoh: "the days of the years of my pilgrimage." And though the Apostle would not say that while we are in the body we are dead, yet he says while we are in the body we are but in a pilgrimage, and we are absent from the Lord. He might have said dead, for this whole world is but an universal churchyard, but one common grave, and the life and motion that the greatest persons have in it is but as the shaking of buried bodies in the grave by an earthquake. That which we call life is but a week of deaths, seven days, seven periods of our life spent in dying, a dying seven times over; and there is an end. Our birth dies in infancy, and our infancy dies in youth, and youth and the rest die in age, and age also dies, and determines all.

Nor do all these, youth out of infancy, or age out of youth, arise so, as a Phoenix out of the ashes of another Phoenix formerly dead, but as a wasp or a serpent out of a carrion, or as a snake out of dung. Our youth is worse than our infancy, and our age worse than our youth. Our youth is hungry and thirsty after those sins

which our infancy knew not. And our age is sorry and angry that it
cannot pursue those sins which our youth did. And besides, all the
way, so many deaths, that is, so many deadly calamities accompany every condition and every period of this life as that death
itself would be an ease to them that suffer them. Upon this sense
does Job wish that God had not given him an issue from the first
death, from the womb. "Wherefore hast thou brought me forth out
of the womb? O that I had given up the ghost, and no eye seen me!
I should have been as though I had not been."

And not only the impatient Israelites in their murmuring
("would to God we had died by the hand of the Lord in the land
of Egypt"), but Elijah himself, when he fled from Jezebel and
went for his life, as that text says, under the juniper tree, requested
that he might die, and said, "It is enough now, O Lord, take away
my life." So Jonah justifies his impatience, nay his anger towards
God himself. "Now O Lord take, I beseech thee, my life from me,
for it is better to die than to live." And when God asked him,
"doest thou well to be angry for this?" he replies, "I do well to be
angry, even unto death." How much worse a death than death is
this life, which so good men would so often change for death!

But if my case be as St. Paul's case, that "I die daily," that
something heavier than death falls upon me every day; if my case
be David's case, "all the day long we are killed," that not only
every day, but every hour of the day something heavier than death
falls upon me; though that be true of me, "I was shapen in iniquity, and in sin did my mother conceive me" (there I died one
death), though that be true of me, I was born not only of the child
of sin, but the child of wrath, of the wrath of God for sin, which is
a heavier death; yet with "God the Lord are the issues of death,"
and after a Job, and a Joseph, and a Jeremiah, and a Daniel, I
cannot doubt of a deliverance. And if no other deliverance conduce more to his glory and my good, yet he has the keys of death,
and he can let me out at that door, that is, deliver me from the
manifold deaths of this world, the every day's death and every
hour's death, by that one death, the final dissolution of body and
soul, the end of all.

But then is that the end of all? Is that dissolution of body and soul the last death that the body shall suffer? (For of spiritual death we speak not now.) It is not. Though it be an issue from the manifold deaths of this world, yet it is an entrance into the death of corruption and putrefaction and vermiculation and incineration, and dispersion in and from the grave, in which every dead man dies over again.

It was a prerogative peculiar to Christ not to die this death, not to see corruption. What gave him this privilege? Not Joseph's great proportion of gums and spices, that might have preserved his body from corruption and incineration longer than he needed it, longer than three days, but would not have done it forever. What preserved him then? Did his exemption and freedom from original sin preserve him from this corruption and incineration? 'Tis true that original sin has induced this corruption and incineration upon us. If we had not sinned in Adam, "mortality had not put on immortality" (as the Apostle speaks) nor "corruption had not put on incorruption," but we had had our transmigration from this to the other world, without any mortality and corruption at all.

But yet since Christ took sin upon him, so far as made him mortal, he had it so far too as might have made him see this corruption and incineration, though he had no original sin in himself. What preserved him then? Did the hypostatical union of both natures, God and man, preserve him from this corruption and incineration? 'Tis true that this was a most powerful embalming, to be embalmed with the divine nature itself, to be embalmed with eternity, was able to preserve him from corruption and incineration forever. And he was embalmed so, embalmed with the divine nature itself, even in his body as well as in his soul; for the Godhead, the divine nature, did not depart, but remained still united to his dead body in the grave.

But yet for all this powerful embalming, this hypostatical union of both natures, we see Christ did die; and for all this union which made him God and man, he became no man (for the union of the body and soul makes the man, and he whose soul and body are separated by death as long as that state lasts is properly no man). And therefore as in him the dissolution of body and soul was no dissolution of the hypostatical union, so is there nothing that constrains us to say, that though the flesh of Christ had seen corruption and incineration in the grave, this had been any dissolution of the hypostatical union, for the divine nature, the Godhead might have remained with all the elements and principles of Christ's body, as well as it did with the two constitutive parts of his person, his body and his soul.

This incorruption then was not in Joseph's gums and spices, nor was it in Christ's innocency and exemption from original sin, nor was it (that is, it is not necessary to say it was) in the hypostatical union. But this incorruptibleness of his flesh is most conveniently placed in that, "thou wilt not suffer thy holy one to see corruption." We look no further for causes or reasons in the mysteries of religion, but to the will and pleasure of God. Christ himself limited his inquisition in that, "even so Father, for so it seemeth good in thy sight." Christ's body did not see corruption, therefore, because God had decreed it should not.

The humble soul (and only the humble soul is the religious soul) rests himself upon God's purposes and the decrees of God, which he has declared and manifested, not such as are conceived and imagined in ourselves, though upon some probability, some verisimilitude. So in our present case Peter proceeds in his sermon at Jerusalem, and so Paul in his at Antioch. They preached Christ to have been risen without seeing corruption not only because God had decreed it, but because he had manifested that decree in his prophet. Therefore does St. Paul cite by special number the second Psalm for that decree. And therefore both St. Peter and St. Paul cite for it that place in the 16th Psalm, for when God declares his decree and purpose in the express words of his prophet, or when he declares it in the real execution of the decree, then he makes it ours, then he manifests it to us. And therefore as the mysteries of our religion are not the objects of our reason, but by faith we rest on God's decree and purpose (It is so, O God, because it is thy will it should be so), so God's decrees are ever to be considered in the manifestation thereof.

All manifestation is either in the word of God, or in the execution of the decree. And when these two concur and meet, it is the strongest demonstration that can be. When therefore I find those marks of adoption and spiritual filiation, which are delivered in the Word of God to be upon me, when I find that real execution of his good purpose upon me, as that actually I do live under the obedience, and under the conditions which are evidences of adoption and spiritual filiation; then so long as I see these marks and live so, I may safely comfort myself in a holy certitude and a modest infallibility of my adoption. Christ determines himself in that, the purpose of God was manifest to him. St. Peter and St. Paul determine themselves in those two ways of knowing the purpose of God, the Word of God before, the execution of the decree in the fullness of time. It was prophesied before, say they, and it is performed now. Christ is risen without seeing corruption.

Now this which is so singularly peculiar to him, that his flesh should not see corruption, at his second coming, his coming to judgment, shall extend to all that are then alive, their flesh shall not see corruption, because as the Apostle says, and says as a secret, a mystery, "Behold I show you a mystery, we shall not all sleep" (that is, not continue in the state of the dead in the grave), "but we shall all be changed in an instant." We shall have a dissolution, and in the same instant a redintegration, a recompacting of body and soul, and that shall be truly a death and truly a resurrection, but no sleeping in corruption. But for us that die now and sleep in the state of the dead, we must all pass this posthumous death, this death after death, nay this death after burial, the dissolution after dissolution, this death of corruption and putrefaction, of vermiculation and incineration, of dissolution and dispersion in and from the grave, when these bodies that have been the children of royal parents, and the parents of royal children, must say with Job, "Corruption thou are my father," and to the worm, "Thou art my mother and my sister."

Miserable riddle, when the same worm must be my mother and my sister and myself. Miserable incest, when I must be married to my mother and my sister, and be both father and mother to my own mother and sister, beget and bear that worm which is all that miserable penury. When my mouth shall be filled with dust, and the worm shall feed, and feed sweetly upon me, when the ambitious man shall have no satisfaction if the poorest alive tread upon him, nor the poorest receive any contentment in being made equal to princes, for they shall be equal but in dust. One dies at his full strength, being wholly at ease and in quiet, and another dies in the bitterness of his soul, and never eats with pleasure, but they lie down alike in the dust and the worm covers them. In Job and in Isaiah, it covers them and is spread under them, the worm is spread under you and the worm covers you. There's the mats and the carpets that lie under, and there's the state and the canopy that hangs over the greatest of the sons of men. Even those bodies that were the temples of the Holy Ghost come to this delapidation, to ruin, to rubbish, to dust; even the Israel of the Lord, and Jacob himself has no other specification, no other denomination, but "thou worm of Jacob."

Truly the consideration of this posthumous death, this death after burial, that after God (with whom are the issues of death) has delivered me from the death of the womb by bringing me into the world, and from the manifold deaths of the world by laying me in the grave, I must die again in an incineration of this flesh and in a dispersion of that dust. That that monarch who spread over many nations alive, must in his dust lie in a corner of that sheet of lead, and there but so long as that lead will last; and that private and retired man that thought himself his own forever, and never came forth, must in his dust of the grave be published and (such are the revolutions of the graves), be mingled with the dust of every highway, and of every dunghill, and swallowed in every puddle and pond: this is the most inglorious and contemptible vilification, the most deadly and peremptory nullification of man, that we can consider.

God seems to have carried the declaration of his power to a great height, when he sets the Prophet Ezekiel in the valley of dry bones and says, "Son of man can these bones live?" as though it had been impossible, and yet they did. "The Lord laid sinews upon them, and flesh, and breathed into them, and they did live." But in that case there were bones to be seen, something visible, of which it might be said, Can this thing live? But in this death of inciner-ation and dispersion of dust, we see nothing that we call that man's. If we say, Can this dust live? perchance it cannot, it may be the mere dust of the earth, which never did live, never shall. It may be the dust of that man's worm, which did live, but shall no more. It may be the dust of another man, that concerns not him of whom it is asked. This death of incineration and disperson is, to natural reason, the most irrecoverable death of all, and yet, "unto God the Lord belong the issues of death," and by recompacting this dust into the same body, and reinanimating the same body with the same soul, he shall in a blessed and glorious Resurrection give me such an issue from this death as shall never pass into any other death, but establish me into a life that shall last as long as the Lord of life himself.

And so have you that that belongs to the first acceptation of these words ("unto God the Lord belong the issues of death"), that though from the womb to the grave and in the grave itself we pass from death to death, yet, as Daniel speaks, "The Lord our God is able to deliver us, and he will deliver us."

And so we pass unto our second accommodation of these words ("unto God the Lord belong the issues of death"), that it belongs to God, and not to man, to pass a judgment upon us at our death, or to conclude a dereliction on God's part upon the manner thereof.

Those indications which the physicians receive, and those presagitions which they give for death or recovery in the patient, they receive and they give out of the grounds and the rules of their art. But we have no such rule or art to give a presagition of spiritual death and damnation upon any such indication as we see in any dying man. We see often enough to be sorry, but not to despair. We may be deceived both ways. We use to comfort ourself in the death of a friend, if it be testified that he went away like a lamb, that is, without any reluctation. But, god knows that he may be accompanied with a dangerous damp and stupefaction, and insensibility of his present state. Our blessed Savior suffered coluctations with death, and a sadness even in his soul to death, and an agony even to a bloody sweat in his body, and expostulations with God, and exclamations upon the cross.

He was a devout man who said upon his deathbed, "Hast thou served a good Master threescore and ten years, and now art thou loath to go into his presence?" Yet Hilarion was loath. Barlaam was a devout man, that said that day he died, "Consider this to be the first day's service that ever thou didst thy Master, to glorify him in a Christianly and a constant death, and if thy first day be thy last day too, how soon dost thou come to receive thy wages?" Yet Barlaam would have been content to have stayed longer for it.

Make no ill conclusions upon any man's loathness to die, for the mercies of God work momentarily in minutes, and many times insensibly to bystanders or any other than the party departing. And then upon violent deaths inflicted, as upon malefactors, Christ himself has forbidden us by his own death to make any ill conclusion; for his own death had those impressions in it. He was reputed, he was executed as a malefactor, and no doubt many of them who concurred to his death did believe him to be so. Of sudden death there are scarce examples to be found in the Scriptures upon good men, for death in battle cannot be called sudden death. But God governs not by examples, but by rules, and therefore make no ill conclusion upon sudden death nor upon distempers neither, though perchance accompanied with some words of diffidence and distrust in the mercies of God.

The tree lies as it falls, it's true, but it is not the last stroke that fells the tree, nor the last word nor gasp that qualifies the soul. Still pray we for a peaceable life against violent death, and for time of repentance against sudden death, and for sober and modest assurance against distempered and diffident death, but never make ill conclusions upon persons overtaken with such deaths; "to God the Lord belong the issues of death." And he received Samson, who went out of this world in such a manner (consider it actively, consider it passively in his own death, and in those whom he slew with himself) as was subject to interpretation hard enough. Yet the Holy Ghost has moved St. Paul to celebrate Samson in his great catalogue, and so does all the Church.

Our critical day is not the very day of our death but the whole course of our life. I thank him that prays for me when the bell tolls, but I thank him much more that catechises me, or preaches to me, or instructs me how to live. There's my security, the mouth of the Lord has said it, do this and you shall live. But though I do it, yet I shall die too, die a bodily, a natural death. But God never mentions, never seems to consider that death, the bodily, the natural death. God does not say, live well and you shall die well, that is, an easy, a quiet death; but live well here, and you shall live well forever. As the first part of a sentence pieces well with the last, and never respects, never harkens after the parenthesis that comes between, so does a good life here flow into an eternal life, without any consideration what manner of death we die. But whether the gate of my prison be opened with an oiled key (by a gentle and preparing sickness), or the gate be hewn down by a violent death, or the gate be burned down by a raging and frantic fever, a gate into Heaven I shall have, for from the Lord is the cause of my life, and with God the Lord are the issues of death. And further we carry not this second acceptation of the words, as this issue of death is a deliverance in death, God's care that the soul be safe, what agonies soever the body suffers in the hour of death.

But pass to our third part and last part: as this issue of death is a deliverance by the death of another, by the death of Christ. "You have heard of the patience of Job," says St. James 5:11. All this while you have done that, for in every man, calamitous, miserable man, a Job speaks. Now see "the end of the Lord," says that Apostle, which is not that end that the Lord proposed to himself (salvation to us), nor the end which he proposes to us (conformity to him), but see "the end of the Lord," says he, the end that the Lord himself came to; death and a painful and a shameful death.

But why did he die? and why die so? As St. Augustine interpreting this text answers that question: because to this "God our Lord belonged the issues of death." What can be more obvious, more manifest than this sense of these words. In the former part of this verse, it is said, "He that is our God, is the God of salvation," so he reads it, the God that must save us. Who can that be, says he, but Jesus? for therefore that name was given him, because he was to save us. And to this Jesus, says he, this Savior, belong the issues of death. Being come into this life in our mortal nature, he could not go out of it any other way but by death. Therefore it is said, "To God the Lord belong the issues of death"; to show that his way to save us was to die. And from this text does St. Isidor prove that Christ was truly man (which as many sects of heretics denied as that he was truly God), because to him, though he were *Dominus Dominus* (as the text doubles it) God the Lord, yet to him, to God the Lord belonged the issues of death. More cannot be said than Christ himself says of himself, "These things Christ ought to suffer"; he had no other way but by death.

So then this part of our sermon must needs be a passion sermon. Since all his life was a continual passion, all our Lent may well be a continual Good Friday. Christ's painful life took off none of the pains of his death. He felt not the less then for having felt so much before. Nor will anything that shall be said before lessen, but rather enlarge the devotion to that which shall be said of his passion at the time of due solemnization thereof. Christ bled not a drop the less at the last for having bled at his circumcision before, nor will you shed a tear the less then, if you shed some now.

And therefore be now content to consider with me how to this God the Lord belonged the issues of death. That God, this Lord, the Lord of life could die, is a strange contemplation. That the Red Sea could be dry, that the sun could stand still, that an oven could be seven times heat and not burn, that lions could be hungry and not bite, is strange, miraculously strange, but super-miraculous that God could die. But that God would die is an exaltation of that. But even of that also it is a super-exaltation, that God should die, must die, and (said St. Augustine), "God the Lord had no issue but by death," and (says Christ himself), "all this Christ ought to suffer," was bound to suffer. God is the God of revenges, says David, he would not pass over the sin of man unrevenged. But then (says that place) the God of revenges works freely, he punishes, he spares whom he will. And would he not spare himself? He would not. Love is strong as death, stronger; it drew in death that naturally is not welcome. "If it be possible," says Christ, "let this cup pass," when his love expressed in a former decree with his Father had made it impossible.

Many waters quench not love. Christ tried many. He was baptized out of his love, and his love determined not there. He mingled blood with water in his agony and that determined not his love. He wept pure blood, all his blood at all his eyes, at all his pores, in his flagellation and thorns (to the Lord our God belonged the issues of blood) and these expressed, but these did not quench his love. He would not spare, nay he could not spare himself. There was nothing more free, more voluntary, more spontaneous than the death of Christ. 'Tis true, he died voluntarily, but yet when we consider the contract that had passed between his Father and him, there was a kind of necessity upon him. All this Christ ought to suffer. And when shall we date this obligation, this necessity? When shall we say that began? Certainly this decree by which Christ was to suffer all this was an eternal decree, and was there anything before that, that was eternal? Infinite love, eternal love; be pleased to follow this home, and to consider it seriously, that what liberty soever we can conceive in Christ, to die or not to die, this necessity of dying, this decree is as eternal as that liberty; and yet how small a matter made he of this necessity and this dying?

His Father calls it but a bruise, and but a bruising of his heel ("the serpent shall bruise his heel") and yet that was that the serpent should practice and compass his death. Himself calls it but a baptism, as though he were to be the better for it. "I have a baptism to be baptized with," and he was in a pine till it was accomplished, and yet this baptism was his death. The Holy Ghost calls it joy ("for the joy which was set before him he endured the cross") which was not a joy of his reward after his passion, but a joy that filled him even in the midst of those torments, and arose from him. When Christ calls his *calicem* a cup, and no worse ("can ye drink of my cup"), he speaks not odiously, not with detestation of it. Indeed it was a cup, a health to all the world. And, says David, "what shall I render to the Lord?" Answer you with David, "I will take a cup of salvation." Take it, that cup is salvation, his passion, if not into your present imitation, yet into your present contemplation.

And behold how that Lord that was God yet could die, would die, must die, for your salvation. That Moses and Elijah talked with Christ in the transfiguration both St. Matthew and St. Mark tell us, but what they talked of only St. Luke. He says, "They talked of his decease, of his death which was to be accomplished at

Jerusalem." The word is of his *Exodus,* the very word of our text, *exitus,* his issue by death. Moses, who in his Exodus had prefigured this issue of our Lord, and in passing Israel out of Egypt through the Red Sea had foretold in that actual prophecy Christ's passing of mankind through the sea of his blood. And Elijah, whose Exodus and issue out of this world was a figure of Christ's ascension, had no doubt a great satisfaction in talking with our blessed Lord of the full consummation of all this in his death, which was to be accomplished at Jerusalem.

Our meditation of his death should be more visceral and affect us more because it is of a thing already done. The ancient Romans had a certain tenderness and detestation of the name of death, they could not name death, no, not in their wills. There they could not say "if or when I die," but "when the course of nature is accomplished upon me." To us that speak daily of the death of Christ ("he was crucified, dead and buried"), can the memory or the mention of our own death be irksome or bitter? There are in these latter times amongst us those that name death freely enough, and the death of God, but in blasphemous oaths and execrations. Miserable men, who shall therefore be said never to have named Jesus, because they have named him too often, and therefore hear Jesus say, "I never knew you," because they made themselves too familiar with him.

Moses and Elijah talked with Christ of his death only in a holy and joyful sense of the benefit which they and all the world were to receive by that. Discourses of religion should not be out of curiosity, but to edification. And then they talked with Christ of his death at that time, when he was in the greatest height of glory that ever he admitted in this world, that is, his transfiguration. And we are afraid to speak to the great men of this world of their death, but nourish in them a vain imagination of immortality and immutability. But (as St. Peter said there) it is good to dwell here, in this consideration of his death, and therefore transfer we our tabernacle (our devotions) through some of those steps which God the Lord made to his issue of death that day.

Take in the whole day from the hour that Christ received the Passover upon Thursday, unto the hour in which he died the next day. Make this present day that day in your devotion, and consider what he did, and remember what you have done. Before he instituted and celebrated the Sacrament (which was after the eating of the Passover), he proceeded to that act of humility, to wash his disciples' feet, even Peter's, who for a while resisted him. In your preparation to the holy and blessed Sacrament, have you with a sincere humility sought a reconciliation with all the world, even with those that have been averse from it, and refused that reconciliation from you? If so, and not else, you have spent that first part of his last day in a conformity with him.

After the Sacrament he spent the time till night in prayer, in preaching, in psalms. Have you considered that a worthy receiving of the Sacrament consists in a continuation of holiness after, as well as in a preparation before? If so, you have therein also conformed yourself to him. So Christ spent his time till night: "At night he went into the garden to pray," and he spent much time in prayer. How much? Because it is literally expressed that he prayed there three several times, and that returning to his Disciples after his first prayer, and finding them asleep said, "Could ye not watch with me one hour?" it is collected that he spent three hours in prayer. I dare scarce ask you where you went or how you disposed of yourself when it grew dark and after last night. If that time were spent in a holy recommendation of yourself to God and a submission of your will to his, it was spent in a conformity to him. In that time and in those prayers was his agony and bloody sweat. I will hope that you did pray, but not every ordinary and customary prayer. But prayer actually accompanied with shedding of tears, and dispositively in a readiness to shed blood for his glory in necessary case, puts you into a conformity with him.

About midnight he was taken and bound with a kiss. Are you not too conformable to him in that? Is not that too literally, too exactly your case? at midnight to have been taken and bound with a kiss? From thence he was carried back to Jerusalem, first to Annas, then to Caiaphas, and (as late as it was) then he was examined and buffeted and delivered over to the custody of those officers, from whom he received all those irrisions and violences, the covering of his face, the spitting upon his face, the blasphemies of words, and the smartness of blows which that Gospel mentions. In which compass fell that crowing of the cock which called up Peter to his repentance. How you passed all that time last night, you know. If you did anything that needed Peter's tears, and have not shed them, let me be your cock, do it now. Now your Master (in the unworthiest of his servants) looks back upon you, do it now.

Betimes, in the morning, so soon as it was day, the Jews held a counsel in the High Priest's hall, and agreed upon their evidence against him, and then carried him to Pilate, who was to be his judge. Did you accuse yourself when you waked this morning, and were you content even with false accusations (that is) rather to suspect actions to have been sin, which were not, than to smother and justify such as were truly sins? Then you spent that hour in conformity to him. Pilate found no evidence against him, and therefore to ease himself and to pass a compliment upon Herod, Tetrarch of Galilee, who was at that time at Jerusalem (because Christ being a Galilean was of Herod's jurisdiction) Pilate sent him to Herod, and rather as a madman than a malefactor. Herod remanded him (with scorns) to Pilate to proceed against him; and this was about eight of the clock.

Have you been content to come to this inquisition, this examination, this agitation, this pursuit of your conscience, to sift it, to follow it from the sins of your youth to your present sins, from the sins of your bed to the sins of your board, and from the substance to the circumstance of your sins? That's time spent like your Savior's. Pilate would have saved Christ by using the privilege of the day in his behalf, because that day one prisoner was to be delivered, but they chose Barabbas. He would have saved him from death by satisfying their fury with inflicting other torments upon him, scourging and crowning with thorns, and loading him with many scornful and ignominious contumelies. But they regarded him not, they pressed a crucifying.

Have you gone about to redeem your sin by fasting, by alms, by disciplines and mortifications, in way of satisfaction to the justice of God? That will not serve, that's not the right way; we press an utter crucifying of that sin that governs you: and that conforms you to Christ. Towards noon Pilate gave judgment, and they made such haste to execution, as that by noon he was upon the cross. There now hangs that sacred body upon the cross, rebaptized in his own tears and sweat, and embalmed in his own blood alive. There are those bowels of compassion, which are so conspicuous, so manifested, as that you may see them through his wounds. There those glorious eyes grew faint in their light: so as the sun, ashamed to survive them, departed with his light too. And then that Son of God, who was never from us, and yet had now come a new way unto us in assuming our nature, delivers that soul (which was never out of his Father's hands) by a new way, a voluntary emission of it into his Father's hands.

For though to this God our Lord, belonged these issues of death, so that considered in his own contract, he must necessarily die, yet at no breach or battery which they had made upon his sacred body issued his soul, but "he gave up the Ghost," and as God breathed a soul into the first Adam, so this second Adam breathed his soul into God, into the hands of God. There we leave you in that blessed dependency, to hang upon him that hangs upon the cross, there bathe in his tears, there suck at his wounds, and lie down in peace in his grave, till he vouchsafe you a resurrection, and an ascension into the Kingdom, which he has purchased for you with the inestimable price of his incorruptible blood. *Amen.*

THE DATES AND
PLACES OF THE SERMONS

1. OF CREATION, THE TRINITY AND THE NATURE OF MAN, I.
   Preached before King Charles I, at Whitehall, probably in April, 1629.
2. OF CREATION, THE TRINITY AND THE NATURE OF MAN, II.
   As above, at some date soon after.
3. ON THE MYSTERY OF THE TRINITY AND WHAT WE MAY KNOW OF THE GODHEAD; A WHITSUNDAY SERMON. *Possibly preached at St. Paul's, 1630.*
4. OF GOD'S LOVE FOR US AND OUR LOVE FOR HIM. *Preached before Queen Anne, Denmark House, Dec. 14, 1617.*
5. OF CHRIST'S CHIEF CARE FOR THE SINNER. *Preached at Whitehall, April 30, 1626.*
6. THE SHOWING FORTH OF CHRIST; A CHRISTMAS SERMON. *Preached at St. Paul's, Christmas day, 1626.*
7. OF HUMAN MARRIAGE AND THE MARRIAGE OF THE SOUL WITH CHRIST; A WEDDING SERMON. *Preached on the occasion of the marriage of Mistress Margaret Washington, Church of St. Clement Danes, May 30, 1621.*
8. OF CHRIST'S COMING TO REDEEM US, IN THE TESTIMONY OF PAUL, I. *Preached at Whitehall, April 19, 1618.*
9. OF CHRIST'S COMING TO REDEEM US, IN THE TESTIMONY OF PAUL, II. *Same day and place as above.*
10. OF GOD AS OUR HELP IN ALL THINGS. *Preached at St. Paul's, Jan. 29, 1625/6.*
11. OF PRAYER, OF IGNORANCE, AND THE MERCY OF GOD. *Date and place uncertain, possibly before 1622.*
12. ON PRAYER, REPENTANCE, AND THE MERCY OF GOD; A

LENTEN SERMON. *Preached before King Charles I, possibly April 20, 1630.*

13. ON THE CONVERSION OF ST. PAUL, HOW GOD MAY STRIKE DOWN A MAN TO RAISE HIM UP. *Preached at St. Paul's, the Sunday after the celebration of the conversion of St. Paul, probably 1624/5.*

14. OF PATIENCE IN ADVERSITY, AWAITING THE WILL OF GOD. *Preached before a congregation of lawyers, at Lincoln's Inn, possibly 1618.*

15. OF CHRIST AS FOUNDATION AND CORNERSTONE. *Preached on February 21, probably 1618/19, at or near Whitehall.*

16. DEATH'S DUEL OR, A CONSOLATION TO THE SOUL, AGAINST THE DYING LIFE, AND LIVING DEATH OF THE BODY. *Preached before King Charles I, at Whitehall, first Friday in Lent, Feb. 25, 1630. Preached shortly before his death, this is often called Dr. Donne's own funeral sermon.*

Format by Morris Karol
Set in Linotype Times Roman
Composed, printed and bound by The Haddon Craftsmen, Inc.
HARPER & ROW, PUBLISHERS, INCORPORATED